Buy Your *Own* Business

Buy Your
Own Business

*The Definitive Guide to Identifying and
Purchasing a Business You Can Make a Success*

Mitchell B. Stern

MACMILLAN • USA

MACMILLAN
A Simon & Schuster Macmillan Company
1633 Broadway
New York, NY 10019-6785

Macmillan Publishing books may be purchased for business or sales promotional use.
For information please write: Special Markets Department, Macmillan Publishing USA,
1633 Broadway, New York, NY 10019.

MACMILLAN is a trademark of Macmillan, Inc.

Library of Congress Cataloging-in-Publication Data
Stern, Michell B.
    Buy your own business / Mitchell B. Stern.
        p.   cm.
    Includes index.
    ISBN 0-02-861476-3 (pbk.)
    1. Business enterprises—United States—Purchasing.   2. New business
enterprises—United States—Management.   3. n-us.
    I. Title.
    HD1393.4.U6S74   1998   98-14235
    658.1'6—dc21   CIP

Printed in the United States of America
10 9 8 7 6 5 4 3 2 1
Book design by Nick Anderson

Contents

Acknowledgments

I would like to express my sincere appreciation and gratitude to the following people: Stephen Pollan for his guidance, encouragement, and support; Betsy Thorpe for her insight and editorial assistance; Deborah Harkins, former assistant managing editor of *New York* magazine, for her creative input and advice; certified public accountants Stewart Bauman and Alan Krasnoff, as well as industrial psychologist and career specialist Chuck Sodikoff, Ph.D., for their professional expertise; and most of all, Dana, my wonderful wife, for her love and unwavering support.

This book is for Dana, Macklin, and Savannah—
the love and light of my life.

Foreword

IF YOU'RE BEWITCHED BY THE PROSPECT OF BEING YOUR OWN boss but bewildered by the complexities of making that happen, then this is the book you must read. The world of the newly self-employed is redolent with opportunity but rife with risk, and in *Buy Your Own Business* Mitchell Stern will show you how, by buying an existing business rather than starting up one of your own, you can maximize the former while minimizing the latter.

In today's marketplace, the threat of downsizing is being offset by the unprecedented opportunities that currently exist for private entrepreneurship, making this a turbulent but exciting time to be at work. Never before has owning your business been a more necessary or a more viable option. But if that's your dream, you need to know what to do to make it your reality.

Now if there's anything I've learned in my thirty years of consulting and advising, it's that no book on earth can instill in anyone the *will* to make such a bold and ambitious move in his or her life;

that has to be generated from within. However, I've also learned that a great many people have that will but don't necessarily know it. They don't know it because it's hiding under a pile of often thoroughly reasonable doubts about their own ability to succeed at such a speculative venture. They see self-employment as hazardous, expensive, time-consuming, and eminently complicated. They want to try it but are paralyzed into inaction by the mountain of obstacles that stand in their way. Instead, they keep slogging through life in one dead-end job or another, unsatisfied, underappreciated, bored, and secretly resentful of those who've gone ahead and done what they themselves have only dreamed of doing.

If you're such a person—or if you've always assumed that launching a startup was your only option—you need to know that your doubts are as reasonable as they are unnecessary. You need to be able to climb your mountain, one step at a time, and discover that with patience, persistence, and proper instruction, your risks can be mitigated and your chances of succeeding greatly enhanced. And this is precisely what Mitchell Stern will help you do. Drawing on his years of experience and expertise, he will reduce your doubts to manageable size by showing you how, for every perceived obstacle to self-employment, there are tested, reliable, dependable correctives.

So if you think you're the kind of person whose passion to take over your own enterprise is stifled by your despair over the enormity of such an undertaking, you're in for a treat. Beginning with a very compelling argument as to why the best way for you to become self-employed is to purchase an existing business, Stern will then take you through a meticulous, entertaining, step-by-step process of identifying, researching, analyzing, financing, and negotiating the purchase of just such a business, followed by a thorough description of how to make and keep it profitable. The creative ideas, the inside information, the compendium of facts, and the lists of resources and support services contained within these pages are enough to ennoble even the most cautious among us to, as Rudyard Kipling said, "dream, but not make dreams our aim." So wake up to your opportunity, and read on.

Stephen M. Pollan

CHAPTER 1

The Prudent Risk-Taker

BEFORE GOING INTO BUSINESS FOR MYSELF, I LABORED TIRELESS-
ly at three law firms. The first two (one in Miami and the other in
New York City), were large practices—among the top-ranked law
firms in the country. I lasted about two years at each job before I
couldn't take the grim routine any longer.

Back then, it wasn't uncommon for me to be at the office until
well after midnight during the week and around the clock on weekends. I'll never forget the time a partner spotted me leaving at
8 p.m.—a very rare and precious occurrence. The next day he called
me into his office and asked me to close the door. He proceeded to
tell me—to shout at me—that the firm didn't pay me to work nine-
to-five and that nine-to-eight was like nine-to-five.

Even before this incident took place, I had decided that I hated
being a lawyer. I *had* to find a different career. Large law firms pay
well, but they chew you up and spit you out; at least, that was my
experience. Brainstorming with friends, talking to career coun-
selors, reading books—even praying—couldn't help me figure out
what else I wanted to do.

In the meanwhile, just to get out from under big-firm domina-
tion, I took a job with a sole practitioner. Though my tenure with
him was barely longer than it had been with the first two firms, the
experience was to prove invaluable. It afforded me the opportunity
to observe first hand the business side of running a law practice. I
still hated law, though—or so I thought—and I remained committed to the unrealistic notion that one day I would come up with
"The Idea " that would change my life.

Around this time my life did change, but not on the career front:
I had the great fortune to meet Dana Pollan, the young woman who
was to become my wife. She was an entrepreneur: For several years
she had been a co-owner of a well-known fitness studio in New
York City. After we had dated for a while, I met her father, Stephen
Pollan, who has written the foreword for this book. Stephen was a
lawyer, but he also had written books and magazine articles, many
of the subjects of which involved changing careers. At Dana's suggestion, I asked her father for a career consultation.

Stephen quizzed me about what I had done so far in the business world. I discussed my experiences with law firms and told him
that I wanted to do *anything* but practice law. He asked what I
thought I might like to do instead. Even though I was prepared for
this question, I had no answers. I knew I wanted to work for
myself—I couldn't bear the thought of having another boss—but I
really had no idea what I wanted to do. The only real work experience I had was as a lawyer.

Stephen listened carefully and then asked if I was ready for his
advice. He warned me that I might not like what I was about to
hear. It turned out that he, too, thought I should go into business
for myself—but not in some yet-to-be found new field; he suggested that I start my own law practice.

I quite heartily resisted that advice. I had dreamed of finding
some great field that would take me as far away from the practice
of law as possible. The reality, however, was that being a lawyer was

something I could do right away. While working for the sole practitioner, I'd had a chance to observe how a small practice was run. I knew I could do it; I just didn't think I wanted to. Eventually, after much soul searching, a few additional consults with my future father-in-law, and some warm support and encouragement from Dana, I decided to hang out my shingle.

That was eight years ago. In those eight years as my own boss, I have found job fulfillment—personal freedom, financial independence, and career satisfaction—that I had only fantasized about when I was working for someone else. While my own circumstances led me to start a business from scratch, the experiences I had working for others (*before* becoming my own boss) are why I relate so easily to the frustration of those people who've only dreamed about being self-employed. Helping would-be entrepreneurs has given me more pleasure than anything else I've achieved in business. In fact, it is the reason I wrote this book.

My practice is centered around advising would-be entrepreneurs and small business owners. That's what I'm comfortable with; after all, a few years ago I, like my clients, was a fledgling getting ready to fly on my own. Now I've been a lawyer and consultant to hundreds of clients on career and business matters, so I have learned a tremendous amount about the process of going into business. In fact, my experience has led to my writing articles for major magazines, making contributions to books, and appearing on national television to discuss topics involving small business and personal financial matters.

In the course of advising clients, writing my articles, and researching this book, I've discovered two things:

1. There has never been a better time for people in this country to go into business for themselves.

2. For most people, buying an existing business is a far better way to become one's own boss than starting a business from scratch.

The Disenchanted Masses

For workers, disappointment and disenchantment are now the order of the day. How often have you heard the phrase "I hate my job," or "I wish I could think of some other way to earn a living," or "My boss is giving me a coronary"? Maybe you've muttered a sentiment like that yourself: I know I did, and so have some of my friends and colleagues and many of the people who seek my advice.

Our grandparents probably never expected to find satisfaction in the work they did. For people who went through the Depression, just *being employed* was privilege enough. But between the end of World War II and the mid-1980s, a booming economy enabled workers to grow secure enough in their jobs to assume that they were entitled to *like* their work. Employers had an unspoken pact with their employees: "Do your job properly and we'll keep you on the payroll till you retire."

Now, however, corporate America is following new rules, rules dictated by an economy that recently has changed as significantly as it did during the Industrial Revolution. Because technology now enables us to communicate instantly with one another, a smaller number of people, either at home or thousands of miles away, can do jobs for U.S. companies that used to require a massive on-site labor force. In the computer age, businesses need far fewer people to complete a particular task than they needed forty years ago. All of this change, which took place during the years America was experiencing a recession, has been responsible for the elimination of a staggering number of jobs, most of which will never be replaced.

The implied contract between employer and employee no longer exists. Today, workers who've been on the job for decades get no reward for their tenure—indeed, older workers, who earn higher salaries than younger workers, are prime targets for downsizing. And, to absorb the tasks of downsized colleagues, many must work at a stressful pace—and yet they can't count on keeping their jobs until they can afford to retire.

Earning a Living in a Changing Workplace

Corporate downsizing, massive layoffs, and the fallout from industries' shift to manufacturing overseas have eliminated jobs from the work force, most of which will never be replaced. However, there are many who seek new careers: All those workers who have fallen victim to the corporate squeeze—from the rank and file to middle management to senior executives. Baby boomers have been especially hard hit. Those faced with the prospect of caring for their aging parents and of paying the high costs of their children's college tuition (an increasing number of American families) have been forced to become two-income households. Many retirees—bored by idleness or unable to survive financially—looking for a second career are often overlooked by recruiters in large companies because of their age. For many, the search for a job has been a lesson in frustration.

Workers have begun to see "quality of life" issues as their primary career concern. They have come to realize that when they're working for someone else they cannot expect their job to fulfill their personal goals. This is by no means a bad thing: Caring about what you do to earn a living will enhance your life, not detract from it, as long as you never lose sight of the need to protect your stream of income. That realization will let you view positively your break from traditional employment, whether the separation was voluntary or involuntary. You will see yourself not as a victim, but as one of the many Americans who are taking advantage of exciting new career opportunities.

Redefining *Entrepreneur*

In the past few years, I have consulted with many who lost their jobs or were in fear of losing them. For the most part, these people were referred by clients I'd helped in the past or through other professionals (lawyers, accountants, and financial advisers) who knew that my practice focused on matters involving careers and small businesses. An overwhelming number of clients had been fired, or were about to be, in that dreaded nineties corporate maneuver known as *downsizing*. (In a true testament to the art of spin control, many companies have heeded the advice of the public relations community and labeled this unpopular tactic *rightsizing*.)

The savvy employee now realizes that all workers these days are "free agents:" Because workers are vulnerable to dismissal whenever a boss decides they have lost their fiscal utility, they are, in effect, working for themselves. Each job is only one among the many a worker can expect to hold down. Therefore, many smart employees have adopted this credo: "I'll do my job as well as I can while I'm in it, but I'll always keep looking for the next job (or business opportunity)."

The term entrepreneur used to be applied only to the trailblazers and risk-takers of the business world. Many books on going into business used to contain elaborate "self-tests" that were meant to tell the reader whether he[1] was daring enough to be an entrepreneur. However, if my experience dealing with today's businessmen and businesswomen has taught me anything, it is that this conventional definition is outdated. It's too exclusive and too elitist. People who want to go into business for themselves these days don't have to be particularly daring. True, they do need courage and a sense of urgency, but they needn't possess a reckless character. Proper planning and hard work are just as important as courage. At the end of this chapter is a questionnaire developed to help you determine whether you are ready to buy a business. The questionnaire was

---

[1] *For simplicity's sake, and because English sentence structure makes doing anything else unwieldy, throughout this book I use* he *when I'm referring to an entrepreneur or to someone who is buying a business. Read that* he *as he or she. The fact is businesses owned by women are a dynamic force behind the economic growth and job creation in our nation today. According to Dun & Bradstreet, in 1994 there were 7.7 million female-owned firms in the United States, employing 35 percent more workers in the U.S. than Fortune 500 companies worldwide.*

prepared for me by Chuck Sodikoff, Ph.D., an industrial psychologist and career specialist, who is himself an entrepreneur. It is designed to let you know whether you fit the profile of the new American entrepreneur—an entrepreneur for the twenty-first century.

Going into business for oneself is a natural solution to today's career conundrum. For anyone willing to prepare well and work hard, self-employment is an opportunity to enjoy the three Fs: *Fulfillment* (personal, emotional, and spiritual); *freedom* (to manage your career—indeed, your life—in the way you choose); and *financial independence* (you alone determine your stream of income, and if you're truly successful, you'll earn more money than you could as an employee).

Fortunately, there has never been a better time to go into business. Small business is the fastest growing segment of American business today. Self-employment and small businesses are "in." The federal government is re-trumpeting the cause of small business and the critical role it plays in helping the United States compete in today's global marketplace. By far the largest single source of federally backed growth financing for small businesses is the U.S. Small Business Administration (SBA, created in 1953 as an independent agency of the federal government to assist the small business community). The SBA has made financing astonishingly easier for small enterprises by offering low-cost, low-documentation loans. Even the home-based business has cachet today. (There was a time when anyone who worked out of his home was thought to be between jobs.)

Technology has made it easier for small businesses to compete with big corporations. The key is one word: access. Customers are less concerned today about where you are as with what you can do and what you can offer. Therefore, what matters most is how accessible you are. The capability of businesses to reach across miles to sell products and services to customers has made the world a much smaller place. Fax machines, modems, e-mail, video conferencing, printed catalogs, and electronic catalogs on the World Wide Web enable small businesses to reach a global audience while at the same time reducing costs for office space and maintaining inventory. For many businesses, an enticing Web page could be more important than a prestigious address or storefront location.

Because of corporations' massive shift away from traditional employment policies, studies indicate that more people are likely to go into business for themselves in the next five years than in the last two decades combined. These hope-to-be entrepreneurs will enter business in one of three ways:

1. Starting from scratch (the stark reality, however, is that the failure rate for business start-ups is enormously high; barely one start-up in ten makes it past the first two years).
2. Buying an existing business.
3. Purchasing a franchise.

Why It's Better Not to Start from Scratch

Peter Caldwell was a systems analyst for a large computer software company in Silicon Valley. For years Peter had been unhappy at his job. His boss was insufferable and the industry had become increasingly competitive and contact with clients and customers far less personal. So, when Peter reached his fifty-fifth birthday and his company offered him early retirement, Peter readily agreed.

After the first year of retirement, Peter realized that he had made a mistake; retirement was not for him. He was bored. But Peter couldn't bear the thought of answering to another boss and was determined to strike out on his own. Although money wasn't an obstacle for Peter—he had accumulated considerable personal savings over the years and had received a handsome retirement package from his former employer—at fifty-six, Peter was reluctant to put his capital at high risk. At the same time, Peter had a dream.

Ever since he was a young man, Peter had boasted about his sartorial splendor. He was a clotheshorse to be sure and had always wanted to own a men's clothing store. Excited by the thought of becoming an entrepreneur, but mindful of reducing the level of risk involved, Peter decided that buying an existing business (with a track record and financials to analyze) rather than starting one from scratch was the way to go. One thing Peter hadn't anticipated, however, was that he was trading one insufferable boss for another—himself!

Peter has never worked so hard. Still, according to Peter, the rewards of entrepreneurship have been worthwhile. The last time I spoke to Peter was on a Sunday night during the Christmas holiday season. He called me on his cellular phone to tell me that he was decorating his store window—and loving it!

Stepping into an existing business will satisfy your desire for career and financial independence yet put you at far less financial risk than a start-up business would. All established businesses have survived for some period of time—and the most dangerous time for a business is the period from starting up to breaking even. Buying an established business is the method of choice of the new American entrepreneur, who is more conservative than his audacious predecessors, more reluctant to put his capital, as well as himself, at risk. The turn-of-the-millennium entrepreneur doesn't start his own business; he looks around for a company with a track record. That means an up-and-running venture with a solid customer and supplier base and a product or service that the market has already welcomed.

However, the biggest advantage in buying an existing business is the fact that it removes the guesswork from entrepreneurship: Buying a business offers a degree of predictability lacking in ventures built from scratch. The entrepreneur can perform a regressive analysis by evaluating the company's past to predict its future. There are operations that can be examined. For instance, what is the business's reputation in the community? Are the employees satisfied? Are they doing a good job and will they stay on with a new owner? Does the business provide a reasonable living for the owners? Is it located in a growing area?

There are benefits as well when it comes to raising capital. Banks are usually more comfortable about lending an entrepreneur money if they can examine financial statements, assets, and cash flow. And the business's assets (equipment, inventory, accounts receivable, etc.) can be used as collateral for bank loans. Another virtue: All existing businesses have one thing no start-up business has—an owner.

Many owners are willing to provide some, or all, of the acquisition financing a buyer needs, often at more favorable terms than those offered by commercial banks. Furthermore, an owner often can be persuaded to stay on for a period of time to help with the transition to new ownership. (You can offer him a deferred buy-out or condition the purchase price on future sales volume; see Chapter 10.) Quite often, the seller's assistance proves invaluable. If properly motivated, the outgoing owner will share his expertise and insight as to how the business was run as well as how things might be done better. What's more, his involvement may help to persuade customers and suppliers to continue to do business with the new owner—you.

Buying a franchise is another way to go into business without starting from scratch. Because franchising is a choice in its own right, we'll discuss it in a bit more detail in Chapter 2.

The First Steps

To acquire a business that isn't doomed to fail, you need to make intelligent preparation. That means finding out all you can about the business or industry you're interested in; maintaining your stream of income until you're ready to take the plunge; and establishing a network of business and professional contacts who can help you when you need help (and you will!). Here are your first steps toward becoming an entrepreneur:

1. ***Don't give up your day job.*** Just because you've decided to go into business doesn't mean it's time to quit your job: I cannot overemphasize the need to protect your stream of income. While you are acquiring the knowledge or experience you need, you must pay your bills. Preparing to shift from worker to business owner may take six to nine months or longer, depending upon your level of business acumen and your knowledge of the industry you've decided to enter. And, perhaps more important, if you're still employed you'll be more likely to take your time looking for the right business rather than jumping at the first thing that comes along. The inability to wait for the right opportunity is a surefire recipe for failure. So remember: If you have a job, your goal is to stay employed until you've acquired the business you hope to own.

2. ***Learn all you can about the business or industry.*** Your first priority must be to learn as much as you possibly can about the particular field you're considering. If the field is new to you, first determine whether the skills you'll need are best obtained through training or developed through experience.

   If you need training, consider going back to school— maybe a night course at a local college or university. This will be particularly fruitful if you have on-the-job experience in an industry but not much of a business background. By taking a few classes in business law, accounting, and marketing, you'll get the flavor of the core courses required at most business schools. However, you'll "graduate" much faster and spend a lot less for your education. Another option is to find yourself a training program. The Small Business Administration sponsors nearly 500 Small Business Development Centers around the country that provide free counseling, courses, and technical assistance to would-be entrepreneurs (see Appendix A, "Source Directory").

Virtually every industry has a trade association or organization. Find out if the trade group in your prospective field holds meetings; if so, attend them. And get on the mailing list if the trade group publishes a journal or newsletter. Another resource is your local chamber of commerce, where you can obtain information on the types of business opportunities available in your geographic area.

3. ***Find a career mentor.*** After you've learned at least the basics about a particular field, seek out a career mentor—someone who has experienced success in the field you'd like to enter. Don't ever be afraid to ask for guidance from knowledgeable, experienced people whose opinions you trust. Choose someone with whom you have a close personal relationship and whose abilities you believe in.

4. ***Networking.*** Every small business owner must put together a network of personal contacts and resources. No one knows everything. I work for myself, yet over the years I have developed strong relationships with many other professionals whose expertise and judgment I admire. Were it not for my initiative in reaching out to these experts for assistance and advice, I wouldn't be in a position to serve all the needs of my clients.

If you're considering buying a business, begin networking now. Make a list of friends, relatives, and business contacts. Call them and tell them (in confidence) that you're interested in buying a business. You're not inconveniencing someone by asking him to discuss his experiences. Business is built on contacts and favors. Someone who helps you today may one day call upon you to return the favor (for instance, you may be asked to help out your contact's friend). That's what networking is all about. Ask if your contacts know anyone who has bought a business. Stress that you're looking for guidance and let them know you're willing to meet with anyone to discuss the process of buying a business and to explore business opportunities. This exercise will come in handy when you actually begin your search for a business to buy. By opening yourself up to exploratory meetings in this way, you are dramatically expanding your network. You may find that your contacts know one or more people who were once in your position. They may even know someone who owns a business he might want to sell.

5. *Moonlight.* If the type of business you're looking for is outside the field in which you've trained, you're going to have to get an entry-level job in the new field. Of course, you should not give up your day job. Therefore, you must be willing to work part-time in your new field while continuing to earn your salary.

What You Will Learn from This Book

In the chapters that follow, I will guide you step by step through the process of buying a small business. First you'll be shown how to select an industry that matches your experience, skills, and personal life-style preferences. Then you'll be shown how to draw up a plan for researching your chosen industry (as well as its geographic location) and how to go about investigating its viability and potential growth.

I will introduce you to several perhaps unorthodox, yet extremely effective, new techniques for locating businesses for sale. I will also help you navigate through traditional search channels such as business brokers and classified ads. You'll be given a set of guidelines on how to finance the acquisition of your business, discussing the various sources of capital available as well as how to prepare for a meeting with a bank officer to request a business loan.

Next we'll examine how to assemble a team of professionals whose job it will be to offer expert advice and guidance and to march you unscathed through the mine fields that lay ahead. Then you'll be ready to learn the tactics you can use when you approach prospective sellers. These tactics range from the very gentle approach you'd use with the owner of a family business to the tougher stance you'd take with a "serial seller."

Then I will demonstrate how to investigate the financial condition of your target business—not only how to read its financial statements but how you can persuade the owner to give you the information you need to perform an effective analysis of the business. You'll also be shown how to look beyond a business's financial statements to determine its true worth. I intend to both demystify the process of valuing a small business and supply you with winning negotiating strategies that will help you buy your business at the best possible price. I'll show you the most advantageous methods of structuring and closing the transaction so that you'll get the best deal possible under the tax laws.

Finally, I will offer tips on how to improve a business after you've taken over. These tips include creating a business redeployment plan that will help you make choices that lead to a successful transition and a promising future for your new business.

By picking up this book you have taken the first step in a process that could change your life forever. By following the straightforward advice set forth in the coming chapters, you will see how easy it is to achieve the fulfillment, freedom, and financial independence that comes with owning your own business. In the next chapter, we'll talk about the crucial first step: choosing the type of business that's right for you.

BUYING A BUSINESS: READINESS SELF EVALUATION

Are you ready to buy a business? What type of business should it be? Answer the following questions about yourself as truthfully as possible. By doing so, your answers will help you identify those areas that may cause difficulties should you buy a business, suggest the kind of business you should consider, and help uncover areas of personal development needs so that you can maximize your chances for success. When you have completed this questionnaire, see "Scoring Key."

Circle the number that best reflects your belief about yourself.

Strongly Agree	Generally Agree	Generally Disagree	Strongly Disagree

1. I think it is important to stick to completion everything I attempt.

4	3	2	1

2. People would describe me as highly flexible.

4	3	2	1

3. I have always been good at identifying creative solutions to difficult problems.

4	3	2	1

4. I get bored easily and need to do many different activities in my day.

4	3	2	1

5. I adapt easily to new situations.

4	3	2	1

6. I believe strongly that the customer is always right.

4	3	2	1

7. I am experienced and confident as a negotiator.

4	3	2	1

8. I have a wide network of friends and business contacts.

4	3	2	1

9. I frequently think about owning my own business.

4	3	2	1

10. I do not need to be directed or motivated by others to work effectively

4	3	2	1

11. I am a natural leader. I have played a leadership role in almost every group to which I have belonged.

4	3	2	1

12. I make decisions easily. I am known for being able to think on my feet.

4	3	2	1

13. I am energetic. I always need something to do.

4	3	2	1

14. I work especially well in high-pressure situations.

4	3	2	1

15. There is a specific business with which I want to be involved. I have done research and am convinced that this type of business will be growing and will be around for a long time.

4	3	2	1

16. I am a strong optimist. I always look at the positive side of things.

    4   3   2   1

17. People trust me because I always deliver on what I promise.

    4   3   2   1

18. I am a strategic thinker. I look at the long term consequences of decisions.

    4   3   2   1

19. I have built many strong, positive relationships with people I have met in my work life.

    4   3   2   1

20. I have never been intimidated by my bosses.

    4   3   2   1

21. I read people well and know how to persuade them to my point of view.

    4   3   2   1

22. People who I have been responsible for hiring, or have recommended for jobs, have turned out to be highly successful.

    4   3   2   1

23. My work life has been a commitment to the delivery of the highest possible quality of products and/or service.

    4   3   2   1

24. I am not a gambler but I am willing to take calculated risks.

    4   3   2   1

25. In my current (most recent) job I was one of the first to work and one of the last to leave.

    4   3   2   1

26. Financial security is the number one priority in my life.

    4   3   2   1

27. I am a hands-on type. I get actively involved in everything related to my work.

    4   3   2   1

28. I am outgoing and enjoy interacting with people all day long.

    4   3   2   1

29. I enjoy planning and organizing. I never start important projects without being fully prepared.

    4   3   2   1

30. I make highly effective presentations and know how to keep the attention of my audience.

    4   3   2   1

Totals _____ + _____ + _____ + _____ = _____ **(Overall Score)**

SCORING KEY

Find your overall score by summing the scores on items 1–25. If your overall score is less than 75, buying a business is a risky option for you.

Items 26–30 provide specific advice on various aspects of buying a business:

If your answer to item 26 is *4*, consider buying into an established franchise.

If your answer to item 27 is *4*, consider buying a smaller business. If your answer to item 27 is *1* or *2*, consider buying an established manufacturing business.

If your answer to item 28 is *4*, consider buying a retail or service delivery business.

If your answer to item 29 is *4*, consider buying a larger, well-established business. If your answer to item 29 is *1*, you will need to develop this skill before buying a business.

If your answer to item 30 is *1* or *2*, you will need to buy a business with an established sales force or hire a skilled salesperson for your business.

CHAPTER 2

What's Your Line?

What Type of Businesses to Go into; and Where

Types of Businesses

WHAT COLOR IS YOUR PARACHUTE? BY RICHARD NELSON BOLLES, has by now guided a generation of unhappy employees into figuring out what kind of work they were meant to do. For disaffected employees who've decided to stop working for someone else and become entrepreneurs, I'd change the metaphor from parachutes to restaurants: Picture yourself at a Greek diner. Look over the whole menu before you choose your meal. Narrow your choice to one food category—say meat, poultry, fish, or pasta—and then order from that section of the menu.

There are basically four business menu categories: retail, service, manufacturing, and wholesaling/distribution. There's also a hybrid, franchising, that we'll discuss at the end of this chapter.

If at all possible, I suggest you avoid researching businesses from more than one category. Let's say you were interested in buying a children's clothing store but weren't sure. You could collect mountains of material to review on a multitude of different kinds of businesses. You could contact a dozen business brokers; speak with friends, relatives, your attorney, your accountant; and scour newspapers and trade magazines. If, after spending all this time and doing all this research, you decide that the *only* thing you want to do is own a children's clothing store (a retail business), you'll have wasted a lot of time and energy. So I recommend you decide on the type of business you want before you start your search. (You will see, in the next chapter, that the work experience you already have will usually determine which type of business you choose.)

Retail Businesses

Retailing is the purchase of merchandise from manufacturers or wholesalers for sale directly to consumers for their personal use, not for resale. Examples include hardware stores, sporting goods stores, and women's clothing stores. However, many service businesses have some retailing elements: For example, most hair salons sell hair care products, and many shoe repair shops sell shoe-related products like polish, laces, and socks. The term *service retailer* is now used to cover the growing number of businesses that sell products related to the services they offer. When we use the term *retail* in this chapter, the advice given applies to the service retailer as well.

RETAILING'S ADVANTAGES

Despite its volatility, retailing remains an extraordinarily popular choice for both would-be and established entrepreneurs. Here's why:

1. *Monetary return.* For one thing, despite the risks and competition, there's still a lot of money to be made in retailing. To illustrate: Virtually all of my clients who own retail concerns complain about business. Yet when I try to reach them on Fridays, they've already gone to their vacation homes for the

weekend. While they often lament that "times are tough," somehow business is good enough for them to afford a nice first home and a second one for weekends and holidays. To be sure, these people work hard for their money, however, at the end of the day many of them have quite a bit to show for it!

2. *Lender friendliness.* Banks and other traditional sources of capital are very comfortable lending to retail businesses. In part this is because banks understand the business of retailing and have become quite good at predicting success and failure.

3. *Built-in vehicles for financing.* Hand in hand with the banking industry's comfort level with retailing is the fact that these businesses have assets that can be pledged as collateral for loans (inventory and accounts receivable, to name two).

RETAILING'S DISADVANTAGES

1. *Markets are very volatile.* Buying habits of consumers can change dramatically as trends come and go. Fashions, designs, and business niches change very quickly. Also, technological changes can have a great effect on what, and how, people buy.

2. *Locations change.* As I'll discuss shortly, most retail establishments live and die on the strength of their business location. Unfortunately, neighborhoods change. Thriving locations can become stagnant. If you buy a business in an area that loses its appeal to customers, there's a good chance your business will not succeed.

3. *You're bound to work long hours.* Retail businesses generally require a long working day: Evenings, weekends, and holidays are the times when retailers often do most of their business (because the buyers are not at work). Would-be retailers must be prepared to make this kind of time commitment.

4. *The competition can be maddening.* Many mom-and-pop establishments have given way to large chain stores, and local

neighborhood stores such as drug and pharmacy stores and home- and office-supply stores have been hurt by the advent of "super malls" and so-called "big box" stores, like Staples (for office supplies) and Home Depot (for home improvement merchandise).

RETAIL LOCATIONS

The three most important factors contributing to the value of a house, experts say, are "location, location, and location." Most retailers would agree that the famous mantra applies to success in retailing as well. (Location is less vital only when the business offers a unique product or service with little accessible competition.) Here are some tips on thinking about location for those who are considering a traditional retail business:

1. *Downtown business districts.* Most small retail ventures choose to locate in a central or downtown business district because it contains a large concentration of potential customers. You'll pay for this feature, so make sure the district is thriving.

   - Remember that business districts aren't particularly attractive for some customers and businesses. Difficulty in parking and overcrowding may keep some customers away. And those who work in a downtown district may not frequent a gardening shop simply because they don't have houses with gardens.
   - Success is very site specific. One side of the street, for instance, may be more desirable than the other.
   - Be sure to check who your neighbors will be. (If you sell children's clothing, you won't want to be next door to a tavern.)

2. *Regional shopping malls.* These centers offer locations with a population density up to several hundred thousand. Also, they

often house major department stores that serve as magnets, attracting large numbers of customers to the center. Rent and overhead tend to be high—too high for small businesses with low to medium sales volume.

3. *Neighborhood strip centers.* These shopping centers are usually located on busy thoroughfares and anchored by either a supermarket or drugstore. They are excellent locations for businesses that sell convenience products. They are generally the least expensive location for a small retail business.

4. *Stand-alone buildings.* These offer excellent access, relatively low rent, spaciousness, and the potential for expansion. But, unless the products the business sells are necessities or are otherwise so unique that customers will make a specific trip for them, stand-alone buildings may not attract enough traffic.

OTHER TIPS

- A good commercial lease can make a retail business; a bad lease can break one. So don't consider buying a particular retail business unless you've analyzed its lease. How long does it last? Is the owner paying a market rent? Is the lease assignable (that is, can the owner turn it over to you), and if you decided to get out of the business, could you sell the lease to someone else? Can it be renewed? (For a more detailed discussion of commercial leases, see Appendix B.)
- Make sure to check the visibility of the store's sign. If no one can see the sign, the store won't get traffic regardless of how concentrated the population is. Check the lease to see what restrictions you'd be under if you wanted to use a bigger sign or move an existing sign to a different place.
- Is there sufficient parking? If not, people will go elsewhere.
- Corner locations are desirable; they draw traffic from both cross streets, thereby doubling walk-in trade.

- Locations near subway and bus stops offer an increased chance for walk-in customers.

WARNING: <u>CLOSEST TO HOME IS NOT ALWAYS BEST</u>

Many first-time business buyers make the mistake of choosing a venture because it is located near their home. Often, the buyer would never have chosen that particular business but for the proximity of its location. This is a cardinal sin in business. Base your selection of a business and a location on sound market and customer analysis, not on personal comfort and convenience.

A final note about the retail business: Don't enter it unless you're a "people person." The personal element—your ability to make people trust and like you—is all important. It's critical that you be honest with yourself here. If you don't have the inclination or aptitude for dealing with customers, suppliers, and employees, retailing is not for you.

Service Businesses

The service business environment has never been better. While the number of traditional service businesses like retailers, restaurants, and hair salons is likely to remain relatively constant, other sectors are mushrooming and probably will continue to do so. The promising fields include telecommunication, technology (including computers), health care, education, travel, and professional services (including law, accounting, and insurance).

A service cannot be seen, touched, weighed, tasted, or smelled in the same way as can a garment manufactured for sale in a department store. Because service businesses' products are typically in the nature of advice and consultation and, therefore, cannot be handled and compared, customers must judge them by a series of perceptions rather than by tangible evidence. And because a service business's distinguishing characteristic is the close personal relationship between the customer and the service provider, customers' perceptions are sometimes superficial (like the provider's appearance). Other benchmarks include the provider's educational background, experience in the field, and who, if anyone, recommended the provider. The selling and marketing efforts of the service business concentrate on the benefits the customer will get from the service as performed by a particular person, rather than on the service itself. Only in a relatively few businesses (possibly, travel agents, insurance salespersons, and real-estate brokers), can the service performed be separated from the owner of the business. Therefore, the service business's reputation and image are the paramount factors that determine its success.

Because the value of the service to the customer depends directly on the quality of the personal relationship between the customer and the provider, you must pay close attention to the nature of that relationship in the business you target. What's more, this evaluation will have an impact on the value you place on the business. The venture may be more likely to flourish—or less likely to succeed—when you are running it than in the hands of the current owner. You must make a calculation about that before you decide what you're willing to pay for the business (see Chapter 9 for more on valuation).

A SERVICE BUSINESS'S ADVANTAGES

1. *The buck stops with you.* That, however, means you have independence; you can control the quality of your work life. People who have gone into a service business for themselves invariably extol the virtues of independence and the quality of life they've attained. While it can be difficult to manage the responsibility of a small service business (assuming you're

the owner and provider), the personal freedom you'll have is hard to match. There'll be long hours, to be sure, but they'll be of your making. And, because you're calling the shots, in most instances long hours can be predicted and planned. More and more people say that "quality of life" is the top priority in their careers. For most people, quality of life means independence (of business thought) and control (of business environment).

2. *The compensation.* Some people may tell you your earning potential is limited. However, I believe that, for the service provider, the sky is the limit. You'll have the flexibility to add or eliminate a service (keeping what's most profitable) or hiring more workers to provide the services, leveraging *their* time to increase *your* bottom line.

A SERVICE BUSINESS'S DISADVANTAGES

Ironically, the two main advantages of the service business also made their way onto the list of disadvantages.

1. *In a small business where you are the "product," the buck stops with you.* While some people thrive on this type of independence and control, to others it can become quite overwhelming.

2. *The compensation.* If you work for yourself, and by yourself some people argue, the business's earning potential is limited by the number of hours you work.

3. *Difficulty in raising capital.* While service business owners can leverage the time of other workers, they normally can't leverage the "products" the business offers. Unlike retailers, manufacturers, or wholesalers, service businesses rarely have hard assets to use as collateral for loans. Therefore, lenders tend to require service providers to put up personal assets (homes, etc.) as collateral for business loans.

SERVICE LOCATIONS

How is the business carried out, and how does the customer choose it? If it's one to which customers come, like a photo lab or dry cleaner, the business needs to be in a location with sufficient traffic and good access and visibility. If, on the other hand, the business goes to the customer, like a contractor, plumber, or window cleaner, you need not be concerned with those things.

After you've narrowed your focus to a particular service business, you'll need to conduct a specific site analysis. Make sure you look at the following factors:

1. *Examine the physical plant.* For land with improvements, investigate the suitability of building placement and design, frontage, access (including parking), and exposure (visibility). For vacant land, check the adequacy of the site itself (for example, confirm the availability of necessary utilities with the local planning department) as well as its size.

2. *Zoning and use restrictions.* Be sure the type of business is in conformity with local and municipal land use and zoning laws.

3. *Community and support services.* Check the availability of police and fire protection as well as the adequacy of street lighting and utilities such as water and waste disposal. To evaluate physical conditions like land and buildings, you should consult with an architect or engineer. For help in analyzing legal and financial aspects of the property, you'll need to enlist the services of a lawyer and an accountant. (See Chapter 5 for more details on how to assemble your team of professionals.)

Manufacturing Businesses

The word *manufacturing* often conjures up the image of large factories with heavy machinery and hundreds of workers. In fact, though, manufacturing businesses run the gamut from a few employees making furniture in the owner's garage to huge automobile companies that produce cars and trucks in factories like the kind people generally imagine.

Manufacturers make products to sell to retailers or distributors. But many also "sell" the products they manufacture (like a restaurant that prepares ready-made meals for sale) or provide a service related to those products (like a jewelry maker who provides repair services).

Three factors—that may or may not appeal to you—are typical in a manufacturing business. For one thing, manufacturers usually have little contact with the consumers of their product. For another, productivity is easily measured. (The number of automobiles put out by a plant can be counted; in a service business, it is the skill and knowledge applied by the provider that is the "labor" itself.) And, finally, quality standards are easier to measure in manufacturing operations (in a service business, the level of quality is a matter of subjective judgment).

Small manufacturing businesses face many of the same problems that large firms face, such as inventory and quality control, personnel training, and equipment and site selection. If you plan to acquire a manufacturing business, you'll probably be dealing with issues more complex than those encountered in selling merchandise or providing a service.

Manufacturing businesses can be divided into three types:

- Job shops involve short production runs where the job may be unique and production setups change constantly.
- Repetitive manufacturing—what we typically think of as mass production—produces standardized products that are made over and over again.
- Batch manufacturing is something of a hybrid of the first two types. Typically, the products produced will relate to each other and use similar production processes, but there will be

more variety than in repetitive manufacturing's assembly line operation.

MANUFACTURING'S ADVANTAGES

1. ***Profitability.*** If the business has good logistic systems in place (for plant, labor, transportation, etc.), manufacturing can be more profitable and efficient these days than ever before.
2. ***Technology.*** Manufacturing businesses are taking steps (as are wholesalers and retailers) to keep inventory levels down. Commercial buying (for wholesale or retail distribution) as well as home shopping and consumer buying on the Internet are becoming increasingly popular. The need to warehouse inventory on a long-term basis is disappearing. This shrinking of the need to maintain large factories and warehousing centers has lowered dramatically the size of the investment needed to get into manufacturing.
3. ***Lender friendliness.*** Like wholesale and retail businesses, manufacturing typically provides greater financing options because there are hard assets that can be pledged as collateral for a business loan.

MANUFACTURING'S DISADVANTAGES

1. ***Volatility.*** Businesses are becoming more and more specialized. As products and markets shift, so, too, can the viability of manufacturing equipment, facilities, and processes. Also, as with retail businesses, products can become obsolete and markets for them can disappear.
2. ***Reliance on labor.*** Traditionally, manufacturing businesses have always relied heavily on the availability of cheap labor. In fact, we've already seen an increased shift to off-site production in remote areas where cheap labor exists. But this can be

risky: Businesses using traditional sources of cheap labor—workers in less developed countries—may be castigated for sweatshop conditions in those factories; in addition, these days Americans are being urged to "buy American."

3. *Environmental concerns.* The public is showing a growing sensitivity to the effect of manufacturing on our environment. Increased regulation of manufacturing practices has been creating roadblocks for many established manufacturers.

MANUFACTURING LOCATIONS

The primary concerns for manufacturers are the amount of space; access to markets and raw materials; proximity to labor supply; zoning restrictions; adequacy and availability of utilities; and reasonableness of local property tax assessment policies, including the availability of property tax relief.

In evaluating a manufacturing site, look for ease of access to its markets and to the raw materials it needs. If the business deals in heavy merchandise or uses large materials (such as lumber), you'll want easy access to a railroad or road, and the plant facility should have a loading dock. If, on the other hand, the business engages in light manufacturing such as jewelry, sunglasses, or cups, all of which can be shipped by common carrier, the facility need not be quite so elaborate.

TIP: EVALUATING PROFITABILITY

To evaluate the potential profitability of a manufacturing business you must examine how the business acquires materials, how its labor force performs, where that labor force is located, and how the business maintains quality control over the products it manufactures.

Wholesaling/Distribution Businesses

Basically, wholesalers, who also are often referred to as *distributors*, act as intermediaries between manufacturers and retailers. They purchase products from manufacturers, mark up the prices, and then sell and deliver the products to retailers. They are essentially the marketing arm for manufacturers.

WHOLESALING'S ADVANTAGES AND DISADVANTAGES

Wholesaling and manufacturing businesses share many of the same concerns in terms of volatility, reliance on labor, and changing views toward the global environment, so I won't list them all again here. But wholesaling is a "clean" industry: You don't produce the goods yourself and are not responsible for their sale to the end user, that is, the consumer. Some people consider this an advantage because you can change the product or customer you deal with easily, with no inventory and no machinery to worry about.

WHOLESALE LOCATIONS

Like manufacturers, most wholesaling businesses need to be concerned with the physical plant facility as well as accessibility to markets and labor. Competition and transportation are the primary factors to analyze in determining the appropriateness of the wholesaler's choice of location. The wholesaling facility must have easy access to transportation because shipment of goods is the main mission of the business. Other aspects of the site, such as appearance, depend on whether or not customers will be coming to the site to buy the goods. If customers come to the location, it will pay to have an effective selling area and certain amenities.

The Hybrid: Franchising

Franchising is an arrangement in which a franchisor—typically a large organization that has developed a product or service—gives a franchisee—typically an independent entrepreneur—the right to conduct a particular business using the franchisor's name, trademarks, products, procedures, marketing plans, promotional materials, and advertising.

For people who are reluctant to start a business from scratch (for financial or emotional reasons or because of a lack of experience) and for those who feel that buying an existing business is like buying a used car, franchising can be the happy medium. Advocates boast that franchises offer first-time buyers the excitement of starting one's own business while reducing the trial-and-error process and, thereby, the risk.

FRANCHISING'S ADVANTAGES

The franchising industry's success continues to astound business experts. According to figures from the International Franchise Association, by 1992 there were 558,000 franchised businesses in the United States, generating $803 billion in sales, and the numbers increase each year. Consider these advantages:

1. *The likelihood that you'll succeed.* If you're dealing with a legitimate franchisor, this is the least risky way to go into business for yourself. Essentially, when you buy a franchise, you are buying someone else's established formula for success. While buying someone else's formula has drawbacks (which we'll discuss), it is also franchising's most significant advantage. A franchise is four times more likely to succeed than a business started from scratch and twice as likely to succeed as a business purchased from someone else. You'll get a proven product, proven marketing methods, and a customer base. In short, franchising dramatically reduces the risk of failure. Statistics show that the failure rate for franchises in the first year of operation is less than 5 percent, while nearly 40 percent of non-franchised start-ups fail during that time. This kind of track record should lead you to give at least some consideration to becoming a franchisee.

2. *A structured environment.* If you view a structured environment as a loss of control, you see it as a negative. However, many people need or want the structured environment, including the standard operating procedures that franchising offers.

3. *Training, management assistance, advertising support, and inventory and supply sourcing.* As a franchisee, you may get the benefit of technical support from the franchisor, in terms of training and assistance, and even may have the opportunity to use the purchasing power of the franchisor to buy supplies and inventory at favorable prices. Other benefits can include cooperative advertising (in which the franchisor subsidizes a portion of your advertising and promotional activities), assistance with appropriate site selection, established systems for accounting and record keeping, and assistance in preparing financing projections to obtain financing.

FRANCHISING'S DISADVANTAGES

1. *Lack of freedom and control.* If one of the primary reasons you're going into business is to "be your own boss," you may not be cut out to be a franchisee. For even on your own premises you'll be a foot soldier, not a general. Franchisors have the attitude, often rightly, that they know best. What they're selling you is their knowledge, expertise, and experience. Consequently, virtually all of the significant decisions to be made—such as how your business looks, what products you sell, how you advertise, what you charge, where you buy supplies, what hours you're open, even what your employees wear—will not be made by you. For many would-be entrepreneurs, this loss of control would be too painful.

2. *Sharing the wealth.* If you choose to become a franchisee, not only will your control over your business be limited, but you'll

need to share quite a bit of the income you make with "big brother." Franchisees typically pay at least two major fees for the privilege of conducting business under the franchisor's name. The first is the initial franchise fee, a one-time fee paid up front by the franchisee for the right to open and operate a business using the franchisor's business ideas and products. The initial fee can run from a few thousand dollars to several hundred thousand dollars.

The second major fee is a continuous operational fee, the most common of which is called a royalty. The royalty fee is generally a percentage of the gross revenues earned by the franchisee. It can be a flat percentage (typically between 2 and 6 percent of sales) or fluctuate depending on the level of sales volume. The other significant operational expense has to do with the lease for the location. Often franchisees are required to sign leases for locations before the franchise deal is consummated. Given the need for site location analysis, lease negotiation, first month's rent, and security deposit, up-front costs easily can skyrocket.

Other franchise-related fees may be more hidden. For example, the franchisee may be forced to purchase all his goods, inventory, and supplies from the franchisor, possibly at inflated prices.

3. *The risk of dealing with an unscrupulous franchisor.* In the 1960s, when franchising was starting to become popular, many franchise operations were, to say the least, shaky. Today, with a few notable exceptions, franchising is a reasonably ethical industry. It's now partly regulated by the federal government, and it has what amounts to a self-policing trade association, the International Franchise Association. The IFA is a nonprofit trade association of more than 550 franchisors that sponsors legal and government affairs symposiums, franchise management workshops, and trade shows. Franchisors are

required to file disclosure statements with the Federal Trade Commission (authorized by the U.S. Congress to regulate the franchise business). These statements contain a wealth of information, including the backgrounds of the franchisor's officers, the franchisor's financial condition, lawsuits filed against the franchisor, and the names and addresses of the company's other franchisees (see "Uniform Franchise Offering Circular"). Yet, despite these safeguards, you'll need to do some legwork yourself before you become a franchisee.

Check out the franchisor thoroughly. To do this, get the names and locations of several franchisees and call—or, better yet, visit—each one. It's best to seek out the owners yourself, as the franchisor will be inclined to steer you toward satisfied franchisees. When you visit these franchisees, ask the owners what they like and what they don't like about franchising in general and dealing with the franchisor in particular. Also, call your state attorney general's office and your city or state's Better Business Bureau or department of consumer affairs to see if anyone has filed a negative report on the franchisor. Obtain a report from Dun & Bradstreet about the franchisor. Have your accountant review the last few years of the franchisor's annual report. You also can contact the Federal Trade Commission in Washington, D.C.; call up references to the franchisor on the Nexis database, if you have access to it; and visit your local library to look up the franchisor in *The Wall Street Journal, New York Times,* and *Entrepreneur* and *Inc.* magazine indexes. All of these business publications include regular features on franchising.

Remember, if you've checked these sources and find nothing, it doesn't mean you have nothing to worry about. It just means that no complaints have been recorded. In the end, your own ability to research and ask the right questions will be the key factors in determining whether to invest your time, energy, and money in a franchised operation (see Appendix C for a franchise evaluation checklist you can use as a guideline).

UNIFORM FRANCHISE OFFERING CIRCULAR

The Uniform Franchise Offering Circular, or UFOC, is a comprehensive disclosure document designed to reveal certain key information concerning the franchise investment. By law, all franchisors must provide one to the prospective buyer in person at their first meeting or at least ten business days before the buyer signs a contract or pays a fee, whichever is earlier.

If you are considering a franchise, the UFOC is required reading. It contains a detailed description of the franchise offering, including a copy of the franchise agreement (e.g., the purchase agreement) and three years of audited financial statements. You'll also get to examine the business backgrounds of the people running the franchise and learn whether the franchise or its management have been involved in any litigation or bankruptcy or have violated any securities laws in the past ten years.

TIP: GET HELP TO REVIEW THE UFOC

Even though the law requires that all UFOCs must be written in "plain English," they are complex documents. Be sure to have your professionals (lawyer and accountant) review the UFOC as well. It is especially important that you review the financial statements with your accountant to determine whether the franchise company is on solid footing.

ADDITIONAL SOURCES OF INFORMATION ON FRANCHISING

U.S. Small Business Administration
409 Third Street, S.W.
Washington, D.C. 20416
SBA Answer Desk: 1-800-8-ASK-SBA
WWW Home Page: http://www.sbaonline.sba.gov.

International Franchise Association
1350 New York Avenue, N.W.
Washington, D.C. 20005
(202) 628-8000

Federal Trade Commission
6th Street & Pennsylvania Avenue, N.W.
Washington, D.C. 20580
(202) 326-2222

Franchise Opportunities Handbook
(Park Avenue Publications; contains more than 1,500 franchise listings;
available in bookstores or by contacting JIST Works, Inc.)
720 North Park Avenue
Indianapolis, IN 46202-3431
(317) 264-3720

Council of Better Business Bureaus, Inc.
1515 Wilson Boulevard
Arlington, VA 22209
(703) 276-0100

American Franchise Association
53 West Jackson Boulevard
Chicago, IL 60604
(800) 334-4232

American Association of Franchisees and Dealers
P.O. Box 81887
San Diego, CA 92138-1887
(619) 235-2556

KEEP AN OPEN MIND AND YOUR EYE ON THE BALL

Sometimes, it can help to have an open mind. Robert Chalfin is a business consultant based in Philadelphia. Chalfin, who teaches a course on buying businesses at the University of Pennsylvania's Wharton School of Business, believes that most people look for a business without having decided on a particular industry or category.

"It's very rare that I have someone come to me and say 'I want to buy a business and it's got to be retail or wholesale or manufacturing'," says Chalfin. Still, he says, "there are certain *characteristics* of a particular business they want, but most are pretty open and willing to listen to any number of ideas."

And while Chalfin acknowledges that certain areas of the country are "hotter" than others (as we'll soon see), he believes that most entrepreneurs who are forced to make decisions concerning geography, base them on lifestyle choices, not on which industry is hot in which area.

As Chalfin rightly points out, some would-be entrepreneurs are flexible and open to working in a variety of industries. However, even these open-minded entrepreneurs should pay attention both to regional dynamics and to whether the industries they're considering contain the characteristics that will enable them to have the lifestyle they want.

Regional Dynamics: Where Should Your Business Be?

In what parts of the country are small businesses most likely to thrive? Entrepreneurs starting or purchasing businesses need to pay attention to regional dynamics—that is, they need to assess the impact of demographics, economic trends, and the political climate on the fortunes of small businesses in various parts of the country.

Suppose you'd like to become the proprietor of a business that sells home furniture and housewares. And say you're willing (or you'd like) to move to a new city or state to find the right one. The last thing you'd want to do is uproot yourself and your family to buy a business in an area where the economy is stagnant, the population is decreasing, and the political attitude toward small business is less than attractive.

And, if you don't want to move, you need to give thorough consideration to the regional dynamics that impact businesses in the area where you live. If you don't normally pay attention to such matters as population trends, the availability of labor, the state of your area's economy, and the political attitude toward small business, you are ignoring factors that may lead to the failure of your new enterprise. Even if the venture you want to buy has a proven track record, it is possible that the market for its products or services may soon dry up. If you consider the demographics and economics of your region as well as its political attitude toward small business, you may discover that it would be foolish to buy the venture you're considering. That is something eminently worth finding out.

The Best Small Business Environments

For the past four years, *Entrepreneur* magazine, in conjunction with Dun & Bradstreet Information Services, has conducted a survey leading to a ranking of the nation's cities that offer the most favorable environment for small business. In the survey, cities are evaluated based on five categories: risk (based on documented success rates), business performance, economic growth, quality of life, and the state's attitude toward small business. The most recent survey appeared in the October 1997 issue of *Entrepreneur*. (For a service charge, you can obtain a copy of the October 1997 issue by writing to Entrepreneur Group, Attn: Back Issues, Morris Avenue, P.O. Box 19787, Irvine, CA 92614-6234.)

According to *Entrepreneur*, in 1997 the top cities in the West for small business included Portland, Oregon; Vancouver, Washington; Seattle, Bellevue, Everett, and Tacoma, Washington; and San Jose, San Francisco, and Sacramento, California. Top Rocky Mountain cities included Denver, Colorado; Las Vegas, Nevada; Salt Lake City and Ogden, Utah; and Phoenix and Mesa, Arizona. Top cities in the Southeast included Raleigh, Durham, Greensboro, Winston-Salem, High Point, and Charlotte, North Carolina; Atlanta, Georgia; Gastonia and Rock Hill, South Carolina; and Memphis and Nashville, Tennessee. Top Northeastern cities included Pittsburgh, Pennsylvania; Buffalo, Niagara Falls, and Rochester, New York; Lawrence, Boston, Lowell, and Worcester, Massachusetts; Brockton, New Hampshire; and Hartford, Connecticut. Top Southwestern cities included Ft. Worth and Arlington, Texas. Top Midwest cities included St. Louis, Missouri; Minneapolis and St. Paul, Minnesota; Kansas City, Missouri; Detroit, Michigan; and Milwaukee and Waukesha, Wisconsin.

What the rankings tell us (not surprisingly) is that economic growth and population growth are good for small business. As populations increase in certain areas, such as the Northeastern and Rocky Mountain regions, so does the need for service-based businesses, restaurants, and retail stores to accommodate the influx of people. Most of the cities listed in the survey also have additional features that impact positively on economic growth and quality of life. They include an availability of labor, a competitive banking climate, and a favorable tax structure. Perhaps the most significant indicator of a city's economy is the attitude of state and city government toward small business. By "attitude" I mean whether or not the state and city government promote collaboration between the public and private sector. For example, according to *Entrepreneur*, Indianapolis's Value Added Committee, composed of government and corporate and small business advocates, "provides entrepreneurs with everything from mentoring and troubleshooting to management assistance and networking opportunities."

Targeting a Business Location

After you've focused your attention on a particular business in a specific locale, you can track business trends by analyzing general market factors within that area: Who buys, as well as why, what, how, where, and when they buy. Then you'll need to examine the specific market for the business's products or services. This involves a process known as *market segmentation*, the method by which small businesses determine on which segment of a population to concentrate their marketing efforts. Most small businesses segment their market on the basis of such demographic variables as age, income, sex, and race. Then they look for a geographic concentration of consumers with the desired characteristics.

There is a plethora of information and data available for this type of research. On the government side, start with the U.S. Department of Census, the Bureau of Labor Statistics, the U.S. Department of Commerce, as well as the various state's Economic Development Authorities. As we will discuss later in this book, the

WARNING: DO YOUR OWN MARKET ANALYSIS

Do not rely on the business owner's market analysis. She will have a lot invested in the market strategies used for the business and will have a natural inclination to sell you on those strategies. Remember, even the owner's methods may be faulty. Before making a decision on buying a business, you need to perform your own analysis of trends and market demographics in the locale you're considering.

Small Business Administration, through its district offices and Small Business Development Centers, also can be a tremendous resource for market analysis. For a more detailed discussion of research sources and techniques, refer to Chapter 3.

So Far, So Good

You've decided to become an entrepreneur the prudent way—by buying an established business. You've reflected on the advantages and disadvantages of the five kinds of businesses: retail, service, manufacturing, wholesaling, and franchising. You've pondered the rewards of each business category in terms of personal freedom, stress, financial risk, contact with the public, and earning potential. You're willing to spend a great deal of time researching your potential field and, after that, investigating the particular business you think you want to buy.

But suppose you don't know what you really want to do. Suppose, after all this pondering, you're not strongly attracted to any kind of business. Does that mean you're not cut out to be an entrepreneur?

CHAPTER 3

Passion Is Not the Point

Pursuing and Satisfying Personal Goals Is

No doubt you're reading this book because you want to be an entrepreneur. But what if you can't figure out what field is right for you? Perhaps you're worried you don't have the kind of zeal it takes to buy and run a business because you can't think of any field that doesn't leave you feeling lukewarm.

Stop worrying. Too many people who want to work for themselves have the idea that they've got to find a business for which they feel passion. I was one of them! But now that I've been my own boss for more than eight years, I realize that simply becoming an entrepreneur will generate passion for your business. If you can find a business in a field in which you are knowledgeable (or in which you can educate yourself) *and* you're reasonably competent in that field and willing to work hard *and* the work affords you a good quality of life and an adequate income stream, you'll feel that passion. The business is yours. You're working for *you*. You'll have the chance to do what no one who works for someone else can— balance your business and personal life as you see fit. You've got no one to answer to but yourself.

You will probably turn out to be the meanest boss you ever had. You'll eat, think, and dream about your business. If that's not passion, what is? If you're among the minority of people who find a business they were "born for," a business that meets their financial needs and is located in a geographic area they like, consider yourself one of the luckiest people in the world. I can tell you from my experience, however, that if you wait around to find a business you'll love, your search is likely to be a lesson in frustration. So don't worry if you're not in love with a particular business. Love isn't nearly as important as living where you and your family will be comfortable and selecting a business in which you have the experience, the skills, the education, and the training necessary to guarantee success.

Remember, the business need only generate a sufficient stream of income to enable you to pursue personal goals.

Go with What You Know

I urge you to focus your search plan on businesses with which you have experience and training. Remember: Unlike the entrepreneur who starts a business from scratch, you won't have a chance to learn on the job; you'll need to step right in and run the business on day one. If you don't have experience in the field you're considering, how intelligently can you evaluate the business you want to buy? You don't have to be an expert in the field you're entering, but you shouldn't be a complete novice. If you haven't worked in a particular industry (which is the best policy), do not consider entering it unless you have friends or relatives in the field who can give you tutorials.

You are likely to find you have more credibility (with people selling a business as well as their vendors and suppliers, sources of finance, and, ultimately, customers) and a greater feeling of security if you concentrate on an industry where you have experience or knowledge. If I can't persuade you to buy a business in an industry in which you have experience, I implore you to find out all you can about the industry before you begin your search for a business to buy. For tips on how to educate yourself and/or acquire background and training, see Chapter 1.

Researching the Field You've Chosen

Industries are always in the process of going up or going down. Even those that appear to have flattened out are typically pausing for advance or decline, so pay attention to the trend in the industry you're considering. If it hasn't been on the way up for at least three to five years, I advise you to pick some other field. This is merely the first of many warning signs that will flash before you finally find the business you should buy. Whenever you get a warning sign, be prepared to walk away—unless you've a solid strategy for overcoming the problem. Somewhere there is a business that really *is* right for you, and you'll need sufficient patience—and optimism—to wait until you find it.

Naturally, it's easier to learn about an established industry's procedures, techniques, and margins than it is to research a developing field. When you investigate an established industry, you can find out what the standard ratios and operating norms are for businesses. Also, you'll be able to get information on how much typically is spent on advertising, marketing, and sales commissions as well as whether sales usually are made directly, through a company's sales force, or through independent sales representatives. I'd suggest choosing an industry that is at least ten to fifteen years old rather than a new or unproven industry.

Another important advantage to selecting an established industry has to do with your ability to sell your business when you're ready to move on. Just as someone who is in the market for a new home must give careful thought to a home's resale value, someone preparing to buy a business must consider what it will bring when it's sold. If you buy a business in an industry that has no proven track record, there may be no buyers when you decide its time to sell. The need for an exit strategy makes it crucial that you choose an established industry.

Here's some advice on how to research an industry for viability, stability, and growth:

1. *Contact a trade association.* Trade associations—a terrific source of information—often have files of extensive data on market conditions, demographics, and technical issues. Many associations do elaborate surveys and statistical studies of their industry. Get in touch with senior executives at an appropriate trade association and ask them what's happening in the industry. They can tell you much about the field you've chosen. You can find the trade association that covers your field by looking through the *Directory of Associations,* available in any public library.

2. *Scan the trade journals ("trades").* You'll be amazed at how much you can learn about a particular industry by reading the many publications that exist in your field of interest. Study the trades carefully. Go back at least three years to track trends. Be sure to look for answers to the following questions: Is the industry growing? What are the key industry issues? How has the industry changed over the past three to five years? What impact has technology and global competition had on the industry? (For example, the use of computers to track and control inventory, as well as to facilitate direct sales to customers, has enabled manufacturers and retailers to cut out many wholesalers and distributors.) What are the industry experts predicting for the industry over the next five years? What are the industry's problems? Can they be solved? How? From what you've read, do your interests and skills seem to fit the requirements of work in this industry?

If you're not familiar with all of the trade journals and newsletters in the field you've selected, you can tap several resources: *The Encyclopedia of Business Sources* lists resources (by industry) such as associations and periodicals. *The Market Share Reporter* presents comparative business statistics on different industries. Both of these directories, published by Gale Research, (800) 877-4253, are good starting points for uncovering data about an industry. They, too, are available at most public business libraries.

3. ***Go to the library.*** Consult the Business Periodical Index (which you'll find in most libraries). This is an extremely valuable resource. It enables you to identify magazine articles relevant to your search. After you do so, it's a rather simple task to obtain a reprint from the magazine that published the article. (You may find the issue of the magazine you want on the World Wide Web.)

Don't be afraid to contact the author of any article that impresses you. I've written magazine articles on many subjects related to small business and personal finance and I've never turned someone away who has managed to track me down to discuss an article.

Other resources available at most public libraries include Ward's *Business Directory* and *Business Rates and Data*, where you'll find over 16,000 different trade journals listed, organized by industry. Also listed next to the name of each trade journal will be the names of people you can contact at the publication (the publisher, senior editor, etc.). Call them and pick their brains. Tell them you're interested in buying a business in the industry and that you're trying to learn everything you can about the field. Ask them for their opinions on general trends in the industry and see if they can refer you to other industry experts. Ask as many questions as you can. Prepare a list before calling. Ask the questions that struck you when you were reading the trade journals and newsletters.

4. ***Do some prospecting on the Internet.*** No doubt each of the trade associations you call for information on your chosen field has a Web site offering useful specifics you can browse through or download. So, when you call, ask for the Web address. Take advantage of federal government's Internet sites as well. For a comprehensive guide to all the Internet addresses you'll find helpful, see Bruce Maxwell's *How to Access the Federal Government on the Internet 1997* (Congressional Quarterly, 1996). Among the worthwhile sites it points you to is the University of Missouri–St. Louis Gopher site, which is chockful of government publications, including *Small Business Administration Industry Profiles* (trends and opportunities in four fields, including restaurants and advertising) and *U.S. Industrial Outlook,* "a 650-page book that analyzes more than 350 U.S. industries and predicts how they'll perform over the short term and through the 1990s."

5. ***Hire a researcher.*** You can always hire a researcher to do some of the legwork for you. Call the Association of Independent Information Professionals at (212) 779-1855. This organization can provide the names of consultants in your area who specialize in business research. You also might try the career counseling or research department at a local business school. Often, graduate students are available for research projects at very modest fees.

Finding a Seller

Now that you've narrowed your focus to a specific type of business in a specific geographic area, you'll need a strategy for targeting candidates for acquisition. Here's how to look:

1. ***Engage a business broker.*** Business brokers function much like real-estate agents, acting as intermediaries between buyers

and sellers of businesses. Like real-estate agents who keep multiple listings of houses, business brokers keep lists of businesses that are for sale. They will work on behalf of an owner interested in selling his company or on behalf of a buyer looking to acquire one. Some provide additional services, such as financial consulting and valuation, renting commercial space for their clients, aiding in the preparation of a business plan, and arranging financing.

Business brokers are often maligned because the field harbors some real duds. If you work with one of those, you'll waste a lot of time looking at businesses that can only be classified as dogs—or ones that simply don't fit your needs. The good news about brokers is that there are some gems out there if you're willing to make the effort to find them. Ask for referrals from your lawyer, accountant, or banker. If you're stuck, you also can check your newspaper and the Yellow Pages, but be sure to ask any brokers you've found this way for references and check them out with your local Better Business Bureau.

If you're looking for a business in your own industry, you probably won't need a business broker because you can use your own contacts. However, if you're changing industries, a broker can be quite useful.

For example, before he retired, my stepfather Harry bought two businesses—businesses he would not have found had he not gone through business brokers because they were outside his own industry. He was successful at both businesses primarily, I think, because after the brokers led him to these ventures he carefully investigated them himself.

Harry had more than twenty years of experience in the appliance business, so that's the field he considered first. However, he had been away from the appliance business for five years, and in that brief period the business had changed dramatically. Owners had formed buying groups that bought in bulk from manufacturers. This purchasing power enabled members of buying groups to buy merchandise for much less than nonmembers. When my stepfather wanted to get back into the business, the cost of becoming a member of the buying group was prohibitive for him. (The group required new members to post large sums of money in escrow to ensure payment to the manufacturers.) In addition, any member of the buying group could veto the admission of a new member. These two problems severely restricted an entrepreneur's entry into the appliance business. Thus, my stepfather was forced to look to a different industry.

Harry was willing to consider many different types of businesses. This made him a natural match for a business broker who had a multitude of candidates from which he could choose.

First, he bought a shirt-laundry business. Dry cleaners and retail stores sent clothes out to his factory. He found it through a business broker who was running ads in the local newspaper. This particular business wasn't advertised, but the broker showed him his "listing book," and Harry did the legwork from there. After a relatively short stint, Harry discovered that running a shirt-laundry plant was not his cup of tea and he sold the business. His next business was selling automotive parts to gas and service stations. Once again he found the business by hooking up with a business broker who was running ads in the classified section.

Harry was careful to spend a lot of time at each of the businesses, both to verify the owner's income quotes and to get a taste of what it would be like to operate that business. That is how he found out that both businesses were solid enough to be worth buying.

When Harry sold his businesses he did not use the services of a business broker. He didn't need to: In both instances he sold to people he had dealt with. One was a customer; the other was the son-in-law of an employee.

Most business brokers base their fee on the selling price; they'll charge anywhere from 5 to 15 percent of what you pay for the business. Be aware that even if the broker tells you the seller pays her commission, *you* are the one who is really paying it because the seller will factor the commission into his asking price. Whether you are asked to pay a percentage of the selling price or whether "the seller is paying the fee," brokers obviously have little incentive to help you, the buyer, acquire the business at the lowest possible price.

2. *Place your own ad.* I say the same thing to every client who wants help in buying a business: "The best business to buy is one that's not for sale." What do I mean by this? In the first place, the majority of sellers do not list their firms with brokers nor do they run classified ads. Selling a business is a delicate matter. Owners don't want their customers or suppliers (or key employees, for that matter) to know the business is for sale. If they get wind of a sale, customers may stop shopping at the store, suppliers may be wary of doing business with the firm, and employees may jump ship.

What is more, many business owners don't know how to go about selling; some don't even suspect there might be an interested buyer. Still others won't acknowledge, even to themselves, that it's time for them to move on. Selling may be in their best interest, but their attachment to the business they've nurtured keeps them in denial. When you're dealing with first-time sellers, you, the buyer, must make the first move. I recommend placing enticing advertisements in regional trade magazines or local papers likely to be read by owners of the kinds of businesses you're targeting.

Your ad must be designed to pique the interest of even the most timid business owner. It should offer the seller wonderful things like long-term financial support, the chance to retire, or employment for his children. The ad should be as specific as possible in terms of what you're looking for and what you're willing to offer. It should run at least once or twice a week for three weeks. Be sure to identify yourself in the ad as a principal, not a broker. You must, of course, include a way for people to contact you. You can maintain your anonymity by having respondents write to you in care of a box number at the newspaper, but that method may put off business owners who might call but won't take the time to write. Instead, I recommend using a direct approach—identifying yourself in the ad and providing a telephone number at which sellers can contact you. Here are some sample ads that are sure to attract attention:

QUALIFIED BUYER. Flexible financial arrangements. Owner to stay on as consultant if desired. Looking for men's clothing store in a major shopping center with a full line of suits, coats and casual wear with annual sales of $250,000 to $500,000. Phone Principal daytime (222) 555-5555.

LET ME HELP YOU RETIRE. I can structure a deal to guarantee you an income for life. If you own an established children's shoe store in a metropolitan area with annual sales of less than $750,000, call (987) 555-3210 in the P.M. I am not a broker.

RETIRE BUT KEEP YOUR INCOME. Bankable experienced buyer wants Greeting Card Store in neighborhood strip center with annual sales of between $150,000 and $300,000. I am placing this ad on my own behalf. Call (123) 555-7890

WANT TO SPEND WINTER PLAYING GOLF? Call me in confidence. Work part-time and sell me your home center and hardware store. We can work out financial terms to meet your needs. Revenues should be $500,000 to $1,000,000. Call principal (333) 555-5555.

I AM A SERIOUS BUYER looking for a landscape business in an affluent suburban area. I am financially secure. If you own a family business, I'm willing to transition you to retirement and keep your family employed. Call (456) 555-0987.

HONEST, HARD-WORKING PERSON wants to buy an established dry-cleaning business with solid customer base. I am interested in retaining you as a consultant and to
buy you out in two to three years. You continue to receive an income and benefits. I
am not a broker. Call (555) 555-7777.

3. **Scan the classifieds.** Most people begin their search by opening a newspaper to the "Business Opportunities" section of
the classifieds. Unfortunately, there are many flops advertised for sale by owners or brokers, and you can waste a
lot of research time before you discover you're looking at
a bad prospect.

If the ad lists a blind box for responses, send a letter simply
saying that you are interested in obtaining more information.
Normally, the seller would then contact you by phone or mail.

Don't answer an ad that's vague. For example, if it says
"retail store, high sales in prime location," you've been told
precious little. What does the business sell? What level of
sales constitutes "high?" What does "prime location" mean?
What price range is the seller asking? You shouldn't waste
your time calling or writing to the person placing this ad.

When you do find an ad that you'd like to answer, be prepared to ask some basic questions, such as: What exactly is the
business all about? How long has the business been in existence? How long has the seller owned it? Where, exactly, is it
located? How long is its lease? What are its annual sales?
What is the asking price?

In general, local newspapers are a good source of leads if
you want to buy a small business like a restaurant or hair
salon. National papers typically have listings for larger businesses. On Sundays, *The New York Times'* "Business
Opportunities" section of the classified ads lists businesses for
sale by owner or broker. On Thursdays, *The Wall Street Journal*
has a similar section. (There are regional editions for those
who want to focus on a particular area of the country.)

Although a relatively small percentage of buyers find their business this way, first-time buyers, in particular, stand to learn a lot by responding to these ads. And you never know—you could get lucky and find a diamond among the shards of glass.

4. *Prospect within your own company.* As Dorothy said in *The Wizard of Oz,* the next time you go looking for your heart's desire, "don't look any further than your own backyard." It's not unusual for a business to be sold to one of its key employees. Such a deal often makes great sense for both sides. The employee knows how the business is run and often has a friendly relationship with its customers, suppliers, and vendors. Furthermore, the employer gets the benefit of seeing his business go to his protégé. When an owner sells to a stranger, he sometimes feels he's abandoning the people with whom he's done business. What's more, when dealing with strangers, sellers can be especially wary of financing the transaction with deferred pay backs. So selling to a trusted hand can ease the emotional jolt for the seller and impel him to ease the financial jolt for the buyer by offering better financing terms than a bank.

While I was researching an article for a major national magazine, I interviewed a young woman whose story I enjoy telling to illustrate how easy it can be to buy your boss' business. Kimberly Hastings dreamed of owning her own firm. After graduating from New York's Fashion Institute of Technology, she worked for a small textile-design company owned by a husband-and-wife team. Having been in the business twenty years, the owners were tired of all the effort that goes into running a small company. Because no family members were interested in the business, they decided to sell. The first thing they did was offer the company to Hastings.

Hastings, just a year out of school, was eager, but reluctant to go it alone. She asked a fellow employee to become her partner. They struck a deal with the owners that required no cash outlay; instead, they paid the owners (their former bosses) a fixed monthly payment based on the company's revenue that enabled them take full ownership in four to five years. And the former owners remained on call as consultants.

Another example is Kate Saunders. For ten years, Kate worked as a hairdresser at a small unisex hair salon in Northern New York State. Kate was ambitious and loved working at the salon, but always had wanted to run her own establishment. She heard a rumor from one of her fellow workers that the owner of the salon was interested in reducing his time commitment to the business to explore other opportunities. Kate and her boss had always gotten along well, and one day just before closing time Kate decided to approach him with a proposition.

Kate told her boss that it had been a dream of hers to own a hair salon and she had heard that he might be interested in selling and, if so, she'd like him to consider selling to her. Because Kate had little capital to invest, she offered to pay for the business over a five-year period based on annual profits. The owner would stay on for a year or so to help with the transition.

Kate also had a plan for expanding the business. She would obtain a diet center franchise and convert the storage area in the basement into a diet center. She would renegotiate a longer lease and get the landlord to fix up the downstairs with an office and waiting room. The landlord would amortize the renovation cost (of "building-out" the space) over the term of the lease (with an interest factor). The landlord would do all the work so Kate wouldn't have to worry about the up-front cost. After Kate shared her ideas for expanding the business with the owner, he was convinced that Kate would succeed and he agreed to Kate's terms. The deal worked out well for Kate and her former boss. She got a business for no cash down and expanded it; her ex-boss phased-out his involvement and, over the course of the next five years, received a fair price for his business.

5. *Network at trade shows.* Trade associations and journals can not only provide vital information on the industry you're considering, they also may lead you to sellers. Trade shows or conferences give buyers an excellent opportunity to network. Attend these programs, mingle with industry leaders, and exchange business cards. You'll get the word out that you're in the market to buy a business. Even if the people you speak with do not know of an opportunity right now, they may learn of one in the future or be in a position to introduce you to someone else who could help.

In "Researching the Field You've Chosen," you've learned how to locate trade associations. Make a list of the appropriate groups and call their executive offices. Try to speak with the head of the association or at least someone who is a leading member, preferably in your area of the country. Tell your contact that you are interested in searching for available businesses in that industry and ask for their advice. They should be able to point you in several directions. At a minimum, they'll tell you what trade journals and other periodicals are available to assist you in your search.

6. *Take advantage of federal, state, and local small business programs.* These are usually thought of as resources for owners of start-up businesses; however, they assist prospective owners as well as proprietors of established small businesses. One particularly helpful program, Small Business Development Centers (SBDCs), provides management and technical advice to would-be and experienced entrepreneurs. Administered by the U.S. Small Business Administration (SBA), the program is a cooperative effort of the private sector, the educational community, and federal, state, and local governments. There are 57 SBDCs in the country, offering expertise at more than

900 service locations, most of them housed in colleges and universities (see Appendix A, "Source Directory").

Another SBA-sponsored program, SCORE (Service Corps of Retired Executives), matches volunteers with would-be entrepreneurs and small business owners who need competent advice. The 13,000 SCORE volunteers, whose collective experience spans the full range of American enterprise, share their management and technical expertise through 383 chapters and 400 other locations nationwide (see Appendix A).

Business Information Centers (BICs) can be an especially valuable resource for the fledgling entrepreneur. BICs (which also are administered by the SBA) offer free access to the latest in high-tech hardware, software, and telecommunications help as well as training and access to research tools. BIC counseling and training are provided by SCORE. There are approximately 30 BICs in service. For further information about these and other SBA programs, contact your local SBA office. To find the one nearest you, look in the telephone book under "U.S. Government" or call the SBA Answer Desk at (800) 8-ASK-SBA. To access SBA OnLine, an electronic bulletin board, go to its home page: http://www.sbaonline. sba.gov.

Your state or local Department of Economic Development can be another source worth tapping. This agency will have information on the various types of industries in your area, how well they've performed, and how to get in touch with them. You also can contact private business schools as well as your state university's business school and ask for a copy of the directory that lists faculty members. Call the appropriate faculty members and tell them you are searching for a business to buy. Because they have the knowledge and resources (that is, enthusiastic students) to conduct research projects, they may be willing to have their students do some research for you.

Lastly, your local chamber of commerce may be able to provide you with a list of contacts and possibly a list of businesses for sale in your community.

7. *Ask your banker.* Local bankers are an excellent source of leads to acquisition candidates. In addition to having close contact with local businesses, they may have made loans to ventures that are struggling or whose owners are searching for an exit. An experienced and trusted banker may be the first to know when a business might be available for sale—even before the owner has officially put it on the market. The banker also may know that a business owner is ill, wants to retire or relocate, or has just died.

Banks' trust departments can be another good source of business leads. These departments typically manage the liquidation of estates upon the death of a client. When a small business owner dies, his or her interest in the business is often placed in trust. (A business might go into trust because the decedent's family has neither the ability nor the interest to run it.) In this case, you may be able to purchase the business from the trust. In a case like this, you won't be dealing with the estate of the business owner but rather the trust officer at the bank or trust company. When you deal with the trust officer, always remember that he or she has a fiduciary responsibility to the decedent's estate. Therefore, even though he or she will be in a position to provide you with information concerning the business, his or her job is to obtain the highest price possible for the business.

8. *Ask a lawyer.* Lawyers can be an invaluable source of acquisition candidates and information. Many attorneys specialize in certain industries: They may know of businesses being sold for any number of reasons (e.g., divorce, bankruptcy, estate divestitures, burn-out, or retirement). I get anywhere from two to three calls a month from clients who want to sell or buy a business. They call me not only to tap my experience as a

lawyer and small business consultant, but to see if I might know of someone who might be interested in buying or selling. And often I do.

One such situation involved a client of mine named Bob Tillman. Bob's business sold roses that were imported daily from Ecuador. His store enjoyed a prime spot in New York City's well-traveled Grand Central Terminal and was literally packed with potential customers seven days a week.

Approximately three years ago, the Metropolitan Transit Authority (MTA, the City agency that operates Grand Central Terminal) began work on a vast renovation project. As a result, the MTA terminated the leases of virtually all small tenant operators in Grand Central Terminal to carry out construction. (Because the renovation had been in the planning stages for nearly 10 years, all leases given by the MTA in Grand Central Terminal had stipulated that the MTA had the right to take back space—including my client's space—for reconstruction purposes.)

Shortly after my client stopped doing business in Grand Central, I got a telephone call from him asking me if I knew of any business opportunities. He said he wasn't necessarily looking for another rose shop (it would be difficult to match the stellar location he had at Grand Central Terminal). Instead, he was interested in a storefront retail space in midtown Manhattan. Although I didn't know of anything at the time, I promised to keep my eyes open. A few days later during a conversation with a commercial real-estate broker who refers work to me, the broker mentioned space he thought was available just two blocks from Grand Central Terminal. I quickly called Bob and gave him the lead. It turned out to be a greeting card and gift shop. Bob approached the owner, who had spoken to a few real-estate brokers but hadn't listed the business for sale. The two worked out a deal for my client to buy the business (subject naturally to a due diligence review of the business operations and finances).

9. *Ask an accountant.* Be sure you don't overlook accountants as conduits to available businesses. These professionals are often the first people to know a company might be for sale. Ask your friends who own businesses what they think of their accountant (it's always best to be referred to a professional by someone you trust; see Chapter 5 for more on this).

The accountants you call may be reluctant to give you a list of acquisition targets for fear they'll lose a client. So assure the accountants you consult that you are merely trying to get the word out about your interest in buying a business. Tell them you are simply asking them to put out feelers on your behalf. It couldn't hurt to promise the accountant that you'll retain him (or her) after you buy a business or even to offer him a finder's fee if his efforts help you. (While finder's fees are negotiable, they typically are based on what is referred to in the industry as a "Lehman Scale," meaning 5 percent for the first $1 million of sales price, 4 percent for the second $1 million, 3 percent for the third, 2 percent for the fourth, 1 percent for the fifth, and one-half of 1 percent for amounts in excess of $5 million.)

10. *Use your personal contacts.* If the key to a retailer's success is "location, location, location," then surely the key to finding a business is "network, network, network." That means—even if you're not the outgoing type—you must tell friends, relatives, business acquaintances, and even people you meet on the street that you want to buy a business.

Look through your Rolodex and start calling. Get in touch with people you talk to all the time as well as people you haven't spoken to in years—pull out your alumni yearbook and contact people you went to school with or professors with whom you had a special relationship. You'll see that the people you reach out to will genuinely enjoy sharing in your excitement. Become active in your church or temple. Join civic organizations and your chamber of commerce. By doing so, you'll come into contact with community members who are themselves active in business and who are likely to give you leads.

Attending local small business conferences and entrepreneurial forums is another way to generate leads in your area. The people attending these meetings may know someone who is interested in selling his business. Indeed, they may even be interested in selling their own.

Conducting a Savvy Search

You've got to be willing to work hard and do whatever it takes to get the job done. However, good intentions and hard work will be wasted unless you have a structured search plan. Here's one:

- First, determine what industry will suit your needs. Take into consideration your experience and training, where you (and your family) want to live, what kind of hours you'd like to work, and how much income you'll need.
- Next, research that industry thoroughly to ascertain its viability, stability, and potential for growth in the region you are contemplating.
- Begin your search for targets:

    (a) Identify the people you want to contact: friends, relatives, business colleagues, business brokers, lawyers, accountants, bankers, etc.
    (b) Read classified ads and answer those that sound promising.
    (c) Actively pursue businesses that are not for sale through conventional channels.

(d) Place your own ads, designed to seduce any owner into thinking about selling.

(e) Reach out to free sources of professional advice like the SBA and the various programs it sponsors. Call the chamber of commerce in your target area and attend conferences and forums where you're likely to meet leaders in the business community. Remember, what's critical at this stage is to choose the industry that's right for you and then target likely businesses. By following these guidelines, you should come up with some attractive leads.

CHAPTER 4

Financing the Acquisition

IF YOU'RE LIKE MOST FLEDGLING ENTREPRENEURS, YOU PROBABLY assume that you should first figure out how much money you can put together to buy a business and, after that, search out a business you can afford.

This may seem like common sense, but it's not good business sense. The smart sequence is:

1. Find the business you want to buy.
2. Put together the financing after you've made your choice.

Say you have $25,000 to pump into a business and you can get another $25,000 from your parents. That doesn't mean you should start scanning the Sunday business section of your local paper to find a franchise available for $50,000. The time to focus on how to raise capital is *after* you've located a business you think is right for you.

Not surprisingly (because they're new to this game), many first-time entrepreneurs don't take into account the fact that they can't prepare a business plan—something essential for financing—unless there is an actual business to discuss (with assets, cash flow, product or service description, projections, personnel, etc.). Another important consideration: Traditional sources of financing for small business owners (relatives and friends as well as commercial lenders, venture capitalists, and government agencies) can't determine whether they should lend to you unless they too have a specific business to analyze. Not only that: The person selling a business is often the person best able to assist with financing. Until you've targeted a particular business, you don't have an owner with whom to negotiate.

How Will You Come Up with the Money?

To finance your business, you'll no doubt need both working capital and acquisition financing (*seed money*). Working capital is the money you must have in the cash register for day-to-day operations as well as the money you'll need to cover seasonal cost fluctuations, finance construction, and provide advances against existing inventory (goods on hand, but not yet sold) or accounts receivable.

Working capital loans typically are paid off as an ongoing expense of a business. They generally run from one to three years and are renewed or renegotiated upon maturity. They may be for a fixed amount or they may involve a line of credit in which funds are drawn down as needed and repaid from cash flow as the business goes along. Acquisition loans, however (which are loans utilized to purchase the business), normally run for a much longer term—from five to twenty years, or even longer.

When most people think about financing the cost of buying a business, they are referring to the other type—acquisition financing. (Some 90 percent of entrepreneurs borrow most or all of the

TIP: CHECK TIME FRAME

Be extremely careful about the time frame over which you agree to repay this loan. If you agree to repay it before your business is profitable enough, you'll have to use working capital—the "muscle" of your business. That's likely to be a big problem for your enterprise.

funds they need to acquire a business.) So, unless you plan on funding that acquisition with your own money (i.e., with personal savings, inheritance, etc.), you'll have to borrow most of the cash needed for the purchase.

Fortunately, funding the acquisition of an existing business is often much easier than raising money for a start-up venture. This is due to three principal reasons:

- *An existing business has a track record.* This provides the element of predictability that potential lenders strongly favor. On the theory that history repeats itself, sophisticated lenders do a regressive analysis when evaluating a business loan—that is, they look to the past to determine how well a venture is likely to do in the future. When they provide money for a start-up, lenders are forced to rely on the skills and aspirations of the entrepreneur. But an existing business already has been tested. This simple fact makes lenders far more knowledgeable about the extent of the risk they're taking and, therefore, more inclined to extend credit.

- *Most existing businesses have hard assets.* Hard assets (such as real estate, equipment, machinery, and/or inventory) can be used as collateral to secure the loan. That makes banks and other traditional sources of capital (including the Small Business Administration) far more willing to finance an existing business than to lend to a new enterprise. I believe that many of my clients who were able to get the loans they needed to acquire a going concern would have been turned down had they been trying to finance a new venture. This is because their financial resources would have been considered too shallow and/or because start-ups come without assets that can be used as collateral.

- *An existing business can attract more flexible financing.* Often the owner/seller is willing to provide all of the financing, or a portion of it, to induce the buyer to consummate the deal. The inducement can come in the form of the seller's letting the new owner pay out the purchase price over a long period of time (a *deferred payout*) or by the seller's accepting little or no cash down. What's more, a seller frequently offers the buyer financing at more favorable terms of interest, or with a longer payout, than a conventional lender. Furthermore, the seller can cooperate in other financial ways as well. By subordinating its loan to the buyer (i.e., agreeing that any loan the buyer gets from a bank must be paid back *before* the seller's loan is repaid), a seller can free the new owner to raise capital from outside sources as well.

Psyching Out the Lender

I remember when I applied for my first loan. It was for a sports car, a brand-new Honda Prelude. When I heard that the bank had approved the loan, I was both ecstatic and mystified. I couldn't believe my good fortune. But during the years I paid back the loan, the name of the bank changed three times and my loan was sold twice. Eventually, that loan ended up being serviced by a credit company in Iowa. It finally dawned on me that the bank hadn't done me a personal favor; it had simply made a business decision. It was in the business of lending, and I had met its criteria for the loan.

Keep my story in mind when you deal with a bank or other lender. You are not arriving as a supplicant, hoping they will like you and therefore do you a favor. Rather, you have applied for the loan because you have come up with a good business proposition and also have the integrity and sober sense of responsibility that justify the lender's trusting you with money that will eventually make them a profit.

First and foremost, you want the banker to respect you. When you sit down for your first conversation, the loan officer will make judgments about your appearance and your manner. You will, of course, dress conservatively, wearing the sort of clothing you'd wear on a job interview.

The loan officer also must attempt to judge your management ability. You will, of course, be courteous, responsive, and confident. However, don't confuse confidence with arrogance. The loan officer is like the police officer who stops you for speeding. The policeman has never met you before, so he has an underlying fear of the situation. Loan officers, like cops, don't like surprises.

Try to develop a rapport with the banker. Do whatever you can to put him or her at ease. When it comes to dealing with people you'd like to be able to influence, the "geometric theory" applies: If $A = B$ and $B = C$, then $A = C$. In other words, if you live in a small community, see if you and the banker know people in common. If you do, talk about them and share experiences; you'll find that your relationship with the banker can be accelerated (see "Lending Criteria" later in this chapter).

You're likely to accumulate the money to buy a business in one of four ways:

- *Using personal funds.* This includes money you've raised and borrowed from friends and family.
- *Borrowing from an institution.* This includes getting a straight loan, bearing interest, from a conventional commercial lender like a bank or getting equity financing from a venture capitalist (agreeing to pay interest on the loan *plus* give the lender partial ownership, a share of the profits, or some other premium—often referred to as a "kicker").

- *Applying for financial backing through the U.S. government or a government organization.*
- *Getting some (or all) of the financing from the seller.*

Using Personal Funds

When I advise clients, I tell them anything goes when it comes to raising the capital needed to go into business. If you use personal funds, you'll need to include every source of capital you can think of—cash savings, proceeds from the sale of personal assets (such as jewelry, art, or collectibles), proceeds from the sale of second homes and automobiles, and portions of pension plans, IRAs, 401(k)s, and Keoghs. (Remember: Under current tax laws, you'll have to pay taxes on withdrawals from certain retirement plans and you'll have to pay a penalty if you are under age $59^1/2$.) Still, having the use of the money today may be worth the substantial tax liability and early withdrawal penalty. Don't be afraid to withdraw some of your retirement money. If your business succeeds, so will your retirement plans. As a precautionary measure, consider leaving yourself a modest cushion in case your venture doesn't pan out. As a general rule of thumb, most personal finance experts suggest holding back 20 to 30 percent of retirement savings to be safe.

Borrowers usually turn first to their friends and relatives. So should you—even if you'd ordinarily feel squeamish about putting a family member or friend on the spot. After all, these are the people who should have confidence in your drive and your ability to succeed. What's more, they are more likely than outside sources to offer lenient and flexible payment terms.

Certainly, before you approach people you know, you'll need to determine, as best you can, that they have the money. (The last thing you want to do is embarrass them or yourself.) What should you do when you simply can't find out if someone has enough money to lend? Figure out what you'll suggest if he (or she) tells

WARNING: USE A SERIOUS APPROACH

Be sure to treat this exchange as a business proposition. Although you don't need to dress up when you make your pitch to family and friends, remember that you must approach them in the same manner you'd approach a loan officer at a bank. You are not a supplicant; you are not asking for charity; you are offering an investment opportunity.

you he can't afford to participate. For instance, if you're dealing with people really close to you, you might suggest that they take out an equity loan on their home that you'll pay off. Naturally, this could be a bit awkward. Taking out a home equity loan carries some risk because you'll be asking this person to gamble on the roof over their head (and the heads of their family members). Not everyone you approach will be willing to take this type of risk. But you won't know until you ask.

You'll get more yes answers if you tailor your proposal to what you believe is your friend or family member's need for return on capital. Expect to encounter signs of aversion to risk on the part of the people you approach for a loan. And the closer they are to retirement, the greater their fear of losing money. Potential lenders who are in their thirties may very well be willing to gamble on getting a share of the profits when you eventually sell your new business. Those in their fifties and sixties are more likely to want some continuing payback, perhaps one combined with a minority stake in the business (5 to 10 percent ownership).

By and large, people in their sixties or older are concerned about the interest income thrown off by savings, pension funds, and Social Security. Often, if you're willing to match the income they derive from these vehicles, may you persuade them to dip into principal to lend you a hand.

Make sure the time frame for payback is stated clearly. Don't promise to pay your lenders back "out of profits." On the other hand, repayment out of a sale of the business is fine—assuming there is a time limit attached.

Your family and friends are sure to want to know how much money you are contributing to the enterprise, so be candid about that. They're likely to be even more preoccupied about the extent of your dedication, so don't go to them with a proposal that could sound like a hobby or a part-time venture. Ask them for money only if you're talking about a business that will consume 100 percent of your working life.

When you approach your parents for help, you may want to point out that if they give or lend money to you now, rather than leaving it to you when they die, they'll have a chance to see the fruits of their gift and to share your enjoyment. (Stephen M. Pollan, author of the foreword to this book, makes a persuasive argument for these psychological benefits in his book *Die Broke*, which was published in 1997 by HarperCollins).

Ray Field is an example of someone who did whatever it took to raise capital. Although he worked for years in the advertising industry, Ray was extremely handy when it came to things like carpentry and electrical work and hoped one day to own his own hardware and home improvement business. While Ray earned a decent salary in advertising, he married at a young age and had three children before he was thirty. Thus, he never was able to amass much in the way of personal savings. He did, however, manage to maintain good credit and faithfully contributed to his company's 401(k) plan. When his children were all in college (they went to state schools, got loans, and worked part-time to pay for tuition), Ray decided to take the plunge.

There was a local hardware store whose owner Ray had known for years. One day, the owner confided to Ray that he wanted to move to Phoenix to make a new start. Seizing the opportunity, Ray asked the owner if he'd be willing to help finance the sale of the business to him or accept payment over time. Unfortunately, the owner needed cash to make his move.

Here was Ray's dilemma: Ray wasn't a good candidate for a loan from a bank because he had no collateral. For the same reason, it was unlikely that suppliers would give him credit, and Ray wasn't eligible for minority funding from the SBA. Because Ray was determined to have this business, he decided to pull out all the stops. He took $75,000 from his 401(k) plan—even though the early withdrawal of these funds subjected Ray to penalties and taxes. He timed things so that he could use his $5,000 Christmas bonus from his former employer. He got $10,000 by using his credit card advance limit. Next, he asked his wife's parents for a $25,000 loan and agreed to pay them interest on the money equal to what they were currently earning. Finally, Ray went to his parents and asked them for a loan as well. After seeing how committed Ray was, his parents decided to take out a second mortgage on the home Ray had grown up in and offered to lend him $50,000. They'd planned on leaving the home to Ray and decided they'd rather see him enjoy some of the money while they were still alive. With a combination of scraping together what he could, tapping into retirement funds, and getting some help from his in-laws and parents, Ray was able to raise enough cash to make his dream a reality.

Borrowing from an Institution

Commercial banks are the primary lenders for small business acquisitions. They supply debt financing; they don't want a share of ownership (equity) in your business. They prefer to lend to businesses with fixed assets that show sufficient cash flow to meet principal and interest payments. They'll want to know how their money will be repaid and almost always want some form of collateral to secure their loan.

The typical bank loan for acquisition financing is a term loan running anywhere from five to ten years. A straight amortization (reducing the loan to zero by means of equal payments of principal and interest) would be too stressful for most businesses because the loan time is so short. Banks know this, so they generally permit the loan to be amortized for up to twenty years, with a balloon payment (a lump-sum payment of the unamortized principal) at the end. Interest rates typically start at prime (a fluctuating rate the largest banks charge their biggest and most secure customers) and go to two or three points above.

Lending Criteria

CASH FLOW

Because banks prefer to lend to borrowers with assets—a house, equipment, inventory, or accounts receivable—these will virtually always need to be pledged. Keep in mind, however, that the bank doesn't really want your assets; it wants your money.

The banker's first concern is to make sure your business can repay the loan. Therefore, she will look for a cash flow profit after taxes that is not only sufficient to pay the required principal and interest installments but leaves the owner with money left over—say, 30 to 50 percent. Be sure to work your loan repayment into your cash flow projections and be prepared to demonstrate how you arrived at your sales and income figures. If your marketing research is sound, you should be able to back up your projections.

CHARACTER AND CREDIT HISTORY

Banks make loans to people, not businesses. They'll want to know who you are, what you'll bring to the business, and how you've handled your financial obligations in the past. What experience have you in the type of business you're buying? The more, the better. If you have little or no experience, do you at least have a general business background of some sort? Having neither may be problematic, although it need not doom your request for a loan. Getting a job (or moonlighting) in the field or taking business classes at a local college or university could help.

Aside from a criminal record, nothing turns a bank off more than a poor personal credit history. Banks judge your *willingness* (as opposed to your *ability*) to pay back a loan by looking at your credit history.

CAPITAL

A bank will want to know how much cash you'll be putting into the business as well as what other equity will be invested and by whom. Your willingness to contribute personal funds demonstrates your true commitment to this business venture, and that willingness to commit is even more important than the amount of money you can contribute.

THE GUARANTEE

In addition to the cash you're investing and the collateral you've provided as security, banks often will ask for a personal guarantee. That means that you (or someone who agrees to stand behind the promises made by your business—presumably, a corporation) agree to repay the loan in the event that you default. Your guarantor might be the proverbial rich uncle who's willing to co-sign your loan or it might be a "professional" loan guarantor like the Small Business Administration.

Borrowing from a Venture Capitalist

Generally speaking, venture capitalists are in the business of investing funds in new businesses in exchange for a piece of the action (i.e., some degree of ownership—anywhere from 20 to 70 percent). Venture capitalists always look for as much return on their investment as they can get. They'll pour money into a business if they believe the idea and management are good and that the venture will grow rapidly and offer substantial profits. The entrepreneur's ability to deliver—and to deliver a good yield on their money—is more important to them than collateral. Accordingly, what they'll examine most closely is the entrepreneur's management ability.

While the influx of funds can be extremely attractive to a fledgling entrepreneur, approaching venture capitalists isn't for everyone. Some of the larger venture capital companies demand as high as a 30 percent return on their investment. And, in some cases, the venture capitalist will demand that the entrepreneur buy out the investment after a certain period of time or that the venture capitalist will sell his share of the business to an outsider. This is called a *put*. This can mean the ruin of the entrepreneur, the demise of the business (as the new owner/borrower knows it), or both.

Borrowers need to be savvy about the preferences of each venture capitalist they approach. Some shy away from a particular industry (e.g., retail) because they believe it is too risky. Others are not as concerned about what kind of product they back as they are with the bottom line.

Venture capitalists come in three varieties: private firms, corporations, and "angels." Private firms tend to look only for companies that can grow big in a short time. Corporations, looking for new subsidiaries, typically make investments in the millions, but they want full ownership. Unless your business has the potential to grow into the next Microsoft, you'll probably deal with the third category.

Angels are wealthy private investors (or groups of private investors) who pump money into fledgling or growth-oriented enterprises. These affluent people, many of whom are in the sports or entertainment fields, have found that investing in a small business is fun, keeps them busy, and is an excellent way to utilize their abilities and business acumen. Your professionals (lawyer, accountant, financial planner, or banker) may know some.

Borrowing (with a Little Help) from the Small Business Administration[1]

Have you ever typed on an Apple computer, sent an important package by Federal Express, or snacked on a triple-decker pepperoni special at Pizza Hut? You couldn't have done any of those things if Apple, FedEx, and Pizza Hut hadn't originally had some help from the Small Business Administration. In fact, during the 40-plus years since it was established, the SBA has played a crucial role in the development of such giants as Intel, Winnebago, America Online, and more than 9 million other enterprises that have reached various levels of success.

The SBA—by far the largest single source of federally backed growth financing for small business—doesn't provide money directly but serves as a kind of rich relative who can co-sign huge loans. Currently, it has a portfolio of some 180,000 companies nationwide that are paying off outstanding loans totaling $27 billion. As recently as 1996, some 55,590 small businesses borrowed more than $7.8 billion with the agency's guarantee—an increase of 52 percent over the number of people who borrowed from the SBA in 1995.

When entrepreneurs apply for an SBA guarantee, they usually do so through a bank or lending institution that has already turned them down. However, if you think you might need the SBA's help, it's probably smart to ask your bank from the beginning whether or not it has worked with the agency. If so, your bank will know the ropes, meaning you'll save time and energy in the application process. Odds are that your bank is one of the approximately 8,000 commercial lenders that have provided SBA financing during the last five years. "Generally," says Mike Stamler, a spokesman for the agency, "the SBA looks for borrowers with good character, management experience, commitment, ability, and willingness to

---

[1] *A portion of this section originally appeared in the October 1996 issue of* Working Woman *magazine. It is being reproduced here with the permission of* Working Woman *magazine.*

repay. Substantial equity in your business is also a plus." The loans take about the same amount of time to process as do most bank applications. However, there's one big difference between them and their garden-variety counterparts: The answer is more likely to be yes.

The SBA does more for entrepreneurs than provide financial assistance. Its Small Business Development Centers offer virtually unlimited technical training and management advice. (There are 57 SBDCs, with a network of more than 1,000 service locations, placed mostly in the offices of local colleges and universities; see Appendix A.) Likewise, a state-by-state list of SBA district office locations can be found in Appendix A. For e-mail addresses and on-line sites from which you can receive additional information regarding other services and programs offered by the SBA, you can log on to the SBA Home Page on the Internet at www.sbaonline.sba.gov. If you're not Internet ready, you can call the Small Business Answer Desk at (800) U-ASK-SBA.

Getting the Seller to Finance Your Purchase

As I've noted above, a seminal advantage of buying an existing business is that the buyer often can persuade the seller to finance some, or all, of the purchase. And the terms generally will be better than those conventional lenders would offer. The interest rate for seller financing is typically one to two points above the prime rate, and the term of the loan is generally five to seven years (or longer); conventional financing is usually prime plus three for a term of two or three years. Many sellers will allow the buyer to acquire the business for little or no cash down if the buyer grants the seller a minority stake with an option to sell after a few years. What's more, seller financing enables for even greater creativity in negotiating the purchase. Perhaps the seller would be willing to take less money in exchange for staying on the books as a consultant on a contract basis. This way the owner retains an income stream after selling the business and the buyer pays less down and can pay off the purchase price from cash flow.

TIP: HOW MUCH IS ENOUGH?

In my experience, virtually all business failures can be traced to one of two factors. First, not all people have the skills, personality, and ability to be a business owner. Second, they haven't enough money. In fact, most experts would agree that undercapitalization is the cause of most small business failures.

Determining how much capital you'll need when you acquire a business requires careful planning. Your financing requirements should correspond to your strategic plan for continuing and developing the business after it's yours. To illustrate: Suppose you can purchase a business for $150,000; your accountant may look at the numbers and determine that an additional $75,000 will be needed for working capital and that yet another $75,000 may be required in the next year or two to replace certain major fixed assets such as machinery or equipment. As you can see, if when you purchased the business you concerned yourself with raising only the $150,000 needed for acquisition, you would have put a severe strain on the business from day one.

Now That You've Found the Money . . .

It's time to put together the team of experts who will turn you into a savvy buyer.

GETTING BANKS TO "SHOW YOU THE MONEY"

Here are several tips to help you obtain the best financing possible for your business:

- Banks often have what's called a split prime rate. The term signals that these banks actually have two prime rates—the advertised prime and a lower prime that's reserved for good customers. You'd be wise, therefore, to apply for a loan at a bank where you've established yourself as a good customer. Even if you're not a customer, don't be shy about asking for a preferred rate. Be as persuasive as you can; offer to do all of your personal and business banking there if you get the loan.

- Because you'll likely be in tight financial circumstances when you take over a new business, try negotiating for a suspension of principal or for a reduced interest rate for an initial period of time, for example, six months to a year. This way you'll give your business an opportunity to get up and running before full-blown repayment obligations kick in.

- As I've said, banks prefer lending to businesses with hard assets. This means that, other factors being equal, you have a better chance of obtaining a loan if you plan to acquire a manufacturing business than if you want to buy a service business. If the business has hard assets, the bank knows that if you default on the loan it can look to those assets for repayment. Banks refer to this as having an exit. If your business has no assets with which to secure the loan, it's unlikely the bank will lend to you unless you make a pledge of your personal assets.

- If you must pledge the fixed assets of your business, try to limit the extent of the security you grant. For example, see if you can avoid granting a security interest (giving the bank a lien) in your accounts receivable. At some later date you may wish to factor them, i.e., sell your receivables to a factor at a discount for cash. Therefore, carving these out (keeping accounts receivable out of any security interest you grant) could prove valuable to your business.

- If you're required to pledge your personal assets, at least get the bank to agree to release those assets when a portion of the loan has been repaid. Also, try to avoid pledging your home. If you have equity in your home, that, too, may be a source of financing in the future.

- Regardless of what you think of your credit profile, it's best to check it with all three of the major bureaus—Experian (formerly TRW), Trans Union, and Equifax—*before* you apply for your business loan. It's quite common for credit reports to contain inaccuracies, such as erroneous past due balances on major credit cards, department store charge accounts, or student loans. If you spot an error, write a letter of explanation to the credit agency, asking it to correct the mistake. It's also possible that you'll see on the report a legitimate debt of which you weren't aware or had forgotten about. If that happens, contact the lender or creditor to set up a payment plan and make sure you get the creditor to submit a clearance letter to the agency to wash away the negative entry from your report. Generally, these problems are relatively simple to correct. Remember, though, that the process can take time—just what you don't have an abundance of when the clock is ticking to close your deal.

The bank will also weigh these factors:
- The borrower's plan to improve the business
- The length and relative market value of the business's lease
- The condition of the business's equipment
- Whether merchandise is up to date and of good quality
- A diversified product line and market base

You are more likely to be able to negotiate for owner financing in the following circumstances:

- *The owner is retiring or does not plan on going into another business.* Owners who want to go into another business will need the cash. But if the owner is retiring or the business is being sold because of a death or divorce, the seller may be more interested in a monthly paycheck than cash up front.

- *You've targeted a service or other business with few assets.* If there are few assets that a buyer can use as collateral to secure a bank loan, the owner may be forced to finance the deal himself.

- *You are a loyal and trusted employee of the business, and the owner has no interested family.* In this case, the owner has an emotional stake in seeing the business continue and will feel good about helping it survive.

- *Economic conditions favor seller financing.* The state of the economy sometimes persuades even the most reluctant owner to provide financing. If interest rates are high or lending practices are restricted, sellers will have no choice but to offer terms to make the deal work.

CHAPTER 5

Assembling Your Team of Experts

Getting by with a Little Help from Your Friends

THIS IS A SELF-HELP, NOT A DO-IT-YOURSELF, BOOK. IF, AS Abraham Lincoln maintained, "any lawyer who represents himself has a fool for a client," any entrepreneur who tries to go it alone has a blockhead for a boss. Buying a business is one of the biggest investments you'll ever make. To negotiate some parts of the process you *must* have the advice of experts.

Your professional team will make sure that you don't blunder into a deal with legal or tax pitfalls, while helping you radiate stability and management skill—something to which sellers, lenders, and investors pay close attention. Polished professionals can pass on their seasoning to their clients. In addition, they have contacts that can help you at each step along the way, and their contacts can become your contacts.

The professionals you engage must be true experts. Someone right out of graduate school may be bright and eager and charge far less, but he or she won't have the wisdom born of experience. You, the entrepreneur, should be the only beginner on the team. Real experts can be costly, but with professionals, as with most things in life, you get what you pay for. Beginner though you may be, however, you're still the captain of the team; you must remain in control. You've got to know when to seek the experts' counsel, when to delegate authority to them, *and,* most importantly, how to choose them.

Before we discuss what you should look for in each type of professional, here are some general rules to follow in assembling your team:

- *Personal recommendations.* The best way to find an expert is through personal recommendations from someone who has bought a business similar to the one you are planning to acquire. Ask friends, relatives, and business acquaintances if they've used a lawyer, accountant, etc. for business transactions, or if they know of one.

- *Professional associations.* If you can't solicit referrals this way, call local professional associations. Explain that you plan to buy a business and that you are looking for someone with expertise in the association's geographic area. Compile a list of at least three candidates for each professional spot on the team.

- *In-person interviews.* Call the candidates on your list and make appointments to interview them. They should be willing to give you a free initial consultation. Don't settle for a brief telephone conversation; it's impossible to tell if someone is understanding and concerned over the telephone. In addition, by interviewing your prospective team members at their offices you can see how organized their operation is and how they conduct themselves in their business environment. Scratch off your list any candidates who claim they're too busy to meet with you. Anyone who won't set aside time for a prospective client isn't going to be there when he or she is needed most. After you're at the professional's office, look around. Don't be too greatly impressed by the number of diplomas on the walls: Every professional has them. Look to see if the candidate has any certificates from professional associations or awards or commendations from peer groups. These show that the professional is admired and respected.

- **Continuing education and experience.** Ask about the candidate's commitment to ongoing education. You want people who stay on top of the latest developments in their field. No one, no matter how experienced, can possibly keep up with the constant stream of technological and legal developments without refresher courses and continuing updates. Question them about their experiences and discuss what you'll expect of them. How many similar clients do they have? How long have they been doing this type of work? Don't shy away from a professional who admits that he or she doesn't know the answer to a question, but promises to find out later. That's an indication that he or she is honest. You may have struck gold. No one knows everything.

- **Communication and commitment.** Listen carefully to their answers. Are they straightforward or vague? Does this candidate exhibit the communication skills you'll need? Look for someone who demonstrates a sincere interest in your situation. Remember, no one who is truly good at his or her profession is in it solely for the money. Your professionals should inspire trust.

- **Fees.** After you've established the professional's experience and character, the last topic you'll tackle in your interview is his or her fee. If it makes you uncomfortable to talk about fees, you're not alone; even professionals often are embarrassed to discuss them. Experts don't want to lose a potential client, but neither do they want to lower their rates. Never characterize a professional's fee as too high: By criticizing the price, you're attacking the person. However, there is nothing wrong with negotiating the fee. If the expert won't lower the price, perhaps he or she can suggest other ways to economize. Offer to do some of the legwork yourself. Perhaps the candidate will agree to take some money now, with the balance paid out over time. At a minimum, get the professional to make a commitment to keep his or her hours lean. Although the discussion can be awkward, you should never leave the professional's office without discussing fees.

- *References.* Before you go, ask for the names of three clients you can call as references. Asking if you can call the three most recent clients whose cases are similar to yours can avoid your being given references who are merely shills. Make sure you call all three. Ask them specific questions regarding how the professional dealt with each phase of the transaction, such as "Did they keep you apprised of significant details? Did they give a timely response when their advice was needed? Did they return phone calls promptly? Were the fees consistent with the initial quote? Were there any problems?"

- *Get it in writing.* Lastly, always enter into an engagement letter with the professional that spells out exactly what he or she will do for you as well as the agreed-upon fee. Include in this letter a mechanism for terminating your relationship should you eventually judge that to be necessary.

What follows is a look at the specific traits and skills you will want from each of your professionals. Although the emphasis will be on your team's major players—your attorney, accountant, and business broker—I will also briefly discuss others' roles in the acquisition. Don't be intimidated: Few entrepreneurs will need to enlist the services of all of these professionals right away. In the early stages of the business, an accountant and an attorney may be all you need. But as the business grows and develops, so will your need for professional help.

Selecting the Right Attorney

Your attorney is probably the single most important professional you will ever hire. He or she will be intimately involved in some of the most difficult and significant decisions and actions in your life, including buying a business. Because of the intimate nature of the relationship, you must find a lawyer you can trust and with whom you have a personal rapport.

The attorney you hire to represent you when you buy a business is a different animal from the lawyer who drafted your will or handled your house closing. She must have a business orientation and have considerable experience in small business acquisitions. If you don't already have a lawyer knowledgeable about buying and selling businesses, you'll have to locate one. The attorney you choose will have to know about business structures and will need to have an understanding of tax law.

An experienced lawyer can lead you to potential acquisition candidates and help you craft a strategy that ensures you'll uncover problems early. She also can help you to accumulate critical information that will lay the ground work for developing an effective negotiation strategy. You'll want to have your lawyer involved early in the process. It's also important that you choose a lawyer when you are in the proper frame of mind to make a calm, well-informed decision. Don't wait until there's a crisis to start your search.

Buying or selling a business is a complex transaction involving various fields of law. Don't expect to find a lawyer who can represent you in every situation. Any attorney who claims to be an expert in every field isn't worthy of your trust or your business. That being said, be sure to use a business lawyer, not a generalist. My clients come to me not because they think I know everything, but because they are confident that I'll do whatever it takes to get them the best possible result. If that means hiring other professionals or referring them to lawyers who specialize in a different area of the law, I do it. Ultimately, you are seeking a lawyer whose judgment you respect and who is predictably competent and trustworthy.

TIP: HIRING THE RIGHT LAWYER FOR YOU

1. Speak with friends, family members, and business associates who are similarly situated and whose opinion you value. The other professionals you employ and trust, such as your accountant, banker, or insurance agent, are also good sources for referrals. In addition, you can contact your local or state bar association and ask for people in your area who are experienced in small business acquisitions. Most bar associations have referral programs. For a nominal fee, you can get the name of a lawyer who is registered with the association for referrals in small business matters. (Although in the past lawyers who registered for referrals tended to be younger and less experienced, many bar associations now require lawyers to demonstrate a minimum level of expertise or experience in the particular area or areas of the law in which they have registered as experts.)

2. After you've developed a list of candidates, try to get as much background as possible on each. Your local law library should have a law directory called *Martindale Hubbell,* which is like an encyclopedia of lawyers. It will tell you the lawyer's education, specialty (if any), and perhaps how the firm is rated by other lawyers in the community.

3. Next, prescreen your candidates by calling each on the telephone. This will help you decide which ones you should interview in person. Ask the following questions: How long have you been in practice? Would you briefly describe your experience after graduating from law school? What do you see as your role in the process of acquiring a business? Tell me about some of the acquisition deals you've worked on. Are you willing to give me the names of a few clients to call as references? Do you expect to be paid for the initial consultation or will it be free? Do you work

with other lawyers on a regular basis and will you be able and willing to make referrals if you encounter a problem outside your area of expertise? Chances are, after listening to the answers, you'll know whom you'd like to meet in person.

4. Conduct the interview at the lawyer's office during regular business hours. This way, you'll have the benefit of observing the office environment. Is the office neat and organized, or are things chaotic? Pay close attention to how the lawyer handles herself. Does she take calls during the interview? Consider constant interruptions a bad sign. If the lawyer won't focus on you during this courtship phase of your relationship, imagine how you'll be treated after she has your retainer in hand.

5. Be prepared to ask some follow-up questions: How long can you expect to wait for a callback if the lawyer can't come to the phone right away? What does she charge for giving you advice on the phone? Will you be billed for a call that lasts less than five minutes? What type of clients does the lawyer represent? What is the ratio of lawyers to support staff (two to one is about right). And, most importantly, who will actually be working on your matter? By that I mean will an associate or paralegal (with a lower billing rate) be assigned to handle administrative or other aspects of the transaction where possible? Will the lawyer be sensitive to the economies of your project?

6. What are the lawyer's fees and billing practices? Generally, lawyers bill by the hour, with the exception of personal injury or professional malpractice lawyers, who charge a "contingency" fee based on a percentage of the amount recovered. In certain circumstances, some lawyers may be willing to charge a flat fee. Even though this arrangement may seem attractive, I advise you not to pay a flat fee: Either you're likely to overpay or the lawyer isn't

compensated fairly. Either way, one side ends up with the short end of the stick, and that leads to resentment. If you follow my advice—or can't find a lawyer to quote you a set amount and you opt for an hourly arrangement—try to get her to cap the fee at a maximum dollar figure.

7. On average, hourly rates run from $100 to $300 (and even higher in certain circles). Whatever method the lawyer proposes, she should be able to provide you with a projected budget for your project and be willing to back it up in writing. This document is called a retainer agreement or an engagement letter. The lawyer also should be willing to discuss strategies for keeping costs down as well as alternative methods of payment. Ask to be billed on a bimonthly basis. This will enable you to keep a close eye on what the lawyer's doing as well as how much her work is costing. If you can't afford this lawyer's fee, perhaps she could recommend a competent colleague who charges less.

Selecting Your Accountant

If there's one professional who will be indispensable to the long-term financial health of your business, it's your accountant. You'd better choose a good one: A bad accountant can break a business.

It's crucial that you have this expert at your side as you develop your strategy on finding and acquiring an existing business. Your accountant will need to review your prospective acquisition's financial records and tax returns for the past three to five years. He or she will try to determine the accuracy of the records and develop a clear picture of the business's revenues, expenses, profits, assets, and liabilities. Your accountant will be in a position to help you make financial projections for the next two to three years—projections that you'll need to show to banks or other investors to obtain financing. He also will be able to help you analyze the business's

WHAT WILL MY LAWYER BE DOING FOR ME?

Your attorney will play a major role in helping you establish the terms for buying the business. Here are some of the issues in which she will be involved:

- Checking to see if all leases are valid and can be assumed by you.
- Protecting you from any claims made by creditors of the former owner.
- Checking on the status of the business's intellectual property and other proprietary information (licenses, copyrights, trademarks, patents, customer lists, etc.).
- Drafting a non-compete provision to prevent the seller from going into business in competition with the one you just purchased.
- Reviewing zoning and business license and permit requirements.
- Making sure the seller guarantees all statements concerning liabilities (especially for sales and withholding taxes), creditors, and accounts receivable.
- Establishing an escrow fund (or *hold-back*) to cover potential claims.
- Setting up conditions to ensure that, after you've signed the agreement to buy the business, the seller continues doing business as usual (up to the date of sale) so that relationships with customers, suppliers, creditors, and employees will not deteriorate.
- Establishing the final terms for the purchase. These include listing the assets, the liabilities to be assumed, and the contracts and agreements to which the business is bound; determining how inventory and accounts receivable adjustments are to be made; and establishing the actual date and conditions for completing the purchase.

cash flow. This will enable you to determine whether it will generate enough cash to meet financial obligations.

It may surprise you to learn that many accountants don't have a clue about how to buy a business intelligently. They have had little or no training or experience in this area. So, how do you find the right one? You need to find someone with both a proven track record and enthusiastic endorsements from entrepreneurs in businesses similar to the one you're looking to buy. In other words, don't assume that just because an accountant gets rave reviews from someone operating a professional service company (say, a dentist), he will do a bang-up job for your retail business. You wouldn't go to a dermatologist to deliver your baby. Neither should you hire an expert accountant unless he is familiar with the complexities and issues of retailing. Ask yourself: What industry am I looking at and can this accountant serve me? Check to see what percentage of the accountant's customer base falls within your industry.

I firmly believe that you should use Certified Public Accountants (CPAs). They cost more, but not only does this designation mean that your expert has passed a strenuous exam (passing also requires a minimum amount of on-the-job experience), it also signifies that he probably is extremely responsible. There is a level of accountability that goes hand in hand with being a CPA. What's more, banks and venture capitalists, in particular, tend to view statements and figures prepared by CPAs with a more trusting eye.

As with all your professionals, keep in mind that the people you deal with in business will likely size you up by looking at your accountant. In particular, banks and investors measure you more by your accountant than by your lawyer. In my own law practice, I share this perception. Virtually without exception, the most astute and intelligent business clients who walk into my office have chosen good accountants.

Your accountant will help you prepare everything from budgets and cash flow statements to your business plan. If your accountant has contacts with financial institutions, that's valuable, but not essential. Accountants are good money raisers, not through banking friends but through other clients. Who knows more about how a business is doing financially than its accountant? Your accountant also should be a good teacher, able to explain complex issues in simple terms. If not, you won't be in a position to make an informed decision.

Just as you wouldn't choose a lawyer over the telephone, neither should you hire an accountant without first meeting him face to face. Also, be sure to ask for several references. If possible, arrange to meet the references in person. You're likely to get a much straighter story that way. Ask the references such questions as: Does the accountant do more than simply prepare your tax returns and keep your books? What are his strengths and weaknesses? Above all, does he respond to you in a timely fashion? One of the biggest complaints about accountants that I've encountered with my business clients is that their accountants don't get critical financial information to them when it's needed. The best information in the world is worthless if it's not available in time for you to use it when making decisions.

Accountants normally charge a yearly fee that can range from $1,500 to $5,000 and up. The fee covers tax preparation and quarterly profit and loss statements. In all other instances (such as when the accountant provides you with financial statements or projections you'll need for loan applications or business plans or for other financial or business advice), he'll typically charge by the hour. These fees can range from $150 to $250 (and up, for larger firms). When evaluating fees, it's important to consider the value—to you—of the services you'll receive. An accountant who plays a vital strategic role in the process of buying your business is worth more than someone who simply acts as a bookkeeper.

Selecting a Business Broker

Like it or not, chances are that you'll deal with a professional business broker sometime during the process of searching for a business to buy. If you're not familiar with the geographic area in which you're looking, if you have few contacts, or if you're unwilling or unable to do the legwork yourself, business brokers can be a valuable search tool. Brokers run the gamut from incompetent and/or dishonest to effective and trustworthy. The good ones typically have a background in small business; many have owned and operated one themselves. However, regardless of the broker's credentials, keep in mind that his incentive is to close the deal, whether it makes good business sense or not. What's more, unless you're working with a specialized type of broker called a buyer's broker, the broker represents the seller and receives a commission only when the deal closes. Therefore, it's to the broker's advantage to persuade you to buy a business—any business. Also, the broker has an incentive to help the seller achieve the maximum sales price for a business because, the more it's sold for, the more the broker stands to make (5 to 15 percent of the purchase price is typical). What's more, unlike real-estate agents, business brokers are not required to meet any state or national qualification standards. Many states do not even require business brokers to be licensed. That's why you must choose your broker carefully.

Here are a few things you can do determine whether the broker you're considering is sophisticated in his field and has integrity:

- Interview several candidates, as you would when choosing any professional. Find one whose expertise is apparent and with whom you can communicate. Ask potential brokers such questions as: How long have you been in business? How many similar transactions have you brokered? Have you ever owned your own business?
- See Chapter 3 for tips on how to locate a business broker.
- There are no multiple-listing books (like those in the real-estate industry) to identify businesses for sale. A brokerage firm is only as good as the individual broker with whom you deal. Look for personalized service: A small firm is fine. Make

sure the broker has considerable experience in the industry you've chosen.

- Don't be shy about asking any broker you interview for references. Good brokers will have several satisfied customers with whom you can speak.

How Business Brokers Typically Work

Good brokers will spend the first few minutes getting to know some basics about you. They'll ask what kind of work you do and what your interests are. They'll also ask about your family. They do this to determine what type of business is best suited to your personality and needs. Eventually, the broker will ask about your finances. Even though you needn't get too specific, you should be willing to give the broker an idea how much (within a specified range) you can afford to spend on your purchase. Without some basic financial parameters, the broker won't know what businesses to show you, and you'll end up wasting both your time and theirs.

Each broker will work differently. Some feel that they must be included in the negotiations, while others feel that by staying involved they will get in the way. If the broker is interfering, tell him that, while you appreciate the introduction, you and your team of professionals will be handling things. On the other hand, with your guidance, brokers can perform much of the legwork in gathering information on the businesses they're trying to sell. You can ask them for information on the company's industry, market, management, and customers. However, do not rely completely on the broker's analysis. The information provided by the broker will be a good basis for your own analysis, but it generally never comes with any guarantee of accuracy. Therefore, be prepared to ask the broker to cite the source of the information so you can go back and check everything yourself.

One potential negative when you deal with a broker is that by doing so you lose some control of the search process. Your attempts to gain information about businesses may be frustrated if the broker insists on filtering information. Brokers often are reluctant to allow prospective buyers to meet with or speak directly to the owner of the business. Many brokers fear that if direct contact occurs in the early stages of the acquisition, they will be cut out of the deal and lose their commission.

TIP: GET THE BROKER TO WORK FOR YOU

Get the broker to do as much legwork as possible to obtain verifiable information on prospective businesses. The best way to do this is to persuade the broker that you're a serious buyer. You can do this by being prepared and having your team of professionals assembled (lawyer, accountant, and banker—if you plan on financing the acquisition). If the broker knows you're for real, he'll work hard for you.

Choosing Other Professionals

Other professional services that most small business owners need include insurance brokers, real-estate brokers, architects/designers/ contractors, marketing consultants, and advertising and public relations firms.

Insurance Brokers

Insurance costs can make or break a business. I am constantly amazed at how many entrepreneurs are either over- or under-insured. Because insurance costs are an overwhelming burden for most entrepreneurs, a savvy business owner cannot afford to make either mistake.

The problem arises, in most cases, when the buyer deals with an insurance person who is more experienced at selling life or auto insurance than at selling business-related policies. It's crucial that you have a seasoned, professional insurance broker (not merely a salesperson). Choose someone who deals with a variety of businesses—preferably a broker with specific experience in your industry. The insurance needs of small businesses are legion—worker's compensation, disability, life, liability, fire, and casualty, to name just a handful. Your insurance broker should be able to look at your business plan and know what types of insurance, and how much, you'll need. What's more, he or she can analyze the insurance coverage that's being maintained by the business you're negotiating to buy.

From day one you'll need adequate coverage. Your entire investment could be at risk if disaster strikes and you're not properly protected. The best way to find an expert insurance broker is to ask your lawyer, accountant, or banker for recommendations. Other business people in the area are also a good source of leads. In addition, you can contact the trade association in your industry and ask if it has an approved list of insurance professionals.

Real-Estate Brokers

In most instances, you will look for a real-estate broker after you've made the decision to target a specific business. Good commercial brokers will know as much about the type of location you will need as you do—perhaps even more than. They'll also be able to let you know whether or not the business is located in an area with growth potential. They can tell you whether the business you're looking at is paying market rent for its space. Their services can be especially useful if the business you're negotiating to buy is not on your home turf.

Architects, Designers, and Contractors

Your decision on these professionals can wait until after you've focused on a specific business. Whether or not you need them during the evaluation and negotiation stage will depend on the space in which the target business operates. If you'd consider the business only if the space could be expanded or renovated, you'd better analyze costs and examine feasibility before making an offer. Because valid cost estimates can be made only after a full set of plans and specifications has been drawn (not an inexpensive proposition), you should make sure you absolutely need these projections before undertaking them at this stage of the game.

Marketing Consultants

From retired executives and business owners to academia and the corporate world, a virtual network of independent consultants is available today. Major corporations and small businesses alike reach out to consultants for expert advice. If you've tried to research the market potential of the target business but you're uncertain of your results, you should consider retaining the services of an independent business or market consultant. Be sure that any consultant you hire has extensive experience in the particular industry in which you will be involved.

Advertising and Public Relations Consultants

As you will see later in this book, when we discuss preparing a business redeployment plan and reopening the business, the image that you and your business present to the outside world can be crucial in the venture's success or failure. At the early stages of operating your new business, it can be extremely expensive to retain high-powered advertising and PR experts. Because your budget may be limited, look for a young, up-and-coming individual or firm. By hiring a recent graduate of a design school and doing some of the legwork yourself, you'll do a competent job and, at the same time, conserve capital.

Seek Out Advice—You Might Learn Something

As we've seen, enlisting the advice of expert professionals is a must. However, they shouldn't be the only ones you reach out to for support and guidance. Experienced business buyers place a great deal of emphasis on listening carefully to the opinions of others, particularly those without a vested interest. You'd be wise to find a few people whose judgment and business acumen you respect and ask them to take a look at what you're doing. If they disagree with how you are approaching a particular part of the acquisition process, the prudent thing to do would be to investigate the issue further. Maybe you'll discover that they're right. Even if they're not, you'll be that much more confident in your position.

Some of the most astute, intuitive, and intelligent advice on business that I've ever received came from my wife, my family, and a few good friends. They can be the best sounding boards you could have. Remember, these people care about you. They have no hidden agendas. They have no vested financial interest in the transaction, and you're not paying them by the hour. Regardless of how insightful you think you are, don't ever close yourself off from those closest to you.

CHAPTER 6

Narrowing the Field and Planning the Attack

LET'S REVIEW: YOU'VE CHOSEN TO ENTER A PREDICTABLE INDUS-try with reasonable growth potential—one in which your experience, expertise, and knowledge will help you succeed. You've decided where you want the business to be located and analyzed business trends in that area. In conducting your search, you've used every resource at your disposal, including business brokers, classified ads, trade associations, professionals who might help you find leads, and the governmental programs set up to assist would-be small business owners.

By now, therefore, you should have a list of solid candidates for acquisition. At this point, you don't know whether the businesses are profitable (you may not even know if the owner has any interest in selling). You simply have prospects—the names and telephone numbers of ventures that seem worthy of further consideration.

Now you have to narrow the list down to those owners who may want to sell (although, as you'll see, even some reluctant owners may be enticed into contemplating a sale). How should you approach the prospects you've targeted?

You'll make the best impression by sending the owner a letter and following it up with a phone call a few days later. It's unwise to call a stranger and say you're interested in his or her business. A letter is less threatening, less startling. Also, when you cold call someone your timing may be off: The owner may be too busy with customers or preoccupied with paperwork to give your call thoughtful consideration. On the other hand, your prospect will open a letter whenever he or she has time to pay attention to it. And, if you send a letter rather than call, you're in no danger of blurting out something that could be misinterpreted, something that could antagonize the seller. To write a letter is to preserve control of what you say.

Make your letter short and straightforward. It should indicate that you are professionally and financially qualified to purchase a business and that you're serious about buying. Try to pique the reader's interest so he or she will want to meet you. Your most important goal, however, is to persuade him or her that you are professional, well informed, and businesslike.

Make sure there are no typos or misspellings. Call the business before you send the letter and verify the address as well as the spelling of the owner's name. Don't skimp on the quality of the stationery you use; heavy stock will help you convey the right message. Mark the envelope "Personal and Confidential;" you don't want the owner's secretary, who often screens mail, reading your letter and throwing it into the wastebasket.

Step One: Sending the Letter

Here are a few sample letters of introduction that you may be able to adapt for your use. Their language varies according to how you, the buyer, were led to the prospective seller.

Tip from a professional

Mr. Roger Caldwell
T & J Hardware
18 Hibiscus Avenue
Coral Springs, FL 33065

Dear Mr. Caldwell:

Our mutual acquaintance and accountant, John Smith, has mentioned you as the owner of one of the better businesses in the area. John tells me that if the right buyer were to surface and propose the right deal, you might be interested in selling your business.

I'm an experienced retailer with broad contacts and solid credentials and I firmly believe that I could continue your company's tradition of providing quality products and top-notch service. I would like to discuss some ideas with you that I know you'd find interesting. Naturally, I will treat all discussions we have in the strictest confidence. Please feel free to ask John Smith about me.

I'll give you a call in the next several days.

Sincerely,

James Tyler

Consultation with a business broker

Mr. Anthony Albert
Al & Tony's Restaurant
101 Main Street
Boston, MA 02101

Dear Mr. Albert:

I've been following the growth of your food establishment for the past few years. I understand, through speaking with Jeffrey Redman, a principal with the business brokerage firm Gallagher, Thomas & Redman, that you plan to relocate to Southern California.

Having spent the last ten years in the restaurant management business, I am presently in the market to buy an established restaurant. Mr. Redman's firm has prequalified me in terms of both business experience and finances.

I would very much like to meet you in person and explore the possibility of a buyout. I'll be in touch with you in the next few days.

Cordially,

James Tyler

Approach your boss

PERSONAL AND CONFIDENTIAL

MEMORANDUM

TO: George Bossman
FROM: Tom Worker
RE: Business Proposition

The purpose of this memorandum is to discuss a matter with you that I believe you will find interesting. I thought it best to write you a confidential memo rather than to approach you at work.

I've worked for you for several years now and, in that time, have had the opportunity to learn a tremendous amount about the retail industry in general and our business in particular. I also have established fine relationships with many of our suppliers and customers.

For some time, I have seriously considered going into business for myself, and it has just come to my attention that you may be considering retirement (although I'm not sure that is something you'd like to do immediately). Mr. Bossman, it seems to me that you and I could work out a situation that might be ideal for both of us. There are many scenarios we could explore, ranging from an immediate buyout—with or without a transition period—to an arrangement that would pass the business from you to me over a period of time, with you remaining as a part-time consultant at a salary. I am open to either approach.

If retirement has crossed your mind, it might be worthwhile for us to explore the possibilities. I will call you at home after work one day early next week.

Response to an ad you've placed

Ms. Katherine Advisor
500 Old Country Road
East Lansing, MI 48823

Dear Ms. Advisor:

I am pleased that you answered my ad in the *Lansing Gazette.* Your business sounds interesting to me, and I'd like to find out more about it—and you. I am searching for a management consulting firm similar to yours. I am most interested in a business with an established client base, a good suburban location, and annual revenues of between $250,000 and $500,000.

I would very much like to sit down with you and discuss your business in greater detail. Perhaps you could be prepared to provide me with some specific information: the exact location of your business, the length of your lease, approximate revenues for the last five years, and the nature of your clientele.

Please be assured that I will keep our conversation, as well as the information you give me, in the strictest confidence. I would be most willing to sign an agreement to that effect before we speak. I will call you within a week to set up a meeting.

Sincerely,

Nancy Classified

A prospect in the classified ads

Ms. Hillary Placer
123 Poultry Lane
Fayetteville, AR 72701

Dear Ms. Placer:

I am responding to the ad you placed in the *Arkansas Herald* concerning the sale of your dry cleaning business. I am a serious and financially qualified individual (not a broker) searching for a business like yours. From the brief description in your ad, I believe that it would be in our mutual interest to meet and discuss your company in greater detail.

So that you can be comfortable with me, I would be pleased to put something in writing to guarantee that our discussions will be confidential. I will also bring with me a brief description of my background and experience in the dry cleaning business.

You can expect a call from me in the next few days.

Sincerely,

Alison Responder

Lead through a trade association

Mr. Richard Houseware
5 Greenwich Street
New York, NY 10004

Dear Mr. Houseware:

Several leading members of the Association of Houseware Suppliers have mentioned you to me as one of the more knowledgeable businessmen in your area. I understand that you may be interested in changing fields and/or reducing your work hours to devote time to other interests.

I am looking to acquire an established, solid business in the industry. What's more, I have several ideas as to how each of us might accomplish our individual objectives. I am enclosing a personal biographical sketch to let you know a little bit about my background and experience.

I hope you will want to meet with me to discuss our mutual interest. I will call you in a few days to follow up.

Sincerely,

Lawrence Subscriber

Third-party referral

Ms. Lisa Robertson
1000 Gateway Plaza
Atlanta, GA 30301

Dear Ms. Robertson:

Please allow this letter to serve as an introduction. Roxanne Golden, our mutual close friend, suggested that I contact you about your business. She tells me that you may be interested in selling your company if the situation is right.

I am a graphic design consultant seeking to acquire a small-to medium-sized textile design company. I have financial resources sufficient to support such an acquisition and would be most willing to discuss the many ways our mutual objectives could be accomplished.

I propose that we meet face to face so that we can discuss more specifically your business, what you want to do with it, and how I might fit into those plans. I will call you next week to find out whether you are interested. Thank you for your consideration.

Sincerely,

Barbara Acquaintance

Step Two: Following Up
with a Phone Call

Your letter promised that you would call the owner within a certain time frame. It's vital that you do just that. If you say you'll call in a few days, don't wait a few weeks: Your credibility—and any positive impression your letter has made—will disappear. At this point, your goal is to persuade the business owner to meet with you. (Be prepared to sell yourself; you may not be dealing with an eager seller. It's all right to be the pursuer at this stage. Don't worry about seeming overanxious. You'll have plenty of time to pull in your reins.)

Decide exactly what you want to say, but avoid sounding as if you're reading from a prepared statement: The conversation should be scripted but not canned. And don't get involved in a long discussion; save that for your meeting.

The more comfortable you sound, the more comfortable the seller will be with you. I have found that the best way to prepare for a conversation like this is to practice on a spouse or friend. Choose someone whose opinion you value and role play with him or her until you feel comfortable.

Be friendly and warm, but don't overdo it. You're not looking to make a new best friend, and neither is the owner. You're simply looking to defuse the owner's wariness and make him or her interested enough to meet with you.

Try not to be put off if owners seem ambivalent or even resistant. Tell them that you understand their feelings and that you share them, but that because they are business people it might make sense for them to check out this opportunity to see if it could go anywhere. After all, what have either of you got to lose? Suggest that each of you invest an hour of time and see what happens.

Step Three: Putting the Owner at Ease

If you play your cards right, the odds are you'll get your meeting. (Of course, when an owner tells you adamantly that he or she doesn't want to sell, there's little point in continuing to pursue matters.)

Before you can find out what you need to know about the business (which is, of course, your mission), you must put the owner at ease. So, at the very beginning of your meeting, acknowledge what is probably his or her primary concern—confidentiality. Bring some form of confidentiality agreement with you (see Appendix D). By offering to sign it at your first meeting, you're giving the owner a powerful signal that you are professional, respectful, and trustworthy.

Another way to defuse some of the owner's apprehension is to share detailed information about your background. By doing so, you've created the model for open communication and set the stage for an atmosphere of trust.

TIP: CREATING TRUST

Pay careful attention to your appearance and grooming; dress neatly and conservatively. Shake hands with the owner and greet her warmly. Look her in the eye and smile. Engage in pleasant conversation by asking questions and call the owner by name. Lean forward when she's talking and acknowledge what she's saying by nodding your head. Be amiable and courteous; keep your conversation low key.

Step Four: Prying Out the Facts

You are meeting with the owner to determine whether the business is worth pursuing aggressively. Your threefold strategy will be to learn as much about the business as you can; to get a handle on the owner's personality (this will help you negotiate effectively if you decide to make an offer on the business); and to establish rapport and build a relationship of trust with the business owner.

Here are the most important things to ask about during this first meeting:

- What, exactly, does the business do? What are its product lines? What services does it offer? What are its main areas of concentration?
- When was it started? Is the current owner the original owner? If not, how long has the owner been running it?

TIP: DON'T BE DISCOURAGED BY THE
OWNER'S LACK OF INTEREST

If you've asked the owner for follow-up information and you don't hear from him for a short time after the meeting, don't take that as a sign that you should walk away. Try as you might to establish a rapport with an owner, a first meeting is just that. Follow up with more than just one letter or phone call and, if you're really interested, be prepared to do some pursuing. You may be dealing with a reluctant seller.

- Has the business always operated at the same location? Does the business own the building in which it is operated? If not, how many years are left on the business's lease?
- What is the approximation or range of sales or revenues generated by the business over the last three to five years? Have revenues increased, decreased, or remained constant over the last three to five years? Has the business ever experienced any severe financial crises or downswing?
- Who manages the business on a day-to-day basis? What is the organizational structure of the business?
- Who are the business's key employees? Are there unions?
- Does the business rely on a few or many suppliers? How long has the business used the same suppliers?
- What is the nature of the business's customer base?
- And, most importantly, why is the owner selling?

Most proprietors will tell you that they are selling because they plan to retire, relocate, or change careers. Few will tell what you need to know—that they're selling because business is bad, new competition is moving next door, or key suppliers are going bankrupt. Somehow, you must find out why this owner is really selling. If, for instance, it's a downturn in business, now is the time to judge whether that downturn is something you can remedy. The issues often are difficult to address because they involve delicate questions. If you've followed the advice previously given about establishing rapport and building trust with the prospective seller, you're much more likely to get information that's of value to you.

TIP: KNOW WHEN IT'S TIME TO MOVE ON

If you can't persuade the owner to give you basic information about the business, you'll certainly have no chance of being introduced to employees, customers, and suppliers—key elements of the due diligence investigation you must later conduct. (Due diligence is explained in Chapters 7 and 8.)

Now that the business has passed these very preliminary tests, you've got to start doing some real digging. I'll discuss this in the next two chapters.

CHAPTER 7

Operational Investigation

Searching Out the Non-Financial
Aspects of a Business

AFTER YOU'VE FOUND A BUSINESS YOU THINK YOU'D LIKE TO BUY, you'll need to evaluate both its financial health and its day-to-day operations. Which should come first? In my opinion, the financial investigation of your acquisition candidate—as crucial as it is— should come only *after* you've completed your evaluation of operational, meaning non-financial, issues. Jumping ahead to read a company's income statement and balance sheet would be like skipping the first eight chapters of this book just to learn the various methods of valuing a business (which is discussed in Chapter 9). That exercise will do little more than enable you to spit out valuation theories.

You, the buyer, must first tenaciously ascertain everything you can about the company's operations—its industry, markets, location, facilities, commercial lease, customer and supplier base, competition, products, services, management, and personnel. Without learning what a company does, who its customers are, who its competitors are, and how it is run, you'll be crunching numbers without a framework from which to properly evaluate them.

As we noted in Chapter 6, you will stand a much better chance of obtaining information about your target business if you've succeeded in establishing a relationship of trust with its owner. However, that's only part of your job. You'll need to know what you're looking for and what questions to ask.

Don't underestimate what you can learn by examining a company's history. By performing what's called regressive analysis (the theory that by examining a business' past you can predict accurately its future), you'll greatly increase the odds that you'll choose a business that will succeed. Find out how long the company has been in business. Is it still being run by the original owner? If not, how many different people have owned it? How long has it been run by the current owner? Has the business grown in size over the years? Have profits risen? Has the business always operated from its present location? If not, where was it previously located and when did it move? Did the move affect profitability? Does the business have long-standing relationships with customers and suppliers?

The Company, Its Products, and Its Services

The best place to start is at the core. The essence of any business is the products or services it produces or provides. Find out what the venture's largest sources of revenue is. This may seem elementary, but it's not. Many businesses have more than one source of income. Retail stores, for example, may offer their customers services that are ancillary to the main business, such as an appliance or electronic store that also offers design consulting services or does repair work. What's more, there's often a wide disparity between the profits generated by the different product or service lines of a business. The financials may not reveal which part of the business makes what profit, and even the owner may not be aware of which area generates most of the profits.

What's more, you should know how the product or service compares in quality to others on the market. If there are problems, you'll need to determine whether they can be eliminated or improved. By discovering which aspects of the business are doing the best, you may determine that (with some strategic changes) the business could be more profitable in your hands than it was under the current owner's control.

Here are some questions to ask to help you evaluate the products or services offered by the business:

- Are some products or services selling better than others?
- What is the percentage increase or decrease in sales volume of each product or service over the last three years?
- Are product lines or services complete? Are more needed?
- Have new product lines or services been added during the last three to five years?
- Are new products or services being planned?
- Are the company's products or services likely to be affected by technological changes? Are any such changes imminent?
- Are the company's products and services legally protected from competitors, that is, are patents, copyrights, and trademarks in place?

The Customers

Customers or clients are the lifeblood of any business. They are the most important asset you will acquire when you become an owner. It often is difficult to find out who the actual customers of the business are before you begin negotiating to buy. Owners generally are reluctant to reveal such information. Recognize, however, that at some point in the due diligence (serious information gathering) process you'll need to get permission to speak with major customers of the business.

However, control the urge to ask the seller for access to key customers the first time you meet. Sellers have a natural fear that, if customers learn that the business is for sale, they'll begin to look for products or services elsewhere. That's why it's best to wait until you've established the trust relationship I discussed in Chapter 6.

You can, however, ask the owner these perfectly reasonable questions about his customer base at an early stage in your discussions:

- What is the demographic breakdown (of individual consumer groups or types of businesses) that buy the products or use the services? How does this compare with the demographics of the business' target market?
- Is the business heavily dependent on one major customer or a few major customers?
- Does any customer or client account for more than 10 percent of the total sales volume? (If so, this might be a problem.)
- What kind of credit and payment histories do significant customers have?
- Are customers under contract and, if so, are the terms favorable? When do they expire?
- Are the major customers likely to remain if the business is sold? (You must discover whether major customers' personal relationships with the seller are vital to the business.)
- Are there signs that the business might lose any major customer?
- How does the percentage of repeat business compare with industry norms?
- How often do customers reorder, and is the rate of repeat business increasing or decreasing?
- How frequently does the business pick up new clients or customers?
- How many active accounts does the business have? What are the pending orders?

Marketing, Advertising, and Promotion

A business that has identified its target market successfully and is communicating to that market the benefits of its products and services brings a valuable asset to a prospective buyer. However, if this targeting and promotion isn't being done well, it's your job to determine whether changes should and could be made in the marketing strategies.

Getting the answers to these questions will prove instructive:

- How are the company's products and services marketed?
- What percentage of total sales volume comes from each sales or marketing method?
- Does the company have any exclusive production or distribution rights to any products or services?
- Are advertising and promotional efforts properly aimed at the company's target markets?
- Are sales made directly by an in-house sales force or through independent sales representatives or distributors?
- Does the company have a planned marketing, advertising, and promotional program?
- What does the company spend on its marketing, advertising, and promotional efforts?
- What is the marketing, advertising, and promotional budget as a percentage of sales? How does this compare to industry norms?
- How does the budget break down by percentage for print ads, radio, television, direct marketing, trade shows, brochures, and co-op ad programs?
- Is an advertising agency under contract?
- Does the company use market research?
- Are there opportunities for exporting into foreign markets?
- Are there opportunities for out-of-state mail order?
- Are there opportunities on the Internet?
- Can the company sell to the government (federal, state, or municipal)?

Competition

Pay close attention to the competitive nature of the business and the industry in which it operates. The business may be profitable and well managed, but if the industry is dying or significant competition is about to enter the marketplace, you could be walking into a minefield.

Interestingly, competition is frequently a subject about which a potential seller has difficulty providing accurate information. Often owners concentrate only on the internal operations of their business, paying too little attention to the external forces acting upon it. This can be a serious mistake.

It is essential to contact competitors. However, owners have justifiable concerns about letting you talk to competitors, just as they do about having you contact their employers, customers, and suppliers. You must, therefore, find a way to get the information you need while at the same time protecting the owner's interests. If you can come up with an approach that will do that and explain it to the owner, you'll usually succeed in persuading him to let you contact competitors. For example, you can explain to the competitor that you're doing research on the industry and you'd like to tap his experience. You also might try telling him that you're thinking about buying a business in his field and that you'd like to get some information about the industry to help make your decision. This approach usually is most effective if you're dealing with a competitor from a remote geographic area.

Contacting competitors directly isn't the only method of gathering information on an industry. As discussed in Chapter 2, trade associations and trade journals track virtually every aspect of industry trends, including which companies are the major players.

Be sure to research answers to the following questions:

- How many businesses directly compete in the company's primary line of business?
- Who are the important competitors?
- What is the competitive structure of the industry?

- How do competitors market, advertise, and promote their products and services?
- Compare strategies and positioning in the marketplace: Is it dominated by a few giants or is it fragmented, with many companies serving specialized markets? Are major competitors expanding or declining?
- What are this company's competitive strengths and weaknesses?
- How can strengths be exploited and weaknesses rectified?
- What changes are needed to maintain or increase market share?
- What expenditures are required to achieve this growth?
- What future competitive changes are foreseeable?

Suppliers

The existence and continuity of quality suppliers can have a dramatic impact on a business. If a business relies heavily on one or two suppliers for a significant portion of the company's needs, then the business is vulnerable to any problems those suppliers might have. If they go bankrupt or if they are unable to deliver product in a timely manner, the business may not be able to meet its contractual obligations.

Try to get a listing of the owner's principal suppliers. How are they paying their suppliers? Find out what terms they offer to your seller and compare those with industry norms. Examine supplier's credit ratings (Dun & Bradstreet is an excellent source).

Check supplier relations as you would a business's relations with its customers. If the business you are interested in has a bad reputation with suppliers, you may not wish to buy it unless you're confident in your ability to turn those situations around.

Here are some items to investigate:

- Who are the company's suppliers?
- Does the business enjoy good relations with its suppliers?
- Do suppliers have a reputation for reliability?
- Are any suppliers "related" in any way to the seller (i.e., are dealings other than arms' length)?
- Does the business rely heavily on a small number of suppliers? If so, are they in good shape financially?
- Has the company lost or gained a major supplier in recent years?
- Could the business survive the loss of a major supplier?
- Is the supplier's industry growing, declining, or stable?
- What payment terms does the business have with its suppliers?

Management

There are two primary reasons for analyzing a company's management. First, you need to know how current management is performing to ascertain its special impact on the company's bottom line. Second, the results of this evaluation will be a key component of your strategy to keep or expand the market share of the business. Understanding the strengths and weaknesses of a company's current management will help you determine what changes are needed—or possible (see Chapter 12).

Your most important consideration: How is the business likely to be affected by a change in ownership? If the current owner is a main reason for the success of the business, the company could be extremely vulnerable to a change in management. Your questions, therefore, should be:

- Who is currently managing the day-to-day operations of the business?
- To what extent is the current owner involved in operations? Is he or she responsible for any special aspect of the business for which a particular skill is required?

- Does the business rely on any key employees and, if so, to what extent? Are they under contract? If not, can these people be persuaded to stay after a change in ownership?
- Have key personnel signed non-compete agreements?
- What is the relationship between management and the current owner—or are they one and the same?

Personnel

Needless to say, sellers usually are reluctant to allow prospective buyers to meet and speak with key employees before there's a signed contract. Yet if you're considering a business that has certain key employees, you'd be foolish to plunk down your money without meeting them face to face. Although this can be a delicate matter, sellers usually agree to employee interviews in the later stages of the due diligence process.

Determine how critical current employees are to the business. Arrange to meet with all key employees. Do certain employees have special relationships with major customers? Would the services of a particular employee be difficult to replace? Unless you have a complete understanding of a business, consider offering financial incentives to key employees to keep them in place—at least during the transition period.

When you do get to meet with employees, here are some tips on what to look for:

- Are they likely to remain if the business is sold?
- Does the business have employment contracts with key personnel?
- Have key personnel signed agreements not to compete with the company should they leave?
- Can the local labor market continue to supply employees for both replacement and future growth?

- Does the company have an employee or operations manual? Is it up to date?
- Are there strong secondary supervisors or personnel?
- How are current employees performing? Are replacements needed?
- Do employees enjoy good relationships with customers?
- Are there good relations between employees and ownership?
- How are key employees compensated?
- Are any employees unionized? If so, when do union contracts expire? Are any problems anticipated?
- What are current payroll procedures?
- What are current practices and procedures for hiring and firing and advancement and promotion?
- How does employee productivity compare with industry averages?
- How do wages or hourly rates compare with industry norms?
- What are standard employee benefits?
- Are there training programs for new employees?

Remember, your goal is a smooth transition. You'll want key employees to stay with you and to stay motivated. To accomplish this, you must determine which employees you are going to meet. In a very small company you should consider meeting every one. Be sure to put the employees at ease. Stress the positive aspects of the potential change and ask for their help.

Next, assure employees that what they reveal to you about the company will be held in the strictest confidence. Ask for their honest opinions. Pay careful attention to what they like and, in particular, what they don't like about the company.

Location, Facility, and Lease

Location may well be most significant factor that determines whether your new venture will succeed. Location is often the most

TIP: OTHER WAYS TO RESEARCH PERSONNEL

If the owner refuses to allow you to contact employees during the due diligence stage—or if you have reason to doubt the accuracy of information you've received from employees—try to locate one or two former senior-level employees. Because they no longer have a vested interest in the business or a fear of losing their jobs, they're more likely to be forthcoming with information—information you might not otherwise be able to obtain from the owner or the company's employees.

crucial element in the success of a retail venture, although it can be crucial in other types of business as well. After you've located a business in which you're interested, the very first step is to evaluate the propriety of the owner's location selection. And remember, even solid market research and a well-negotiated lease are no guarantees that the location is perfect. Neighborhoods can change, and with them, customers and buying habits. Other key location factors, such as the existence of competition, also are susceptible to change. The last thing you'd want would be to buy a business with little or no competition in the area and suddenly learn that the "big boys" were moving in. When you evaluate a business location, be sure to look inside as well as outside. Determine whether the way the space is being used properly promotes the business's products and services. Are the facilities well kept and organized? Is the space adequate for the volume of customers and staff it must handle?

A favorable lease can make or break a business. What's more, a typical commercial lease will represent a long-term commitment of any business you consider buying. Therefore, you must check whether the lease is assignable. If not, the owner of the business you're considering may have precious little to offer. See when the lease expires. Can it be renewed, or the term extended? Is expansion a possibility? Next, find out if the business is paying a market rent for its space. Consider retaining the services of a local real-estate broker to assist you in this regard. An hour or two of his time should be enough. Make sure the zoning in the area permits the premises to be used for the business being conducted. Lastly, because the lease should be signed by your corporation, not by you individually, find out whether the landlord will require your personal guarantee in exchange for allowing the seller to transfer (assign) the lease to you. (For a detailed discussion of commercial leases, see Appendix B.)

CHAPTER 8

Financial Analysis

Getting Down to the Nitty-Gritty

ALTHOUGH YOU'D NEVER RISK BUYING YOUR TARGET BUSINESS without leaning on the expertise of a canny accountant, you need to understand at least the basics of its financial condition. During the financial investigation you and your accountant must conduct, you'll discover some good things and some bad things—indeed, you may find flaws so significant that you'll have to back away from the deal. But, on the plus side, your research also may show you that the current owner has overlooked significant ways in which the business could be made more profitable.

The four most important objectives of the financial investigation are to verify the accuracy of the seller's statements about the condition of the business; to enable you to project its future profitability; to give you an idea what the business is worth; and to provide clues on how you could improve it.

You must go *beyond* the numbers to get a clear picture of the company's financial health.

The Basics

At a minimum you should examine the financial statements, as well as the federal and state tax returns, of the company for the past three to five years. If the owner says there is no financial information for you to review, or if the business's records consist of a shopping bag filled with slips of paper, your best move is to walk away. If, in such a case, you are determined to proceed anyway, you'll need special assistance from your legal and financial experts. Be prepared to rely heavily on their advice.

A common problem is the buyer's inability to gain access to the seller's financial information. Many potential acquisitions are aborted because the issue of access is not handled properly. Typically, business owners are highly sensitive about their financial affairs. If the buyer hasn't laid the proper foundation by establishing a relationship of trust with the seller (see Chapter 6), the seller may view the request for financial information as an unjustified intrusion.

Your job is to convince the seller that you are qualified to buy the business and that you have sufficient interest in making the acquisition to justify his releasing the information. If you offer to sign a confidentiality agreement up front, even a reluctant seller should be willing to grant you access to his books and records. (A form of confidentiality agreement can be found in Appendix D.) It's often helpful to have your accountant make the request: The seller may be more comfortable that matters will remain confidential if the information goes directly to your accountant. What's more, sellers know that accountants charge a fee for their services. Involving yours will demonstrate that you have a legitimate interest in the business. If the seller still refuses to turn information over to you, I strongly urge you to forget this deal and move on.

The Financial Nitty-Gritty

Financial statements (financials) are the various accounting reports that present a picture of the financial condition of a business. A complete set of financial statements includes a balance sheet, an income statement, a statement of cash flow, and footnotes.

The Balance Sheet

A balance sheet represents a snapshot of the financial condition of a business at a particular point in time. It profiles a company's assets and liabilities and owner's equity as of a particular date—typically, the end of a company's fiscal year (which may or may not be the end of the calendar year). It also can cover periods ending quarterly, semiannually, etc.

The first item listed on the balance sheet is *assets*—that which the company owns. Then comes *liabilities*—that which it owes. The difference between the two, called *owner's equity*, is next. Owner's equity is sometimes also listed as *stockholder's* or *shareholder's equity*, *net worth*, or *book value*.

Both assets and liabilities, as they appear on the balance sheet, are further organized into the categories *current* and *long-term* (or fixed). Each is ranked by its *liquidity*, meaning nearness to cash. Assets are considered current if they're either cash or can be turned into cash within twelve months (i.e., cash, accounts receivable, inventory, and prepaid expenses). Long-term, or fixed, assets are more permanent in nature. They are intended for use in the business rather than for sale: Examples are machinery, vehicles, equipment, buildings, and land.

The same time-frame categories apply to liabilities. Debts or bills due to be paid within twelve months are current liabilities (for example, the accounts payable incurred in the ordinary course of business). Those liabilities due beyond the twelve-month time frame are considered long-term (for instance, a note that's not payable within one year).

The significance of categorizing an asset or liability as current or long-term has to do with the concept of cash flow (which we'll come to shortly) and with whether or not a business is generating enough capital at times when money is needed to pay bills and debts.

Here's a list of the items you'll see on a typical balance sheet, along with some tips and questions that will enable you to look beyond the numbers to gain valuable insight about the business:

SAMPLE BALANCE SHEET
XYZ BICYCLE MANUFACTURING COMPANY
DECEMBER 31, 1997

ASSETS	DOLLARS ($)
Current assets:	
Cash	50,000
Accounts receivable	95,000
Inventory	215,000
Other current assets	20,000
Total current assets	**380,000**
Fixed assets:	
Land	75,000
Gross plant and equipment	750,000
Accumulated depreciation	(375,000)
Net plant and equipment	375,000
Total fixed assets	**450,000**
Patents	50,000
TOTAL ASSETS	**880,000**

LIABILITY AND EQUITY	DOLLARS ($)
Current liabilities:	
Accounts payable	75,000
Accruals	25,000
Interest payable (on credit line)	40,000
Total current liabilities	**140,000**
Long-term notes payable	200,000
Total liabilities	**340,000**
Equity:	
Common stock	75,000 (owner's investment)
Retained earnings	70,000
Total stockholder's equity	**395,000**
TOTAL LIABILITIES AND EQUITY	**880,000**

ASSETS

Cash

- How much cash does the business have on hand?
- Does the business have sufficient working capital?
- Has working capital changed significantly? If so, find out why.

Accounts Receivable

- Are levels unusually high? Whether the levels of accounts receivable are high will depend on what's normal for the particular type of business you're evaluating.
- Have accounts receivable increased? (If so, this could indicate mismanagement.) Look back at balance sheets from the last three years for a comparison.
- Is there any one dominant customer? If so, pay particular attention to that customer's payment history. If any major customer or customers have been dragging their feet, that could signal that the business will be strapped for cash or that these companies may be in trouble.

TIP: WHO'S PAYING?

Get an accounts receivable aging analysis from the seller. (This is a list of the company's accounts receivable broken down by the length of time they've been outstanding.) The "aging" report will tell you two things: First, you'll see whether (and which) customers have been paying their bills. Next, it will tell you the collection period on accounts receivable (i.e., how long its takes to collect the money that is owed to the company for the goods or services it has provided to its customers).

- Are any accounts more than 90 days old? If so, be wary: Lenders may not accept them as collateral for financing. Examine the credit rating for customers with significant receivables.
- Is the percentage of bad debts reasonable? Every business has a percentage of accounts receivable that don't get paid and must be written off. Therefore, the business should reserve (i.e., allow) for a reasonable amount of uncollectible accounts and deduct for those on the balance sheet.

WARNING: GET A TRUE PICTURE OF NET WORTH

If the business hasn't adequately allowed for bad debts, the accounts receivable will be overstated, as will the total net worth of the business. Have your accountant compare the amount reserved on the balance sheet with the *actual* bad debt history of the business from prior years.

- Are any receivables in collection? (i.e., with a collection agency) If so, are they collectible?
- Are any receivables factored or pledged as security for business loans? If the business factors its accounts receivable, that

means it has sold its receivables to a "factor" for cash on a discounted basis. Have your accountant review the factoring arrangement carefully if you're dealing with a business whose receivables have been factored.

INVENTORY

What is the value of the inventory listed on the balance sheet? The actual current value of the inventory may not correspond to the figure attributed to inventory on the balance sheet. What appears on the balance sheet is the amount the company paid for the inventory, not what it could be sold for now. That could be more, or less, than the amount stated. Find out the following:

- What was the original cost of the inventory?
- What is its fair market value?
- What is the condition of the inventory? Is it obsolete, out of style, or slow moving?
- How much of the inventory represents raw materials, work in progress, or finished goods? The answer to this question could be significant. The value of raw materials, such as uncut rolls of fabric or textiles, isn't nearly as great as the value of a finished dress or sports coat. A completed garment need only be sold. Raw fabric would have to be cut, dyed, and sewed— meaning that you'd still have to incur the expense of converting the fabric into finished goods.

Make the same kind of analysis for equipment and machinery:

- Check the value of the equipment and machinery listed on the balance sheet against its fair market value.
- Is the equipment up to date with current technology?
- How is equipment depreciated?
- Have inventory and equipment been pledged as security for business loans?

LIABILITIES

Liabilities are claims on the assets of a business. The company must use cash (or other assets that will be converted into cash later) to pay these liabilities.

Examining the liabilities listed on a company's balance sheet will tell you certain things about a business. Looking beyond those listed items and asking more questions, however, can tell you much more about the business. Be sure to find out what the accounts payable of the business consist of. For example, to whom does the business owe money? What types of expenses does the business incur?

Because you won't find these on the balance sheet, you'll need an accounts payable analysis from the seller. When you get the accounts payable analysis, examine the following:

- What are the amounts due and the terms?
- What are the names of, and amounts due to, specific suppliers?
- Is there a key or dominant supplier? Are key suppliers family members of the seller? Do they have a special relationship with him? (If so, you'll need to check them out as well. If they went out of business, could you find other supplier sources?)
- Is the business paying its trade debts (i.e., debts to vendors and suppliers) on time?
- Are any trade debts in collection?
- Are loans current?
- What are the rates of interest and remaining terms of the company's long-term liabilities (business loans)?
- How will a change of ownership affect the company's loan obligations? That is, will a change of ownership trigger a requirement that the outstanding balance be paid immediately?
- What is the company's credit rating?
- Does the company have significant accrued liabilities, such as unpaid vacation and sick pay, unpaid sales taxes or withholding taxes, and underfunded pension plans? If so, watch out.

- Have these accrued liabilities built up in recent years?
- Are tax obligations current? (It's not unusual to find that the entrepreneur of a troubled business has been using sales taxes collected by the business to keep things afloat.)

When it comes time to sign a purchase agreement for the business, you can protect yourself properly from these liabilities only if you have prized out this information. What's more, if you're buying a business owner's stock (as opposed to the business's assets), you'll need a special understanding of the nature and extent of the business's liabilities. Why? Because they'll be yours! (See Chapter 11 for more on this subject.)

NET WORTH/OWNER'S EQUITY

This section of the balance sheet includes the amount of money the original investors contributed to the business (or the amount put in later if the business needed an infusion of capital; referred to as *paid-in capital*) plus any earnings that have been retained in the business over the years (called *retained earnings*). Ask the following questions to get a clearer picture of how the net worth increased:

- What is the business's net worth?
- How much capital did the owners contribute to the business when they started it?
- Have there been recent contributions to capital (i.e., loans by shareholders or partners)?
- What are its retained earnings?

Answers to these questions will be crucial if you're buying the stock of a company, rather than its assets. Even if you buy assets, you'll need to consider how the business was capitalized by its owners to make proper decisions (and projections) about whether the debt of the company will increase or decrease in your hands. For example, say the practice of the current owner has been to infuse the business with capital to keep things going. If you, on the other hand, have to take out a big loan for working capital, then, unlike the seller, you'll need to factor in that debt service to your expenses for operating the business.

The Income Statement (or Profit and Loss Statement)

While the balance sheet represents a snapshot of a company's numbers at a specific point in time, the income statement, also known as the profit and loss statement (or P&L) is a summary of what the business has done over a period of time—normally a month, a quarter, or a year.

The income statement is perhaps the most important element of a company's financial statements because its analysis will enable you (and anyone who might consider lending you money) to see what the business has done in the past and to project future profitability. The income statement is broken into four parts: gross sales or revenues; gross profits (margins); expenses; and net profit (or profitability).

I'll show you how to get to the bottom line when you look at the income and expense statement. Starting with gross sales or revenues, a deduction is made for the cost of making those sales; the amount you've deducted is known as *the cost of goods sold* (or *the cost of sales*). Typically, those terms refer to the cost of the materials and labor that went into making and/or selling the products sold by the business. This deduction gives you a figure known as the *gross profit*. When you hear the term *gross profit margin,* it refers to gross profit as a percentage of sales. For example, if a company has annual sales of $1 million and its cost of goods sold is $600,000, the company's gross profit margin would be 40 percent. Margins vary depending on the type of business you are examining. For instance, the gross profit margins of a manufacturing business will normally be higher than those of a retail business with a high sales volume, and virtually always higher than those of a service business. In a service business, labor is the main expense (not labor *plus* materials, as it is in manufacturing).

Margins are particularly critical in a retail business. A business can have an incredibly high level of sales, but if it pays too much for the merchandise it buys, for labor, and for other expenses (such as rent, insurance, and office systems), its profitability won't reflect its sales success.

TIP: CHECK THE GROSS PROFIT MARGIN

Compare the gross profit margin of the business you're examining with industry norms. You can get information on industry margin averages from Dun & Bradstreet, as well as trade associations and trade journals. If the margins vary a great deal from the average you'd better find out why.

EXPENSES AS A PERCENTAGE OF SALES BY INDUSTRY

The table below shows a breakdown, by industry, of typical expenses of a business, along with an average percentage those expenses (ratios) should represent of the business's revenues. It is based on a nationwide study by Bauman & Krasnoff, CPAs, of companies in each industry with sales ranging from $500,000 to $2,000,000

	Retail	Wholesale	Service	Manufacturing
Rent	9.3%	3.0%	6.8%	0.4%
Payroll*	19.4	23.0	38.9	33.3
Utilities**	2.3	2.0	2.1	0.2
Insurance†	1.9	3.2	2.8	0.4

Excludes officers' compensation.

**Telephone and electric.*

†*Includes health, office, liability, workmen's compensation, and malpractice (service only).*

LOOKING FORWARD

It is especially important to look at the income statement with an eye toward how you might do things differently if you were in control. That is what's known as rescheduling, or recasting. Keep this in mind when you go down the list of income and expense items. Here is a list of items you'd find on a typical income statement, along with some questions to ask about the numbers attributed to each:

Under "Income"

- Are sales increasing or decreasing?
- In general, do they fluctuate (i.e., are they seasonal) or are they steady?
- How are sales divided among product lines?
- Do sales depend on one or more key customers?
- Does the sales total include any extraordinary or non-recurring items? If so, you'll probably need to back-out those numbers to get an accurate picture of what the business actually is generating in the way of sales.

Under "Expenses"

- **Salaries.** Be wary of excessive salaries, as well as salaries for "phantom" employees. Many a business owner has been known to have his children or other relatives on the payroll.
- **Advertising.** Does the business spend enough on advertising, and is the money it does allocate spent effectively?
- **Insurance.** Examine the policies carefully. Make sure there has been adequate coverage that will protect the business. Is there officer's and director's liability coverage? It's not cheap, but you may want to increase this number. At the same time, there might be an opportunity to cut costs here. Insurance has become a big overhead item for most businesses (5 to 15 percent of sales is not unusual). Increasing deductibles is one way

of slashing premiums. You'll want to be certain that coverage is adequate, but not excessive.

- **Rent.** Is the business paying a fair market rent? If not, why? If you're not sure, consider retaining a real-estate broker or appraiser to analyze your lease costs. The need to review carefully the terms and conditions of a business's commercial lease cannot be overstated (see Appendix B for a detailed discussion).
- **Repairs, supplies, taxes, telephone, and utilities.** Examine these items over the last three to five years and look for any significant changes.

Statement of Cash Flow

The third major section of the financial statements, statement of cash flow, or cash flow statement, is the most commonly used tool for understanding a firm's cash position over a given period of time. The cash flow statement reflects the movement of cash in and out (for payment of suppliers and other operational expenses of the business) over the fiscal year. In a sense, it's like a checking account ledger.

Simply put, cash flow is the difference between what you take in and what you pay out. Obviously, if a business pays out more than it takes in, it will be short of cash. By measuring the cash flows in and out, you can monitor the financial heartbeat of any business. Without cash on hand, a business will die regardless of its sales level or profitability.

TIP: CHECK THE CASH FLOW

Because a shortage of cash is responsible for the failure of the majority of small businesses, be sure to have your accountant make a monthly analysis of the cash flow of the business you are considering.

Footnotes

Make sure you scrutinize the footnotes (or "notes") to the financial statements. They are an inseparable part of the financial report. Footnotes provide the fine print that goes along with, and explains, how certain of the numbers you see in the balance sheet, income statement, and cash flow statement were derived. These explanations will be critical to your financial analysis.

There are basically two kinds of footnotes. The first identifies and provides an explanation of the accounting practices of the business. For example, the footnotes will identify the company's depreciation method (i.e., accelerated or straight line). Depreciation is the annual deduction that can be taken by a company for a fixed asset.

The second kind of footnote provides additional disclosure regarding line items that appear in the main body of the financials. For example, the maturity dates, interest rates, collateral, and other details of the long-term debt of a business (i.e., business loans) are presented in the footnotes. There also will be a discussion about the existence and status of major lawsuits and legal actions against the company. Details about stock options and employee stock ownership and retirement and pension plans also are disclosed.

Using Ratios to Analyze Your Business's Financial Health

Ratios point out the interplay between the various components of the financial statement. Often, these ratios actually can tell you more about the business than the financial statements themselves. Ratios derived from a given year's financial statements can be compared with ratios from prior years' statements to determine the trends for that business. What's more, you can compare your business's ratios with those of similar businesses. This is an extremely valuable device for detecting problems and judging future profitability. Two of the better source books for ratio comparison are *Industry Norms and Key Business Ratios* (Dun & Bradstreet) and *Annual Statement Studies* (Robert Morris Associates). You can find these in most public business libraries. Various trade associations also compile key ratios for their member businesses.

Because every business has its own unique characteristics, calculating and comparing financial ratios isn't an exact science. Nevertheless, comparative analysis can be used as an approximate guide. In fact, banks often use ratios when evaluating business loans.

Typically, ratios fall into one of three categories: liquidity, solvency, or profitability. Here's a brief look at each.

Liquidity

Liquidity ratios tell you how easily the company can convert its assets into cash. When we discuss *liquidity* here, we are referring to the capability of a business to pay its bills. Common ratios that give an indication of the liquidity of a business include current ratio, quick ratio, day sales receivable, and stock to sales ratio (also called turnover or cost of goods sold to inventory).

Current ratio is the ratio of current assets divided by current liabilities. The number that results from this calculation is considered low (meaning, unhealthy) if it's between 1.0 and 1.5, whereas a current ratio of 2 or more usually signals a healthy company. *Quick ratio* is similar to current ratio, but excludes inventory in the calculation of current assets—under the theory that inventory is not usually as easily converted into cash (as are accounts receivable and notes).

Day sales receivable, or *sales/accounts receivable,* is a measure of how quickly the company is able to collect from its customers. The ratio is calculated by dividing net sales by trade accounts and notes receivable. The higher the resulting number, the faster accounts receivable are being turned into cash. This is important because the slower that receivables are turned into cash, the greater the cash drain on the business.

For those businesses with significant inventory, *stock to sales ratio* is a key liquidity ratio. Businesses can experience cash flow problems when they are forced to stock inventory. The longer inventory sits unsold the more likely it will spoil, become obsolete, or have to be sold for a lower markup. What's more, cash tied up in inventory could have been used elsewhere. The $100 it cost you to buy stock could have been put into the bank, where it would have earned interest. It also could have been put to use paying another bill. This is called the opportunity cost of money.

This ratio measures the number of times during the year that inventory turns over. In general, the more often you turn your inventory over, the better off you are. Again, you'll need to examine industry norms to compare how many times inventory is turning over in the type of business you're analyzing. The ratio is derived by dividing the cost of goods sold by the inventory. A high number (higher than the norm for the industry in question) indicates that the company turns over its inventory quickly. A low number means the inventory isn't moving. You actually can pinpoint the average time an item of inventory sat on the shelf by dividing the number of days in the year by the turnover ratio.

Solvency

The solvency analysis indicates whether the company is over-leveraged, that is, whether it has borrowed too much relative to the amount of equity that has been contributed by investors. This ratio is derived by dividing current liabilities and long-term debt by equity capital and total liabilities. The ratio should be significantly less than 1.0.

Profitability

Profitability, or *return on investment* ratios, indicates how effectively management is using the money invested and how much cash the business is generating. Profitability ratios are especially important to buyers because historical profits usually are accurate portrayals of future profits. By dividing profit by sales, you arrive at a ratio that measures profitability. By dividing profit by net worth, you measure a return on investment. Generally, the larger the number the better.

WARNINGS: BEWARE OF FINANCIAL COVER-UPS

Just as public relations firms use language to create an image they wish to portray, an ambitious seller can use financial jargon to neutralize or enhance his business's financial condition. You'll need to know what to look for and what questions to ask to recognize misinformation. The following sections list some pitfalls.

PHANTOM INCOME

Have your accountant examine at least three to five years' worth of financial reports—audited (meaning "certified") reports, if they're available—and review income tax returns. Don't be surprised if the profits look thin; owners often minimize stated income to hold down their taxes. This is nothing new or nefarious. Many big companies quite legally report one profit number to shareholders and another, much lower, number to the IRS. However, if the potential seller claims additional income over and above what's shown on the return, watch out. Any suggestion that the business generates more money than the records indicate usually is false (and if it were true, that practice would be illegal).

INFLATED EQUIPMENT VALUE

Never accept an owner's statement about what her equipment is worth without obtaining independent appraisals. Following this advice saved a client of mine from drastically overpaying for a manufacturing and packaging business. At my suggestion she hired an appraiser, who assessed the equipment she was going to buy at less than 30 percent of the value listed on the seller's books. Confronted with this discrepancy, the owner explained that he had inflated the equipment values to maintain operating lines of credit at the same levels as when the gear originally was appraised by the bank—more than ten years earlier.

DEFERRED MAINTENANCE

Not only might a business owner inflate equipment value, he or she might defer key equipment maintenance, much as a homeowner might put off replacing a roof when hoping for a quick sale. Examine all maintenance and service contracts; ascertain the efficiency and life expectancy of equipment and review operating records.

INFLATED INVENTORY VALUE

Even though a business may appear amply stocked, the merchandise could be obsolete. Examine it closely to see if it is well balanced and up to date. Are the goods clean and functioning properly? If it's an apparel retailer, are sizes varied and in style?

CAMOUFLAGED COLLECTION PROBLEMS

Business owners often are reluctant to admit to problems with accounts receivable. To get the actual picture, review invoices to identify late payers. If they make up a significant portion of the company's sales (10 percent or more), you could have a chronic cash flow problem. Also, because sellers have been known to postdate invoices to obscure the age of receivables, be sure to review invoices going back several months. If you see more invoices than payments, or payments for less than the invoice amounts, the seller may be trying to foist a credit problem on you.

TIP: DON'T TAKE FINANCIAL STATEMENTS AT FACE VALUE

This applies in particular to financial statements that have not audited. These types of statements, called "compilations" and "reviews," have been prepared with numbers provided by the seller—so, buyer beware! Be sure to be especially vigilant when a company's financial statements contain the following items.

CONTINGENT LIABILITY

This is a claim or circumstance that may cause future expenses to be incurred—for example, a lawsuit against the company. These must be stated on the balance sheet. In reality, however, the company's accountant makes a judgment regarding the likelihood of payment being made. If payment of the contingent liability is determined as unlikely (remote), it need not be listed at all.

GOODWILL

In many instances companies are remarkably fuzzy in the way they put a valuation on goodwill. Goodwill is an intangible asset. If goodwill is listed on a company's balance sheet, that means that sometime in the past the business purchased an asset for an amount in excess of its fair market value. Things like reputation and covenants not to compete (two common "intangible" assets) are not hard, quantifiable assets. They are non-corporeal (i.e., they can't be touched). The real value of goodwill can be stated as the difference between the fair market value of a company's tangible assets and the actual cost of what a buyer paid for the company. In effect, a company's goodwill is a measure of the buying prowess of the purchaser—something difficult to convert into true value.

CHAPTER 9

Valuation

How Much Is Your Target Business Worth?

BEFORE WE EVEN GET INTO THE NITTY-GRITTY OF THE VALUA-
tion process, let's examine what the objectives are of valuing a business in the first place. You, the prospective buyer of the business, are
seeking to learn two things: Will the purchase of this company be
a sound investment? What is the current market price for the business? Only by knowing the latter can you make a proper initial offer
and negotiate a final price.

What Constitutes a Sound Investment?

Compare this business acquisition with other investment options.
Buying your target company must be a better investment than
other, more traditional, investments and also must promise a better
return on your capital than the other two methods of going into
business we've discussed (starting a new business and purchasing a
franchise). To properly judge the quality of your investment, you
must weigh two factors: the investment's rate of return (i.e., how

much money you'll earn on the amount you've invested) and its measure of risk.

To illustrate, say you've got $100,000 to invest in your new business. Now, suppose you took that same amount of capital and bought U.S. Treasury notes instead. That investment, too, will bring a certain *rate of return* on your capital over the next five to ten years (depending on the maturity date you choose). You must ask yourself: How do the projected earnings (see Chapter 8) of your target business compare with the earnings you can expect if you invest in U.S. Treasury notes?

Perhaps the projected earnings of your target business would far outstrip the projected earnings of the Treasury notes. But how does the *measure of risk* you'd run in acquiring the business compare with the risk involved in buying Treasury notes?

U.S. Treasury notes are conservative investments. They tend not to be volatile; even more important, they are perhaps the *safest* investment anyone could make because they are backed by the U.S. Government. However, as you already know, buying a business (even a business with an established track record) involves an element of risk. So you must carefully ponder whether the superior rate of return of your target business justifies the financial risk you'll run in buying it.

Valuing Your Target Business

Business valuation is the murky process by which various parties try to determine the worth of a business or interest in a business (see "Acquiring Minority Business Interests" later in this chapter). Coming up with an accurate valuation is arguably the most important—and vexing—step in the acquisition process. Even most experts would agree that small business valuation is far from a precise science. Texts the size of phone books have been written on the subject. How, then, can you know whether the seller's asking price is fair?

Don't be daunted. You don't need to read a textbook to learn what you've got to learn. The purpose of this chapter is not to turn you into a business appraisal expert or investment banker but to help you establish, within a realistic price range, the market value of the business.

To lower the odds that you'll overpay for your target business, you must value the business yourself and determine that it will generate a profit for you. Although your accountant can be an invaluable resource, it is essential that you become familiar with the most common methods that sellers, banks, investment bankers, and business brokers use for valuing a small business.

This chapter will focus on valuing a business for acquisition purposes, that is, for helping the buyer determine whether the seller's asking price is fair so that he can negotiate a realistic purchase price. Business valuations also must be made for the following reasons:

1. A seller needs to establish an asking price for his business.
2. Shareholders of a corporation need to agree on a method for establishing a buy/sell price for a business to get parameters for remaining, outgoing, and incoming owners of the business.
3. A couple is divorcing and the husband or wife owns an interest in a closely held company. A valuation must be put on the business to establish an equitable divorce settlement.
4. Someone is making a gift or bequest (upon death) of an interest in a business; naturally, he or she must try to minimize the gift or estate tax consequences.
5. Someone is preparing for a bankruptcy reorganization.

So how do you put a value on the business? You educate yourself in the criteria that go into business valuation. Unfortunately, it's not as easy to come up with a business's value as it is to determine the value of a house. Real-estate appraisers can relate the value of land and buildings to construction indexes and local market conditions and can compare the sales prices of similar homes. However, such

WARNING: WRONG-WAY THINKING

A common but misguided valuation approach is to assume that a buyer can put a proper value on his prospective business by starting with the seller's asking price and then negotiating downward. Some buyers figure that if they've gotten the seller to slash his price by 20 to 30 percent, they've got a bargain. Do not fall into this trap! If the seller has grossly overpriced the business, even a 30 percent price reduction may not reflect proper value. What's more, the seller is probably the person least qualified to determine a "fair" value for his business: He's got too much invested emotionally and too much to lose financially.

comparative methods are inappropriate for valuing a business—mainly because no two businesses are the same.

The type of business (retail, manufacturing, wholesale, personal service, or professional practice) will have a significant impact on the valuation approach you use. For example, a small- to medium-sized retail business that owns a large inventory (with an easy-to-identify market value) should include that inventory as part of its valuation picture. Similarly, businesses with the bulk of their assets in real-estate, machinery, and equipment must include the appraised value of their assets as part of the total picture. On the other hand, services businesses (e.g., insurance agencies, real-estate agencies, and repair businesses) and professional practices (e.g., lawyers, accountants, doctors, and financial advisers) usually do not have much in the way of hard assets or inventory. Therefore, valuing those businesses requires an entirely different approach. The following sections describe the three most commonly recognized valuation methods (each of which has many variations).

The Market (or Comparison) Approach

This method attempts to determine a business's *fair market value.* This term refers to the price at which a business would change hands when there's a willing seller and a ready, willing, and able buyer. Under this definition, fair market value refers, not to a specific seller and buyer, but to the hypothetical parties involved in an average, arms'-length transaction.

Reducing this concept to its simplest terms, if you wanted to purchase 100 shares of IBM, you'd calculate its value by going to the stock market and seeing what IBM is worth that day. Then you'd call a broker and have her get the best deal for the stock. The price she came away with would be the stock's fair market value.

The same concept holds true for buying a small business. If you're considering acquiring a computer technology company, you'd compare it with other computer technology companies and come up with a value based on what those other companies are selling for. Optimally, you'd attempt to find an exact mirror or mirrors of your target business for comparison. By mirror, I mean a company in a similar industry, in a similar location, of a similar size (in terms of volume and profitability), in business a similar length of time, and so on. Look at what price those businesses are selling for.

However, as we've discussed, the problem with this approach is that no two businesses are exactly alike. Because the individual characteristics of businesses depend on so many factors (unique talents of the owner and key personnel, sales volume, expenses, and competition, to name but a few), companies rarely have sufficient points of similarity to support credible comparisons. Not only that: It's unlikely that you'll find a large number of recent sales of businesses that are similar. And, while the selling price of a house is a matter of public record, there's no central repository where records of business sale transactions are maintained. Therefore, even finding out what a "similar" business sold for could be problematic, if not misleading.

One exception to this is franchised businesses, particularly new ones. Franchising is based on uniformity in terms of operating procedures, and conformity in terms of products, suppliers, and pricing—including comparable sales, expenses, and operating cost data (see Chapter 2). Thus, franchised operations more readily lend themselves to accurate comparison.

The Asset Approach

This is perhaps the most popular way to value a business when the business is asset intensive (primarily involved in selling tangible assets) and has many hard assets that can be sold. In such a case, you'd start by getting an expert to value the assets of the business, meaning inventory, furniture, fixtures, machinery, and equipment. To illustrate: If you have a lumberyard, you count how many pieces of wood there are and attribute a value to them; that's the value of the business.

When we speak of attributing a value to assets, we're referring to their market value, the price you'd expect to pay if you were to buy each asset or piece of equipment on the open market at a price experts in the industry would agree is reasonable. In a strict asset value approach, you are assuming that the value of the business is equal to what the assets are worth. If the business you're considering has a great many fixed assets and much equipment, it would be wise to have an appraisal done. Be sure to hire a professional appraiser with experience in your particular industry.

Valuing a business by the sum of its hard assets, however, has inherent limitations. Besides assets, inventory, and fixtures and equipment, which can be appraised, virtually all businesses include intangibles that must be included in the valuation. These intangibles (goodwill, customer lists, covenants not to compete, location, and things of that nature) have a more elusive value. Still, the value of goodwill (the anticipation of future profits) and other intangibles often exceeds the value of tangible assets. Thus, they should be included as part of any prudent approach to valuation.

Another problem: The asset value method assumes that all, or a significant portion, of a company's assets could be liquidated readily if so desired. This approach is fine for secured lenders who are assessing the value of collateralized assets. However, it's suspect when it's used to put a value on a business for acquisition purposes. The fundamental problem with an asset value approach is that it looks at a business's assets as valuable in and of themselves, without regard to the impact of those assets on the capability of a going concern to generate future income. Accordingly, valuations for the purpose of acquiring a business are better made with valuation methods that reflect future benefits to the investor (i.e., buyer) in the way of earning power (see "The Earnings Approach").

THE NET ADJUSTED ASSETS METHOD

A more accurate, more refined variation of the asset approach is the *net adjusted assets method*. In this method, the buyer values the assets and liabilities of the business, subtracts liabilities from assets, and adds on a value for intangibles (goodwill, customer lists, location, and the like). Here is an illustration of how the asset approach and net adjusted assets methods work:[*]

XYZ COMPANY SCHEDULE OF BOOK VALUE

Balance Sheet Category	Dollars ($)
Cash	160,000
Fixed assets	233,000
Accounts receivable	84,000
Inventory	266,000
Accounts payable	<75,000>
Accrued expenses	<13,000>
Equity	<655,000>
Calculation (equity method) equity	655,000
Goodwill (assuming two times earnings of $210,000)	420,000
Net book value	1,075,000

[*]*The illustrations appearing in this chapter were prepared by Bauman & Krasnoff, CPAs, an accounting firm based in New York City.*

The Earnings Approach

The last—and, I believe, the best and most widely recognized method—is the *earnings approach*. This method presumes that a business's value is based on its earnings. Here, because we are assuming that earnings dictate value, the key is to measure those earnings accurately and to determine their "worth" to you as a buyer. If, for instance, a company is going to generate a $100,000 profit for the next ten years, what you're willing to pay the owner should be based on that return and only on that return. The following sections discuss the three most common methods used in the earnings approach.

CAPITALIZATION OF EARNINGS METHOD

This approach places no value on the equipment or other fixed assets of the business. Instead, the value of the company is based on its capability to create earnings—the stream of income for which you are buying it. The business's assets are considered only incidental to that future income stream.

The capitalization of earnings approach presumes that the value of the business is based on its earnings *at a specific capitalization rate* (i.e., yield). A capitalization rate (cap rate) is a percentage that you plug into your valuation formula.

To make your calculation, you assume that the business's future earnings will be the same as its past earnings. So, go back a minimum of three to five years and write down what the after tax profits for the business were for each year. (Note: Using a time period any shorter than three to five years could be deceiving. The business could have had an extremely good year or bad year. You're looking for a weighted average.)

After you have this figure, multiply it by a *capitalization rate*. That will give you a value for the company. The key factor here—determining what capitalization rate to use—is what makes valuing a business so difficult. Here's where you (depending on your ability and willingness to properly research industry norms) and/or your

XYZ COMPANY CAPITALIZATION OF EARNINGS

	1996	1995	1994	1993
Weight *	4	3	3	2
After tax profits	$210,000	200,000	190,000	180,000
Weighted average	4/12	3/12	3/12	2/12
Net weighted average profits	$70,000	50,000	47,500	30,000

Weighted average adjusted after tax profit: $197,500
Capitalization rate: 8%
Value of business: $1,580,000

*Weight refers to the valuation strategy by which more importance is given to current and recent years' figures, under the theory that those numbers are more indicative of how the business actually is performing.

accountant will need to perform some legwork. Typically, a capitalization rate will be anywhere between 8 and 15 percent, depending on the industry. The above table provides an illustration of this approach.

In determining capitalization rate you look at factors such as whether the company (or industry) is risky or not, its profitability (historically) and earnings potential (in the future), the length of time the current owner has owned the business, whether its customer base is growing, whether competition is intense, etc. Depending on the answer to these questions you might need to make adjustments in the cap rate used for a particular business. For example, you'd be willing to use a lower capitalization rate for a business that's highly profitable than you would for a business that barely makes a profit.

THE RATIO MULTIPLIER METHOD

Industry multipliers are formulas that apply to specific industries. Because these are essentially "rule of thumb" valuation formulas, they are provided here with a big word of caution. The actual value of specific businesses within those industries may be very different. And although this method can be accurate, it's extremely simplistic and frequently unreliable. The reason is that these multipliers only consider sales and disregard profits. And because profits of a business rarely coincide with sales, relying on a measurement of sales volume can be misleading. A business with substantial sales may have substantial losses, whereas a business with a smaller sales volume may have a big profit margin. Still, industry multipliers can be useful in arriving at a ballpark figure, particularly when you're trying to take a quick first look at how a business is being priced.

Industry multipliers most often are used to value service businesses, particularly professional practices (lawyers, accountants, doctors, engineers, architects, insurance agencies, etc.) Essentially, the approach consists of multiplying the revenues generated by a business times an industry-accepted percentage (see accompanying chart). The normal range of multipliers is anywhere from 50 percent of revenues to two times revenues. Although this method isn't the most accurate one we've discussed, it's widely used because it is so simple.

INDUSTRY MULTIPLIERS

Industry	Multiplier
Service	1 times gross annual revenues
Manufacturer*	37 times gross annual revenues
Wholesaler*	$^1/_3$ times gross annual revenues
Retailer*	$^1/_3$ times gross annual revenues

*Although good for quick, seat-of-the-pants valuations, according to Alan Krasnoff, CPA, industry multipliers most often are used for service businesses—and have less utility in these industries.

One problem with industry multipliers is that they can be significantly affected by the terms of sale. For example, if a seller allowed a buyer a five-year payout, a higher multiplier might be appropriate because the buyer actually was able to use the revenues generated by the business to buy the original owner out. In this situation, the buyer might be willing to use a high multiplier because he'd be able to acquire the business without a significant cash outlay. Seventy-five percent of revenues to one times revenues is the most commonly used ratio, although factors such as location and competition can push these ratios up or down.

DISCOUNTED EARNINGS (DISCOUNTED CASH FLOW) METHOD

This is similar to the capitalization of earnings method, except that instead of using historical earnings, you use projected future earnings—typically, over a three- to ten-year period. In calculating future profitability, you'll need to make certain adjustments. For example, you may add certain expenses that the former owner didn't have which you might incur (like adequate insurance). And you may plan to reduce or eliminate other expenses, like certain advertising and promotional activities. Then you discount those projected earnings at a specific *discounted rate* (or *factor*). Discounting future cash flow reflects the fact that a dollar coming in tomorrow is worth less than one in your pocket today. It is a *time value of money principle*. (You'll read more on this concept in Chapter 10.) Like capitalization rates, the choice of discount rate will be the key to any valuation based on discounted earnings. The discount rate generally is determined by the return required on the assets, equity, and debt of the business and by its degree of risk. Obviously, this is quite complex. If you use this approach, you'll need to rely heavily on a professional experienced with business valuations based on discounted cash flow. The following table shows how this approach works.

XYZ COMPANY DISCOUNTED EARNINGS

Year	Projected earnings	Low risk present value discounted at 10%	Medium risk present value discounted at 12%	High risk present value discounted at 15%
1997	242,457	220,415	216,479	210,832
1998	278,825	230,434	222,278	210,832
1999	320,649	240,908	228,232	210,832
2000	368,746	251,858	234,345	210,832
2001	424,058	263,307	240,622	210,832
2002	487,667	275,275	247,067	210,832

Using this valuation method, the business would be worth $1,482,197, $1,389,023, or $1,264,992, depending on the degree of risk assumed. That's an average value of $1,378,737.

WARNING: USE REALISTIC PROJECTIONS

As you can see, the earnings forecast is critical when you are buying a business. Approach this important task with objectivity and care. A lack of objectivity in forecasting can be fatal. Many businesses fail because the buyers are too optimistic when they make projections.

Historical profits should be considered, but not relied upon exclusively. Even if the seller's statements regarding profitability are accurate (they often aren't), future profits may differ dramatically when the business is in your hands. Nevertheless, regressive analysis (i.e., an examination of the business's past) can help you define certain ongoing costs and expenses—and that, in turn, will help you forecast future profits more accurately.

ACQUIRING MINORITY BUSINESS INTERESTS

If you are considering acquiring a minority interest in a business, as opposed to the entire business, you'll need to discount your valuation by anywhere from 20 to 35 percent. Even the IRS recognizes such discounts for income, gift, and estate-tax purposes. By doing so, the IRS is acknowledging that a partial interest in a business (or an asset) has far less appeal in the marketplace, in part because the owners of minority interests have virtually no power or control over the company's affairs—a distinctively unattractive feature for most entrepreneurs.

The Bottom Line

Perhaps the most important thing to remember in the valuation process is that you must remain objective. Certainly you shouldn't rely on what the seller or business broker tells you about the business. Both have a financial stake in the deal. The more you pay, the more they stand to make, so both will be biased. (In fact, the broker will get paid only if you go through with the deal.) Instead, involve your professional team in this process. Their knowledge and experience may prove invaluable. And, because they don't have a financial stake in the transaction, they should be reliable sounding boards for your ideas and concerns.

A Final Word of Advice

In small business valuation, there's no such thing as an accurate rule of thumb. It sounds clever to say that service businesses should sell for one times annual earnings. However, you can't stop there. The formulas provided in this chapter are merely a starting point. And there's no one way to value a business. I believe that the best approach is to use all three methods. Determining value based on the different approaches will provide a check and balance to your analysis. While I would suggest giving more weight to the earnings approaches we've discussed, it's best not to put all your eggs into one basket.

CHAPTER 10

The Negotiation

Happily, you do not need a lawyer to conduct your *price* negotiations—indeed, in most instances, your lawyer shouldn't do the negotiating. When attorneys enter a room, the participants' mood, which should be collegial, quickly turns adversarial. Lawyers want to win, but you are not necessarily trying to win: You merely are seeking to acquire the business at a price both you and the seller see as fair.

You should talk to your lawyer about other matters, however, before you go into the bargaining session. He or she will focus your attention on two crucial issues: terms of the transaction that might expose you to personal liability and the importance of getting the consents you'll need to conduct the business successfully.

With respect to the latter, for example, you must be sure that the landlord will consent to the seller's transfer of the lease (on the business's location) to you. It is absolutely vital to get the seller's assurance that the lease is assignable (otherwise you may not be interested in the business at all), to find out what kinds of permits and business licenses might be needed, and to confirm that they too are transferable. A lawyer with experience in your target industry will be especially helpful on issues like these. (For instance, a lawyer who frequently handles the buying and selling of restaurants will be well versed in the intricacies of getting a liquor license.)

As Stephen M. Pollan points out in his book, *The Total Negotiator*, the price the seller first asks for her business is not a statement of value, but merely an invitation to buy. "Sellers rarely base their numbers on some exact mathematical formula," Pollan writes. "Instead, their numbers are generally hopeful guesses at what someone will be willing to pay." What's more, the terms of payment can be just as important as the dollar figure in persuading the owner of a business to sell.

That's why you also should consult your accountant before you get to the negotiating table. An accountant will know of ways you can make the transaction attractive to the seller even if you're unable to bargain the price she expects to receive down to the top price you're willing to pay.

And remember, you must never exceed that top price. Don't be seduced into paying more, even if you're convinced that the business you're trying to acquire is perfect for you—indeed, meant to be yours.

The negotiating tactics you'll use will depend on whether the owner you're dealing with is the proprietor of a family business, a serial seller, or what I'd call a "selling sophisticate." By the time you get to the negotiation stage, your research will have enlightened you as to which sort of seller you're dealing with, so you'll know what psychological skills you should bring to bear as well as what kinds of concessions are most likely to be fruitful with this particular seller.

Whatever the seller's personality, though, be careful not to let your ego take over during the negotiations. One party's lust for winning routinely kills deals that would have been advantageous to both buyer and seller. The fact is that you and the seller are not adversaries. As a potential buyer you have only two objectives: to pay no more than market value for the business and to structure the deal so that the payment is as easy on you as possible.

Don't let yourself become consumed, as far too many buyers and sellers do, with getting everything you want. If the business you acquire is right for you—gives you an adequate income stream and enhances your quality of life—you have come out a winner.

Enticing a Reluctant Seller

Anyone you are asking to sell a family business must be handled with particular delicacy. This is not the average salami negotiation, in which you slice at the meat with such cunning that the seller can't keep you from winding up with the bigger share. An owner who is letting go of a beloved family firm feels as if she's selling you a part of herself, so you must convince her that she can trust you. (In Chapter 6, we discussed strategies for establishing trust.) Of course, you'll need fewer powers of persuasion when the family business owner has put the company on the market. Still, you must negotiate with tact, for in the seller's mind, you are, in effect, asking to join her family.

Handling a Serial Seller

Restaurants, diners, bars, and mail order houses are the kinds of ventures that attract serial sellers—entrepreneurs who start them up, operate them for a couple of years, put them up for sale, and then start another business. Serial sellers are experts at bringing a company up to break even and then selling it to someone who, they hope, will pay too much.

Don't deal with a serial seller unless you've researched his business so thoroughly that you aren't as naive as he hopes you will be. Your negotiating tactics will be different from those you use with a family business owner. You'll be courteous, but you can show some

<u>**TIP:** DON'T WAIT FOR A BUSINESS TO GO ON SALE</u>

Don't be afraid to approach the owner of a business you think is an attractive buy even if she has not put it up for sale. Owners will always listen to a pitch. Even if they haven't given much thought to selling, they'd like to know what sort of value a stranger would put on their enterprise.

---

sharp edges. Remember: The last thing this sort of owner wants is to see you walk out. Therefore, if he continues to ask a price you think is too high, it's okay to bring him up short with a question like "Is your business for sale or not?"

The ability to walk away from a deal is the strongest tactic a buyer can deploy. However, you should never come across as hostile; you merely need to make it clear to a serial seller that you intend to stick to whatever top price you previously determined to pay. (If you don't, you risk making the worst kind of mistake—a knowing mistake.)

With a family business owner you'd be careful not to disparage anything about the business. But with a serial seller you want to point out the negatives, factors that should make him lower his price. You needn't be belligerent. You should, however, be firm and direct. For instance, "I can't pay that price because there are a lot of things I'm going to have to fix." (And then you enumerate them: "I'm going to have to spend a lot of money on marketing," etc.)

The Sophisticated Seller

This owner just wants to get out. He's not emotionally attached to the business, and you can't lure him with the offer of an annuity or a consultancy (see "Sweetening the Deal"); he wants only to get out quickly, get the best price he can negotiate, and get cash.

Because the sweeteners mentioned later in this chapter won't be attractive to the sophisticated seller, the only way you can acquire his business—if you can't pay enough to meet his bottom line—is to out sophisticate him by buying less than the whole company and giving yourself an option to buy the rest of the business later. You and the seller can agree up front that at a specified future date, you'll buy him out of his remaining interest in the business at a set price (this is called a *put*).

Purchasing less than the whole company can still be a good deal for a buyer: If you own more than 50 percent of a business, you control the way the company is run. If you can't afford to buy the whole thing, why not acquire 51 percent?

Negotiating 101

When you and the seller sit down to negotiate, you'd be wise to know how to perform that delicate dance of offer/counteroffer called *incremental negotiation*. This is the bargaining technique often used in real-estate transactions.

Suppose (to keep the illustration simple) the seller is asking $100,000, and you think the business actually is worth around $65,000. Your first offer should be somewhere around $50,000. If the seller really wants to sell, he will signal his seriousness by taking a giant step downward, reducing his price to, say, $75,000.

Most people in America believe in "splitting the difference" when we're conducting a negotiation. Clearly, the seller has already done that. He's chosen the middle between $100,000 and $50,000 for his counteroffer. So should you split the difference between his $75,000 and your $50,000 by offering $62,500? Definitely not. You, the buyer, will create the "lowest possible middle" by making your increments of price increase small. Any price raise you offer tells the seller two things: that you're willing to negotiate and that there's a limit to how far you're willing to go. Your aim is to inch the seller down toward you.

What the seller has indicated, by reducing his price to $75,000 after you've offered $50,000, is that he's willing to settle at a figure near $62,500 (for he expects you, too, to split the difference). Don't do what he expects. Say, "Look, when I said $50,000, I really meant $50,000. Maybe I can do $55,000." (If you're dealing with a family business owner, you'd convey the same idea, but more gently. Sometimes, all you can do is ask the seller if he could possibly lower his asking price because you can't afford to go any higher.) You're not going to be as generous to him as he has been to you. And your next incremental increase should be even smaller. Naturally, you'd modify your tactics according to how much you believe the business is worth. If you think it's worth your while to get closer to his figure, then your increments should be bigger. Once again: You are not trying to win a game; you are trying to acquire the business for a price you feel comfortable paying.

And now for the psychological dynamics. When you make a counteroffer, always explain why you've made your bid this low. You must be sure that your counteroffer isn't perceived as an insult, particularly when you're dealing with a family business owner. You must not seem to be saying "You're asking too much for your business." If there's a good reason why your bid is so low, explain why gracefully. If you can't find a realistic reason, then say, "I'm afraid I can't afford to pay that."

My experience with negotiating sessions has shown me why pride is one of the seven deadly sins. Because I know how easily a tactless remark can provoke hostility, even intransigence, I'm careful to be temperate in the way I phrase things. And you should be just as circumspect.

Sweetening the Deal

Needless to say, before you go into the negotiating session, you must carefully research the firm you want to buy and do a valuation analysis (see Chapter 9). However, to achieve your ultimate goal (which is to purchase the business at the low end of the range of prices identified as reasonable in your valuation analysis), you must understand the ways in which a deal can be sweetened for the seller (or made more palatable to you, the buyer) if he refuses to come down to your top price. Here are a few such strategies:

1. ***Structure the deal so the seller pays a capital gains tax rather than ordinary income tax.*** According to Stewart Bauman, CPA, "The characterization of income as *capital* or *ordinary* and the differentiation between long term and short term capital gains and losses is required for proper structuring—from a tax perspective." (More on this in Chapter 11.) A *capital* gain arises from the sale of a capital asset. Some examples of capital assets involved in the sale of a business are the sale of stock, fixed assets (such as real-estate), and goodwill. Capital gains are included with a taxpayer's other income but are subject to a maximum tax rate of 20 percent (recently lowered from 28 percent). Income from other than a capital gain is considered *ordinary* and is subject to a maximum tax rate of 39.6 percent. Your accountant should be able to suggest ways to structure the deal so that the tax consequences benefit the seller and, by extension, you the buyer. In this instance, careful structuring, from a tax perspective, could help bridge the gap between seller and buyer in the negotiation over price.

2. ***Propose an installment sale.*** According to Stewart Bauman, another way to bridge the gap between seller and buyer is to have an installment sale—that is, you offer to structure the deal so the seller receives the purchase price over several years. This will enable the buyer to spread out the payments, with interest, over a stipulated period of time. The advantage to the seller is that he can prorate, over the installment sale period, the taxable capital gain he's required to pay on the sale.

3. ***Propose that a significant portion of the purchase price be allocated to fixed assets or a consulting agreement.*** If the seller is stuck on his price, the buyer should consider structuring the deal so that a significant portion of the purchase price is allocated to fixed assets (which can be depreciated faster than, say,

goodwill) or a consulting agreement with the seller (which can be expensed currently). By structuring the deal this way, you'll be able to meet the seller's price and, in turn, reap a financial benefit through significant tax write-offs early on. (For a more detailed discussion of allocation, see Chapter 11.)

4. *Pay more—but over a longer period of time.* Suppose, after you've bargained awhile, the owner is still insisting on an unrealistic price. You may sense that because his ego clearly is involved and he'd consider a lower price an affront to his business, you should stop making counteroffers. Don't give up. Even in such a situation, you may be able to make the deal. You could, for instance, agree to pay the price he asks—as long as he gives you more time in which to pay him. If he'll give you the time, you can afford to give him the money, especially if the projections you've made indicate that you'll be able to generate that extra money out of company profits.

Let's say the owner is asking $500,000, all cash, and you've decided that you should not go above $400,000. Before you came to the negotiating session, your accountant should have taught you that money diminishes in value when you wait to pay it. So you agree to the seller's $500,000 price, but you'll add two conditions: that you pay that extra $100,000 in five to ten years and that you'll pay the extra money only if your revenues exceed a certain dollar figure.

In any decision where the timing of costs to be incurred or revenues to be realized varies, the *opportunity cost* of spending or receiving funds at an earlier or later date (a concept known as *the time value of money*) is an important consideration. The easiest method of incorporating the time value of money into the decision involves the use of present value formulas.

Here's an example: Say the current rate of interest that you can comfortably earn on your money is 8 percent. If you agree to pay $100,000 more than you expected to pay, but don't make that payment until a year from now (investing the money instead), that extra $100,000 will really only cost you $92,592.60. Why? Because $92,596.60, invested today at 8 percent, would give you $100,000 at the end of the year. Therefore, for purposes of our discussion of price, when you pay over a longer period of time, the significance of the extra amount of money you're paying is diluted.

5. *Persuade the seller that his life's work will live on through you.* Before you go into the negotiation, prepare a business redeployment plan that will show this reluctant seller how you can make his business grow (see Chapter 12). When you show him the plan, you are letting him know that you are not merely buying a business, you are continuing his dream.

6. *Let the seller know that the family member you retain will help carry on his legacy.* Sometimes, offering to let a family member stay on is a very effective tactic. If the owner has, say, a daughter working in the business, he may be thinking, "Omigod, what will she do now?" If the negotiation is going badly for you, you might consider saying, "Well, I've been watching your daughter, and she's really doing a nice job. Do you think she might want to stay on?"

7. *Offer to let the seller retain a portion of the business or be kept on for a circumscribed period of time as a consultant.* If the deal threatens to fall through, you might offer the seller a small partnership interest for a short period of time. Make this sound like a wonderful deal for him: "What if I offer you the best of all possible worlds—this price plus an equity position? Let's say that for the first five years, you get 5 percent of the profits after I've made my payments to you and taken a salary for me." However, make such a suggestion only if you've done your homework well and have good reason to believe that future profits will make such a partnership interest feasible.

8. *Offer to close very quickly.* A business sale often takes a very long time. For one thing, a typical buyer spends a lot of time on his due diligence research (see Chapters 7 and 8).

However, a buyer who has experience in the field or who already has done his homework may be able to close more quickly than normal. Also, if the buyer doesn't need financing because he can pay cash or has prequalified for a loan, that buyer, too, can close quickly. And sometimes a quick closing is important to a seller.

The Letter of Intent

After you and the seller have come to an agreement on major issues, you should draw up a simple *letter of intent* describing the matters on which you and the seller have agreed. This document should clearly state that it does not obligate you to buy the business, but, rather, that any sale of the business will be contingent upon the signing, by you and the seller, of a mutually agreeable formal document called a *purchase agreement*. This document, which will be far more detailed (see Chapter 11), will be drafted by both the buyer's and the seller's attorneys.

Your goal, in drafting the letter of intent, is to get down on paper, as soon as possible after the negotiating session, the specifics of what you and the seller agreed to in that session. The document should cover the price and terms agreed upon as well as a discussion of the kind of access you will have to the seller's business premises, financial records, key employees, customers, and suppliers. If the seller balks at giving you the access you need to his premises and his records, you'll know this is a troubled business—not the business for you to buy.

Now it's time for your lawyer and the seller's lawyer to get together to draw up the purchase agreement.

CHAPTER 11

Structuring the Transaction and Closing the Deal

So FAR YOU'VE SUCCESSFULLY NAVIGATED THE SEARCH PROCESS, compiled a list of potential candidates, and located a business that's right for you. You've researched the operational and financial aspects of the business to ascertain its current condition and potential for future growth. You've used the valuation formulas we discussed in Chapter 9 and consulted with your legal and tax experts to determine a proper value for the business. You've made an offer to the seller and, with the help of the negotiating strategies we discussed in Chapter 10, negotiated price and payment terms you consider fair. After all that, your offer has finally been accepted. What's left? Structuring the transaction and closing the deal.

When they "structure the transaction," the buyer and the seller take into account the tax and legal considerations that arise in the transfer of a business from one party to another. Many legal texts and other how-to books on buying a business suggest that deciding how you, the buyer, want to structure the deal should come before the negotiating session. It's unwise, they suggest, to go into a negotiation if you haven't figured out the tax consequences of the way the deal will be structured or if you haven't decided whether to buy the stock of the business or just its assets (a choice we will discuss in detail).

The authors of these texts don't state this outright, but I gather that they believe that buyers and sellers are well enough versed in complicated matters like tax law to deal with these factors during their negotiating session (either that or they're suggesting that lawyers and accountants should negotiate price and terms, which, as you know, is contrary to my advice). However, virtually none of the buyers I've encountered in my practice have the expertise to negotiate the tax and legal issues that arise in the transfer of a business, so it is difficult for me to picture most buyers taking this on themselves. Although you, the buyer, should think about these issues before the negotiating session, I advise you not to bring them up when you're negotiating with the seller. It's the professionals—the buyer's lawyer and accountant and the seller's lawyer and accountant—who should structure the deal. What's more, I see a psychological advantage to the buyer in leaving the discussion of deal structure until after the seller has agreed on price and payment terms.

After the buyer and seller themselves have agreed upon a value for the business, it is easy for them to step out of these discussions (at least, the initial discussions) and let the experts bang heads. In my experience, a seller who has gotten to this stage of a transaction won't let the deal fall apart over tax and legal considerations, provided, of course, that the deal structure the buyer is asking for isn't completely unreasonable.

As you'll discover later in this chapter, after the buyer and seller have come to terms about everything, including how the transaction shall be structured, they sign a purchase agreement. This document contains all of the terms to which the parties have agreed. It sets forth the obligations of the parties toward each other, spells out the manner in which all financial and other issues have been resolved in the negotiation process, states how the deal will be structured, states how the closing is to be handled, and binds the seller and buyer legally.

Structuring the Deal: Buy the Assets or Buy the Stock?

The seminal decision, for some, at this stage of the business acquisition is whether to purchase the assets or the stock. (If the seller is a sole proprietor or the business is conducted as a partnership, you have no choice; all you can buy are the seller's assets.) Assume that the seller conducts her business as a corporation and that the corporation owns all of the business's assets. There are two possible ways to buy the business: You can buy the entity itself, by acquiring the corporate stock from the corporation's owners (its shareholders), or you can buy the business's assets.

When you purchase the stock of a business, everything the business owns (and owes) becomes the property of you, the new owner. That means that all of the assets, as well as all of the liabilities, of the company are transferred to you. If, on the other hand, you purchase only the assets of a business, only title to those assets enumerated in the purchase agreement will be transferred to you; the seller retains the liabilities, unless you specifically agree to assume them. For this reason (and others that we will discuss), sellers usually prefer to sell the stock of their business, and buyers usually prefer to acquire only the assets.

Often, whether you buy the stock or whether you buy the assets will have an impact on the amount of money you'll be willing to pay for the business. If the seller won't sell her business unless you take on her liabilities by purchasing the company's stock, but you want to buy only the company's assets, you may be able to resolve the issue by taking the stock but paying less than you had negotiated in the negotiating session. Or you might offer to take only the assets, but pay more than you'd agreed to pay in the negotiating session.

Therefore, while I believe they should not take place first, discussions regarding how the deal is to be structured should follow closely on the heels of your price and terms negotiation.

Advantages and Disadvantages of Acquiring the Assets

Most buyers prefer to buy the assets of the company for two basic reasons: tax benefits and protection against lawsuits and claims for unpaid taxes (particularly sales and withholding, which are personal liabilities) provoked by the actions of the previous owner.

The Advantages

1. *Tax benefits.* When you purchase the assets of a business, you'll immediately begin to recover a portion of your investment through tax deductions for the inventory and depreciable property. But heed this warning: Don't inflate the fair market value of your business's assets. (Some buyers do this to increase their expense write-offs.)

   Prior to the Tax Reform Act of 1986, assets could be bought and "written up" to fair market value without incurring a tax liability. (What's meant by written up is that the assets actually have a lower value because of depreciation than buyers reflect on their tax forms. Instead the buyer will value these assets as if they were still worth what they'd cost new.) Under current law, however, if the assets are written up in value after the purchase, the buyer must pay a tax. And if the IRS believes that you've valued the assets above their fair market value, they may take the position that the excess amount is attributable to goodwill.

   To skirt this tax trap, it's wise to allocate all, or a significant portion, of the purchase price to a non-compete agreement or a consulting contract (see item 4 under "The Purchase Agreement: Protecting the Buyer"). Either of these will provide you with tax-deductible expenses that more often than not won't be challenged by the IRS.

2. *Relief of liability.* Suppose, on the day after you've bought the business, one of the customers files suit against you claiming he lost thousands of dollars as a result of a late delivery by the former owner. If you've purchased only the assets of the business, you're off the hook. On the other hand, if you had bought the stock, you would own the entity that contracted with the injured customer, and any damages would be paid from your business.

The problem of unknown or contingent liabilities is one of the main reasons sellers want to sell stock and why buyers prefer to buy assets. Sellers want to know that, when they turn over the business, they're done with it. They can walk away without worrying that an old problem could come back to haunt them at some later date. Naturally, buyers want just the opposite: They want to know that they'll receive only that for which they've bargained—what's disclosed on the business's balance sheet and income statement.

The Disadvantages

1. *The sales tax.* In most instances, people who buy a business's assets are required to pay a sales tax, just as do people who buy personal assets or property like clothing, furniture, cars, etc. Therefore, state and local sales taxes will effectively increase the purchase price of the business.

Advantages and Disadvantages of Acquiring the Stock

The Advantages

1. *It's easier to persuade owners to sell a business's stock rather than a business's assets.* Sellers generally prefer not to sell assets because they must pay two tiers of tax on an asset sale. First, the business pays a tax (at the corporate level) on the sale of the assets. Then the business makes a liquidating distribution

WARNING: THE BULK SALES PITFALL

Virtually every state has a law—triggered by the sale of all, or substantially all, of the assets of a business—that is known as the Bulk Sales Law. It comes into play only if the sale is an asset sale. The purpose of bulk sales laws is to give some protection to the creditors of a business whose assets are being sold (assuming that the business being sold has inventory, although the requirement that the business has inventory to trigger the bulk sales law varies from state to state). Here's how it works: The buyer must notify all of the seller's creditors (from a list given in a sworn affidavit by the seller) of the intended sale no less than ten days before the sale. If the buyer fails to do so, the seller's creditors can later make a claim against the assets sold to the buyer. (If the seller fails to list any business creditors on the affidavit, the seller remains liable for claims from that creditor, not the buyer.)

Because bulk sales laws protect the buyer, not the seller, sellers often attempt to persuade buyers to waive compliance with the law. If the seller tries this, she'll usually offer her indemnification of liabilities as a substitute. Do not be persuaded by the seller to waive the notification requirement. If you do, and problems with creditors surface later and the seller doesn't have the money to pay or can't be found, you'll be stuck.

(of the amount paid by the buyer) to the shareholder/owner, who must pay tax (at the personal level), on the dividend (assuming there is a gain).

When it's a stock sale, however, the seller has only one level of tax to pay—a capital gain on the difference between the sales price of the stock and its original basis, that is, its value when the seller bought it. Therefore, the capital gains rate may influence the desire of the seller to sell either stock or assets, particularly because the rate was recently reduced from 28 to 20 percent.

2. *A stock sale is faster.* Acquiring the stock of a business is less time-consuming than acquiring the assets because selling stock is much easier for an owner than selling assets. To sell her stock, the individual seller need only endorse her stock certificates over to the buyer and resign as an officer and director of the corporation. That's all. However, in most states, when assets are sold, all of the creditors of the company whose assets are being sold must be given prior notice of the pending sale. This process (a bulk sales notice, which we've touched upon earlier and will discuss in more detail later) can be cumbersome. What's more, because a sale of assets is a corporate action, the transaction must be approved by shareholders' resolution and officer and director meetings.

3. *A stock sale can overcome restrictions on the transfer of a valuable right or asset.* When the corporation being sold owns a valuable right or asset essential to the conduct of a business, and that right or asset cannot be transferred, the buyer may have no choice but to buy the stock of the business from its owners. A classic example: The corporation holds title to the business's commercial lease as tenant and "the tenant's interest cannot be assigned or sublet." This lease restriction, however, doesn't always prohibit the shareholders of the corporation from selling their stock. When they do so, the buyer and seller will have been able to circumvent the transfer restriction contained in the lease. Similar examples include the transfer of a liquor license (in the restaurant business) or the transfer of a broadcast license (by a radio station).

The Disadvantages

1. *Vulnerability to lawsuit.* This is a serious drawback to buying a business's stock (see item 2 of the advantages under "Advantages and Disadvantages of Acquiring the Assets").

2. ***Possible pension liabilities.*** If the seller has instituted a qualified pension or profit sharing plan for her employees under ERISA (Employee Retirement Income Security Act of 1974), the seller was required to make annual contributions to the plan. The purpose of annual contributions is to ensure that sufficient funds are available to pay employees' pension benefits or meet their share of the profit sharing plan. If your seller is behind in those payments, or if significant future payments will be required, you'd better make adequate provision to cover those liabilities. Before buying a company with such a plan, make sure that you have an ERISA expert determine the plan's funding status.

3. ***Conflicts with the employees' union.*** The other common area of concern is dealing with unionized employees. In a stock transaction, the new owner's relationship with the union (good or bad) will be the same as the previous owner's (i.e., by law, you must honor the union contract). However, if you buy assets of a unionized firm, you will not be required to recognize (comply with the terms of) the collective bargaining agreement with the union. If you plan on retaining most or all of the union employees, however, the law prohibits you from disavowing the agreement.

The Purchase Agreement: Protecting the Buyer

The purchase agreement is one of the most important documents you'll ever sign. It is the cornerstone of the business acquisition, both intellectually and legally. A good contract will reflect your hard work, taking advantage of your thorough investigation and protecting you from known and unknown risks. A bad one will waste your good efforts and leave you exposed by making the seller's problems yours.

This is where your choice of a savvy attorney will really pay off. Many of my fellow authors suggest that the buyer's lawyer be the one to draft the purchase agreement. However, your attorney may not get the chance to do so. In the real world, it is usually the seller's attorney who is charged with the responsibility of preparing the agreement. This isn't necessarily a bad thing.

If your attorney is skillful, she will be able to use the role of "receiver" (of the seller's draft agreement) to her advantage. While the drafter of the agreement lays the groundwork, the responding attorney is free to attack what's been written and to add items that have been left out.

Although your attorney will be in charge of responding to the agreement (or, on rare occasions, drafting it), you should know what sorts of things to watch out for. Here is a list of the provisions that appear in a typical asset purchase agreement, along with some tips on what issues each should address:

1. *The parties.* The first section sets forth the names of the parties who are to be bound by the terms and conditions of the agreement. Because you're buying the assets directly from the corporation that owns them, the corporation must be named as a seller. But that's not enough: You'll need to go one step farther.

   Be sure to have the *individual shareholders* of the corporation named as well. Because you're buying all the assets of the corporation, there may be nothing left to sue for in the event that the *corporate* seller fails to live up to the representations, warranties, and other obligations in the agreement that continue beyond the closing. (In fact, most selling corporations are dissolved shortly after an asset sale.)

2. *Assets and liabilities.* Whether the deal is structured as an asset purchase or as a stock purchase, this section is especially

critical. You need to know exactly what it is you're buying, and therefore the seller is going to have to list *all* of the assets being sold (including equipment, machinery, furniture, inventory, accounts receivable, leases, contract rights, licenses, goodwill, trademarks, copyrights, and patents). Make sure that the seller represents that all of the assets are owned by the seller and that they will be conveyed to you free and clear of any debts, liens, or encumbrances.

In addition, the seller must be required to disclose all of its liabilities or obligations, and the agreement should state which, if any, will be assumed by the buyer. If the seller fails to list a liability, the buyer won't be bound by it. Remember our discussion on bulk sales (which we'll discuss further later in this chapter).

3. *Purchase price.* This section will state how much the buyer is to pay for the business, and should set forth the terms of payment, that is, how much of a deposit is to be paid when you sign the purchase agreement (typically, 5 to 10 percent of the purchase price), how much the buyer will pay at closing in cash, and how much is to be paid by promissory note (if the deal involves seller financing—and most do). The terms of the promissory note are typically not set forth in the agreement; instead, the promissory note itself will be prepared and attached to the agreement as an exhibit.

4. *Allocation of purchase price.* How the purchase price is allocated among the assets being bought can have significant tax ramifications. Typically, a buyer will attempt to allocate as much of the price as possible to depreciable assets to gain a high beginning *basis*. Because a future sale of the business will be taxed on the *gain* over and above the buyer's basis, this allocation favors a buyer. Conversely, if the assets have been substantially depreciated over the years by the seller (on his tax returns), the seller stands to get hurt by this allocation because he may realize a significant taxable capital gain on the sale of

those assets (when he receives much more than the depreciated value). You should consider allocating a significant part of the purchase price to an agreement not to compete, or a consulting agreement, with the seller. That's because by doing so, you'll receive write-offs much faster than you could from any assets you buy. (You can amortize the payments over the term of the agreement, which typically runs from one to five years, as opposed to allocating price to land, inventory, and goodwill, which cannot be depreciated or amortized at all.) Because this section of the agreement is primarily tax driven, be sure to have your lawyer consult with your accountant so the allocation will be structured to your advantage.

5. *Closing date.* Contrary to what you might think, the date set forth in the agreement for closing is not chiseled in stone. Instead, it is a target date, and both parties have the right to postpone the closing for a reasonable period of time. What's reasonable depends upon the particular circumstances and varies from state to state—although about 30 days is a typical time-frame. The one exception is where the agreement specifically states that "time is of the essence" with respect to the parties obligation to close on a certain date (the "magic" language varies). When that language is used, the parties have, in effect, drawn a line in the sand. The downside of using this language is that it's very risky for both seller and buyer. If a party becomes ill, has a death in the family, or is otherwise unable to attend the closing on a specific date, the deposit could be forfeited, in the case of the buyer, or the deal could be lost, in the case of the seller.

6. *Representations and warranties.* The section that sets forth the seller's representations and warranties is the meat and potatoes of the purchase agreement. In this section, the seller promises you that certain matters are true and accurate. The seller may have painted a rosy picture of his business during the negotiation stage; that's merely puffing. However, if he

fudges on any representations, he has breached the agreement and he'll suffer the consequences (which we'll discuss shortly). Here's a list of the most important representations to get:

- The seller is a validly existing corporation (if it is a corporation), is in good standing, and has the authority to enter into the agreement.
- The agreement has been entered into with the approval of the seller's board of directors and shareholders (if there are shareholders).
- The seller owns the assets outright, and the assets will be free and clear of liens and encumbrances at closing.
- On the date of closing, the lease covering the seller's location will be in full force and effect (with no defaults by seller).
- The equipment, machinery, furniture, inventory, and other tangible assets will be in good working order on the date of closing.
- The seller has no subsidiaries or interest in other businesses that conduct part of the seller's business.
- The seller has no business dealings or interests in any customers' or suppliers' businesses that aren't at arm's length.
- The financial statements (given to you previously) are complete, accurate, have been prepared in accordance with generally accepted accounting principles applied consistently, and fairly present the financial condition of the seller for the periods covered.
- All taxes, including income, sales, and withholding taxes, have been paid in full.
- There are no claims or legal proceedings or judgments against the seller, its officers, directors, employees, or assets.
- The seller has not violated any laws, regulations, or ordinances applicable to its business.

- The seller has disclosed (by attaching a schedule to the agreement) a complete and accurate list of all contracts to which the seller is bound.
- After the agreement has been signed, and prior to closing, the seller will conduct its business in the ordinary course, maintain its assets in good condition, use its best efforts to maintain good relations with customers, employees, and suppliers, and refrain from taking any actions that would be adverse to the buyer's interests.
- The buyer and the buyer's representatives shall be given full access to the seller's employees, books and records, and contracts. The seller and its accountant shall cooperate with the buyer and supply such information as the buyer may reasonably request prior to closing (naturally, the buyer should promise not to disclose any such information prior to closing other than to his/her professionals).

TIP: INCLUDE APPROPRIATE BELTS AND SUSPENDERS

Buyers will want to add certain other representations and warranties, depending upon the type of business and assets being acquired. For example, in a retail business the seller should be required to warrant inventory levels and collectible accounts receivable. Because it would be impossible to attribute a precise value to these at some future date (i.e., in advance of the closing), the seller might ask that the warranty be limited to a specified value range. If so, make sure you're comfortable with the range warranted and never compensate the seller dollar for dollar for receivables. They may be uncollectible. If possible, make collection the seller's responsibility.

What will you, as the buyer, be asked to represent and warrant? Unless the seller provides financing, all a buyer typically is required to represent and warrant is the existence of the new corporation formed to acquire the assets and its authority to consummate the transaction spelled out in the purchase agreement. If the seller is providing financing, the buyer normally will be asked to represent and warrant its financial condition. If the buyer is a new corporation with no financial history, the seller will want this to be a personal representation and warranty from the buyer's principal—you.

7. *Conditions to closing.* Along with the two sections that follow (indemnity and escrow or holdback), this section of the purchase agreement is as important as any other. If any of the matters set forth in this section occur or, if required, fail to occur before the closing, the buyer can walk away from the deal. In effect, this provision is the buyer's escape clause. Not surprisingly, the attorneys for the buyer and seller usually spend quite a bit of time negotiating this section. As a buyer, your lawyer should attempt to protect you by making the conditions as broad as possible. At a minimum, you'll want your obligations conditioned on the seller's representations and warranties' being true and correct; the seller performing all of its obligations (as set forth in agreement); no material adverse change having occurred (financial or otherwise) in the business or its assets; and the seller having obtained all required consents for the transfer to the buyer of all leases, licenses, contracts, and permits reasonably necessary to conduct business at the current location. The seller should not resist these. If he does, that could spell trouble.

8. *Covenant not to compete and consulting agreement.* You'll want to make sure the purchase agreement contains sections regarding the seller's covenant not to compete. This means that the seller won't set up shop down the street and continue to do business with his old (your new) customers, employees, and suppliers. It also includes the seller's promise not to use or disclose proprietary information or trade secrets of your business.

Assuming the seller is going to stay on for a period of time to train you or to facilitate transition, you'll also want those obligations carefully spelled out in a consulting agreement.

While both of these issues can be handled within the four corners of the purchase agreement, in most instances the purchase agreement will simply make reference to them. Separate agreements will be prepared, negotiated, and attached to the purchase agreements as exhibits, as we'll see later in this chapter.

9. *Indemnification.* The indemnification section is crucial to the buyer. It is the teeth behind the seller's promises. Even though you'll hold back money at the closing to cover unknown, undisclosed, or contingent liabilities or debts, the amount held back could be insufficient to cover what might arise. What's more, as we'll see, you'll be entitled to hold back your money only for a finite period of time, so you'll need additional protection to safeguard against problems that surface after the holdback period expires.

In effect, in this section the seller is agreeing to reimburse you in the event that you suffer a monetary loss due to a breach by the seller of the representations and warranties made in the purchase agreement. Of particular concern to the buyer are the promises that relate to the extent of the seller's debts and liabilities, financial condition (meaning what's on the balance sheet, tax returns, etc.), and the existence of any claims, suits, or judgments against the seller not disclosed in the agreement.

The Holdback: Protection Against Unexpected Problems

You will recall that in Chapters 7 and 8 we discussed the procedures for investigating the operational (non-financial) and financial

TIP: CHECK THE INDEMNITIES CAREFULLY

First, be sure the seller's indemnities cover the costs you'd incur in enforcing the agreement. In other words, if you have to sue the seller, you should recover what you're forced to spend to do so (legal fees, etc.). Next, make sure the seller's indemnities run to the seller's individual shareholders *personally*. As we've discussed, most corporations are dissolved shortly after they've sold all their assets, so you'll want the shareholders of the seller/corporation on the hook personally in the event you have to sue.

---

affairs of your target business. Despite its importance, this earlier investigation is only a preliminary procedure to assess potential pitfalls. It does nothing to protect the buyer legally from hidden liabilities, whether known by the seller (but not disclosed) or unknown, nor does it afford the buyer any opportunity for recourse against the seller should problems arise at a later date.

Along with a device known as *setoff* (which we'll discuss later when we look at the promissory note), the best method of protection available to a buyer is the requirement that a portion of the purchase price be held back and placed in *escrow* to satisfy later claims. In effect, the holdback provision amounts to a pool of funds that are set aside to pay debts not disclosed by (or that were unknown to) the seller. The three most important issues involving the holdback are how much, how long, and who holds it. How much is normally a function of the size of known liabilities and the likelihood of risk from unknown ones. A minimum of 10 percent of the purchase price is a ballpark rule of thumb, although I've seen as much as 50 percent in certain instances. In terms of how long, the amount held back should be kept for at least six months (which, in most states, is the period of time in which a creditor of a business that has changed ownership is required to make a claim).

As far as who holds the money, the seller will want his attorney to be the escrow agent, and you'll want yours. Because the escrow agent should be acting merely as a stakeholder, my feeling is that you should be more concerned with the amount of the hold-back and the length of time the money is to be held rather than with who holds it. If the seller's attorney is holding the money, you'll want to be sure he is not allowed to release the funds without your written consent.

Other Ancillary Agreements

There are issues related to the purchase of a business that are so critical that it may not be sufficient simply to deal with them in the purchase agreement. The three most significant issues are the covenant not to compete, the consulting agreement, and the promissory note and security agreement.

The Non-Competition Agreement

Say you've just bought a pizza shop in a thriving business district. Business people flock to your location because there's no other pizza place in the neighborhood. How would you feel if, on the day after you bought your business, the former owner opened up a pizza place down the street? To avoid this kind of disaster, you'll need to get the seller to agree, in writing, not to compete with you after the sale. Don't be influenced by the seller's assurances that he's "leaving town" or "quitting the business." Even if that's true today, what if he changes his mind in a month or a year? Without a non-competition agreement you'd be stuck.

The agreement must be ironclad and must protect you for a sufficient length of time. It also must cover a specific geographic territory so you'll be assured that your customer base will remain intact. The duration and geographic scope will depend on how unique the business is and on the impact your business would feel from competition with the former owner.

The agreement should state that the seller will not compete with you directly, indirectly, or through anyone else, in any capacity whatsoever. It also should state that the seller will not use or disclose any information that is proprietary to your business (i.e., trade secrets, customer lists, supplier lists, and the like). Finally, it should prohibit the seller from enticing your employees, customers, or suppliers to change affiliation. And the consequences of violating the agreement must be severe—such as monetary damages, an injunction (where a court steps in and says "stop"), and/or the release from payment obligations under the promissory note. See Appendix G for a form of non-competition agreement that can be adapted for almost every situation.

The Consulting Agreement

Before turning our attention to what a consulting agreement should say, let's examine why you'd want one. There are three excellent reasons why you should consider keeping the seller involved in the business for a period of time after the acquisition. For one thing, such an arrangement will often help induce the owner of a business to sell to you in the first place. As discussed in Chapter 6, owners sometimes need (for financial reasons) or want (for emotional ones) to remain active in the business they're about to sell. Some need the continued stream of income. Others desire the comfort of a "place to go" where they can continue to feel important and productive. For example, if you are attempting to buy a "mom and pop" or family-owned business, your willingness to "adopt" the owner's son or daughter may clinch the deal, especially if you're dealing with a reluctant seller.

A second reason is that the continued presence of the seller in the business often is needed to effect a smooth transition after the acquisition. The presence of the previous owner can pave the way for good relations with customers and key employees and suppliers. Depending on the nature of the business you are buying, and your level of knowledge and experience, the transition period might be as short as a week or as long as several months.

The third reason is that with a properly crafted consulting arrangement, the money to be paid to the seller (in the form of a lump sum payment or salary) will be considered an expense paid by the buyer for tax purposes. Therefore, the payment will be deductible as a business expense.

Assuming you'll need the seller's involvement for some period of time, the arrangement should always be put in writing. The seller's verbal promise to "help out" is not enough. This promise can be included as part of the purchase agreement or, as is more often the case, may be embodied in a separate document called a consulting agreement. The agreement should address a few key points:

- How long must the seller be available? I recommend 30 days as a bare minimum. Often, a longer period of time is appropriate, particularly if the seller is to provide training or if the business you're buying relies heavily on the personal contacts of the seller (as it would for a service business).

- What time commitment must the seller make? The agreement should specify the amount of time the seller must put in. Will she be expected to be at the business location a few hours per week, a few hours per day, or full-time? You may wish her to be there full-time initially, then less over time.

- What duties is the seller to perform? In addition to general consulting, the agreement should specify the nature of what the seller is to do. If you expect the seller to introduce you to customers and suppliers or to actively pursue maintaining existing clients or customers, the agreement should spell out those responsibilities.

In terms of compensation, the preferred method of structuring your payments to the seller for her consulting services is to "back out" an agreed-upon amount from the purchase price of the business; this amount will be paid if the seller provides the services specified in the agreement. By exchanging money for performance, you'll know the seller will deliver what you've bargained for. (See Appendix H for a form of consulting agreement.)

The Promissory Note and the Security Agreement

Because most small business acquisitions involve some amount of seller financing, the odds are that two of the documents you'll be asked to sign at closing will be a promissory note and a security agreement. A promissory note is a written document that is legal evidence of a debt in which you're promising to pay a sum of money at a specified future date. A security agreement is the document in which the buyer agrees to pledge certain assets (of the business) as security (or collateral) to assure repayment of the amount the seller has agreed to finance.

In addition to setting forth the terms of repayment (i.e., what interest rate is to be charged as well as when payments are to be made and for how long), the promissory note also should contain some protections for the buyer. Make sure that the promissory note (and the security agreement) provide for the right of *setoff*, meaning that, if the seller defaults under the purchase agreement, the monetary amount of the default can be set off (i.e., deducted by the buyer from the amount he is due to pay the seller).

Also, be sure the security agreement covers only your hard assets, not your accounts receivable, and that the seller will agree to "subordinate" his security interest in those assets to superior financing. This language means that if you want to get a loan from a bank, you'll be able to pledge your assets to the bank. If you can't pledge the assets, you'll never get the loan. The seller may want to limit the subordination to loans of a certain size. If you agree to this, be sure that the amount is high enough to give you the flexibility to borrow what you're likely to need in the future.

Finally, make sure the promissory note and the security agreement both contain clauses that require the seller to send you a written notice if he claims that you are in default and that you're given a reasonable opportunity to cure the default before the seller can accelerate, or *call*, the loan (i.e., demand payment in full) or put a lien on the assets you've pledged as security.

The Closing: Passing the Torch

The big day has finally arrived. It's time to close on the acquisition of your business. The closing is the ceremony during which ownership of the business is legally transferred from seller to buyer. What happens at the closing? If the buyer and seller, and their respective attorneys, have done their jobs properly, the closing itself should be straightforward and uneventful. Everything that goes on at the closing has been agreed to in the purchase agreement we discussed in this chapter. Still, the closing is complicated and more than a bit intimidating.

There will be quite a crowd sitting around the table at the attorney's office (yours, your bank's, or the seller's). Present will be you and the seller, the attorneys for both sides, your banker and/or your bank's counsel (unless your money is coming from another source), the seller's bank if he is paying off any business loans, the business broker, who helped the buyer and the seller find each other, and perhaps a creditor or two who may have liens against the seller's assets.

The key to a successful closing can be stated in one word: *preparation*. Adjustments, or prorations, are payments you will be making to the seller for expenses, such as rent, security deposit, premiums for transferable insurance policies, etc., that the seller has paid for but which you will benefit from. Often these adjustments can be the last stumbling block in a difficult negotiation. Calculating adjustments should be left to the attorneys on both sides. These calculations should be made and agreed to before the closing, so the parties aren't left scrambling around to figure them out on the day of closing.

Adjustments aren't the only problems that come up during closing. Anything that happens that is inconsistent with the terms of the purchase agreement is a problem. These problems are serious because, the moment title to the business changes hands, the purchase agreement ceases to exist and has no value at all, except with respect to portions of the agreement that were expressly made to "survive the closing." (You'll see this language in the form of the purchase agreement in Appendix F.) If anything goes wrong before the actual transfer of title and you still proceed to close, the seller is under no obligation to fix the problem—unless, as we've said, provision has been made in the agreement for the obligations of the purchase agreement to continue. Keep in mind, however, that the only workable agreements that survive the closing are those that are backed up by financial incentives or penalties.

Go over everything with your attorney before the closing. Consider having a pre-closing to familiarize yourself with the process and to make sure you are informed and prepared. Bring to the closing a checklist of things that have to be picked up from the seller. Your list should include ownership papers or lease agreements for all assets included in the sale, customer lists, business licenses, and transferable insurance policies. Of course, don't forget to get the keys to all doors to the business's commercial space from the seller!

Going Forward with Your Own Business

A Game Plan and a Fresh Coat of Paint

Part I. The Business Redeployment Plan

YOU'VE JUST LEFT THE CLOSING TABLE AFTER CONSUMMATING the acquisition. The business is finally yours. You have great ideas, competent employees (you hope), and sufficient start-up capital (if you've followed my advice). What else could you need? A business plan.

Newlywed couples often are asked how they met. Although the story might be interesting, even amusing, it's not particularly relevant in terms of whether the marriage will succeed. The same goes for the business you've just acquired.

The key to the success of any business is how you grow it, not how you got it. So whether you buy an existing business or acquire a franchise (or even, for that matter, if you've started a business from scratch), you must have a plan to take you through the next three to five years.

One of the most important managerial tools for anyone who's buying a business is a document we'll refer to as a *business plan* or *business redeployment plan.* Some people mistakenly believe that you don't need a business plan if you don't intend to borrow money or bring in a partner. It's true that a business plan may help you get financing for your business, but you'll need one for other reasons as well. The business plan states your company's mission clearly, explains its marketing strategy, and outlines its financial history and projections. An effective business plan is essential if you are to achieve your business goals. Here are the three main reasons why:

1. A business plan will give you a blueprint and a focus for your company. It's a way of organizing your thoughts about your business. In fact, you'll find just the exercise of putting things on paper invaluable. Doing so forces you to take an objective, critical, and unemotional look at your new business in its entirety; it's a way of committing yourself to the way things are going to be. And, because each section of the plan will contain facts about the business, the plan will make you crystallize your thoughts about your company and its products and services as well as your customers and competition. According to Josselin Charas, a business consultant based in New York City who specializes in writing business plans, "writing a business plan will force you to ask the questions you might not otherwise have thought about—like where you are going to buy the cartons, or how the packaging is going to look, or how much it will cost to market your product."

2. Your business plan will provide you with a road map for your company. It can be used to check actual performance against projections. It also acts like a beacon pointing toward the future. For instance, the financial projections both show where you want your business to be three years to five years down the road and give you checkpoints along the way. Naturally, your numbers should be fine-tuned periodically (at least each year, and more frequently if any significant changes have affected your business). That's because a major change,

such as the addition of a new product or employee, could create a ripple effect on your numbers, and your projections must be adjusted accordingly.

3. There also are the external uses for business plans, like raising capital or finding an investor or buyer for the business. The harsh reality is that you won't get bank or other financing without a solid business plan.

Some experts suggest preparing a business plan before you've actually targeted a business and negotiated its acquisition. While there is some merit to this advice (without a written plan, most investors wouldn't touch you), it's virtually impossible to write an effective plan until you've focused on a specific business. What's more, if you've followed the advice I've given, you've already evaluated the company, its industry, and its products and services in detail and made careful financial projections as a part of your acquisition analysis. Therefore, this chapter focuses on the best way to reopen the business and how to re-engineer it to increase profitability. In effect, your plan will be a redeployment plan.

Although no single formula for a business plan exists (because no two businesses are exactly the same), experts generally agree that a plan should have three basic components:

1. A general overview of the business and its key personnel.
2. A discussion of how the business will create and maintain customers.
3. A set of financial projections that detail expected profitability for the next few years.

Here's a layout of a typical business plan:

1. *The table of contents.* This should list each section of the plan, using easy-to-read topic headlines.
2. *The executive summary.* The function of the executive summary, which is generally one to two pages long, is to describe

your business as you would if you had less than a minute to tell someone about it. The summary should provide a clear, concise description of your business, its reputation, its customer base, its targeted markets, its competitive advantages, how it is financed (or how you'd like it to be), and a brief word about management.

Be prepared to discuss the background of the business's key people. This may be just you. If so, stress your accomplishments and any past experience in the kind of business you'll be operating as well as any other relevant experience. Consider attaching a personal resume as an exhibit.

Spend a lot of time on this section. Make sure that it's tight and that it reflects the research that went into preparing your business plan. I always recommend writing the executive summary after you've completed the rest of your business plan; this will help you write a clear, straightforward statement. Remember, because the executive summary is the first thing people will see (should you ever need financing for your business), your aim is to make sure anyone who looks at it will want to keep on reading.

3. *The description of the business.* This section will contain a description of the business and an overview of your concept for running it. Here you'll identify why you've acquired the business and what you expect it to become in the next three to five years. You'll not only state your objectives but describe how and when you plan to achieve them and who will be involved in your venture.

Start off with a brief history of the business to demonstrate how it has gotten to this point. Then describe exactly the core of the business, that is, identify the market opportunities it seeks to exploit. A sample description: "The business produces computer-based labeling technology that assists garment businesses in tracking merchandise throughout the world."

Next, state your objectives in specific terms, for example, "to have sales of $1 million, a net worth of $250,000, and to be recognized as a leading provider of security software to the garment industry." Do you plan to expand your business or its location? Would you like to acquire an additional business or to franchise your venture in five years? If so, those goals need to be stated.

Lastly, consider ending this section with an organizational chart. Even though you've already named the individuals who will be a part of your business, now's the time to illustrate their roles in its operation.

If you're basically a one-man shop, you'll still need to indicate if other people will be employed on a part-time or seasonal basis or describe the sort of person you'd look to hire if the business grows. If you have a partner, then you'll need to indicate how the work and responsibilities will be divided between you.

4. *The marketing plan.* This section will describe your marketing efforts. You'll identify:

- The products or services you offer.
- The types of customers you attract (and those you intend to target) and in what geographic areas.
- The facility from which you operate your business, including its location (and whether it is appropriate for your needs or whether you plan to expand or relocate).
- The competition and their strengths and weaknesses.
- The industry's trends (the U.S. Department of Commerce and the Bureau of Labor Statistics are good sources of information; see Chapter 2). Discuss the history of the market, its changes and growth rates, projections for the market, factors relating to growth or decline, the sensitivity of the market to external factors, and local factors affecting your sales (assuming that your market is not national).

- The objective of your marketing efforts. For example, for a hotel: "Our goal is to operate at 80 percent capacity, or to average 120 guests in occupancy during the first two years of operations."

5. *The financial projections.* The business plan for an existing business, unlike that for a new venture, will contain historical financial statements, income statements, and balance sheets reflecting the business's operations under the former owner, your seller. That's your starting point.

Because you are going to use this plan as a blueprint of your business's growth—and as a checkpoint to monitor performance—this section of the business plan will reflect the financial projections you made when you were valuing the business.

However, because you also will be using this section as the basis for financing, you must indicate whether the business will need additional capital at a later date (if, for example, you intend to expand operations by adding a new facility, expanding the existing one, adding a new product or service line, or increasing marketing efforts). This section should indicate when these events are likely to occur, the amount of money they require, and how it will be financed (i.e., through institutional lenders, outside investors or by bringing in new partners).

Allies

The Small Business Administration, through local Small Business Development Centers and SCORE (see Appendix A), is an especially valuable resource for free training and advice on how to write a business plan. If you choose to hire someone to prepare the business plan for you (there are business consultants who specialize in writing them), you can expect to pay from $2,000 to $10,000 (or more). Regardless of who prepares the plan, you should be actively involved in putting together the final documents.

Summing Up

Remember, the compilation and presentation of the data in your business plan will say a great deal to others about your business skills and knowledge of the business. Although I encourage you to use your professionals—business consultant, lawyer, accountant, and others—to help you (especially if you have little or no experience in writing a plan), I urge you not to completely remove yourself from the process. Not only will you need the skills necessary to write the plan to run your business, but when it comes time to persuade a lender to pump capital into your firm, you'll need to be able to discuss the plan intelligently and coherently. If it's not written in your voice, that will be especially difficult.

Part II. The Makeover and Reopening: A Fresh Coat of Paint

The next part of going forward involves re-engineering the business to make it profitable (the way large companies attempt to do when they acquire smaller businesses). Here are fifteen ideas on how to improve upon what the old owner was doing:

1. *Expand into a new product or service line.* Ask yourself the following: Do your research and observations lead you to believe that the products or services offered by the business are appropriate to the group of customers served? Are changes in order? Perhaps it's possible to add a new product or service that's complementary to the existing core of the business. Take real-estate consultants, for example (agents and brokers). Many real-estate agencies offer mortgage financing and insurance services. These ancillary businesses are a natural because most

home buyers need financing and virtually all buy home-owner's insurance.

Conduct market surveys; then, if necessary, modify your existing products or services. When a business is sold, the buyer often finds that the seller hasn't exploited all existing markets, to say nothing of entering new ones. Nearly all business failures can be traced to poor marketing.

The critical test is this: Are the business's products or services appropriate for the demographics (age, sex, income level, and education) of the general customer group?

At a minimum, consider conducting an informal verbal customer survey. Ask the following questions: What do you like about my business? What do you think about the quality of my products and services? What do you dislike? What would you like to see changed or done differently?

One of my favorite success stories is how Jack and Naomi Anderson turned an underperforming photocopying and printing business into a virtual gold mine with some solid marketing research and clever advertising. Photo-Plus, a small copying and printing business, was located in a thriving downtown business district in New York City. Even though Photo-Plus had a great location, over the last three years revenues were stagnant, primarily due to the increasingly competitive nature of the business. Not only were large stores like Kinko's invading their turf, but it seemed every retail store in the area now had a copy machine.

Jack and Naomi were looking for a retail service business in lower Manhattan. After researching businesses in the immediate area, they discovered that more than 50 percent of the businesses in the office buildings neighboring Photo-Plus were occupied by law firms. Because Jack had practiced law at a large Wall Street firm, he came up with a brilliant idea. Why not buy Photo-Plus, change the name to Lawyer's Copying and Printing Service, and specialize in providing services geared to the needs of lawyers? When Jack was a young lawyer, he had spent countless hours at the printing store down the street from his firm waiting for massive public offering and private placement documents to be copied and bound. The idea of tapping into this market made Jack and Naomi see dollar signs. They would buy Photo-Plus, change the name, and completely redo the storefront. The space would include fax machines with modems, several telephone lines, and comfortable furniture. They'd purchase high quality binding machines so that printing jobs would look sleek and classy. They'd run off fliers advertising their business and canvass the area targeting law firms that did securities work, mergers and acquisitions, and complex litigation. In no time, Lawyer's Copying and Printing Service became *the* place where law firms outsourced their copying and binding jobs. Jack and Naomi had taken a stagnant business, discovered a market niche, and increased revenues exponentially.

2. *Rethink your location.* Most business locations need not be chiseled in stone. In fact, one of the advantages of owning a small business is the ability to change directions. Just because a business has been at its existing location for a number of years doesn't mean that a change is out of the question. Ask yourself the following:

- Is the present location the best one in terms of customer accessibility, where competitors are located, traffic flow, and cost?
- Is the business visible to the kinds of people it seeks or attracts?
- Is location important to this business? If it isn't (for many service businesses, it's not), you might consider relocating to more cost-effective space.
- Does the neighborhood and general setting match the business's clientele?
- Would another location be better?

- Is the building being maintained properly? If not, will contacting the landlord help?

3. **Redo the existing location.** Say relocating your business is impractical. You should consider making modifications to improve your existing space. Perhaps the size of the selling area could be increased. Try reorganizing merchandise so that complementary items (shoes, laces, socks, slippers, sneakers, sandals, etc.) are kept together. Consider redecorating—adding a fresh coat of paint or some new furnishings.

4. **Give marketing materials and brochures an image makeover.** Effective marketing materials and brochures are one of the best methods for starting and maintaining contact with customers. Perhaps the promotion techniques used by the former owner are out of date. Maybe the format and look of these materials haven't changed in years. A makeover (format, color scheme, size, and shape of materials) could breathe new life into a stagnant marketing program.

5. **Change sales strategies.** Proper sales techniques can vary greatly, depending on the nature of your business and your customers. If you just bought a restaurant or a clothing store, personal selling is something you'll need to do well. If, on the other hand, you've purchased a newsstand, grocery, or convenience store, you'll need to do relatively little selling in its true sense. Keeping track of how customers respond to the manner in which you sell is the key to testing the success of your business's sales strategies.

Because your goal is to build customer loyalty, a key time in the personal selling process is after you've made a sale. Use the following techniques:

- Ask the customer for feedback, both positive and negative.
- Keep in touch after the sale. Communicate regularly with customers, informing them of upcoming sales or promotions.

- Make each customer feel special.
- Ask for referrals (meaning, ask the customer to refer other customers to you).

6. *Deal creatively with complaints.* Turn a bad situation into a good one: Respond to customer complaints by demonstrating how deeply you care about what has gone wrong and how committed you are to making things right. Do whatever it takes to rectify matters. Then, follow up to make sure things were indeed straightened out.

Most entrepreneurs instinctively follow these personal selling guidelines. However, even the best personal selling style may not be enough if you're the only person in your business who is following these rules. Work closely with your employees. Explain how you expect them to conduct themselves and why. Be sure to reward good performance; refuse to tolerate bad.

7. *Personal selling training.* Successful entrepreneurs know there's no more powerful marketing device than personal selling. They recognize that the only way to keep customers is to provide quality products and superior service. If your business is one in which the capability of your sales force is crucial, you should consider training (or retraining) your sales team in the art of personal selling. Here's what you should be telling them:

The key to personal selling is creating trust. Here are some tips on building trust:
- People instinctively trust someone they believe cares for them. In demonstrating you care, you'll accelerate the environment of trust.
- Dress neatly. Pay careful attention to your personal appearance and grooming. Keep your workplace clean and comfortable.

- Getting off to the right start is crucial. Greet customers warmly. Look them in the eye and smile. Shake hands, if that's appropriate.
- Engage the customer in pleasant conversation by asking questions.
- Call the customer by name. Introduce yourself before asking for his or her name.
- Lean forward when the customer is talking and acknowledge what they're saying by nodding your head.
- Treat telephone communications as you would face-to-face meetings: Be warm and cordial.
- Always say please and thank you.
- Come across as natural.

8. ***Learn all you can about your competition.*** Make sure you check out your competition. Visit as many of those businesses as possible and buy something. Talk to their customers and listen to what they say. Look around and note your impressions about decor, location, parking, customer service, pricing, product presentation, and quality. Analyze competitors the way you did the business you just acquired. By comprehending your competitor's strengths and weaknesses, you'll learn a lot about how to improve the way your business has been operating.

9. ***Consider overseas opportunities.*** Our economy is becoming increasingly global. Exploring overseas opportunities can be an extremely effective method for expanding markets. The U.S. Department of Commerce has many resources to help small business owners investigate foreign opportunities. For a list of helpful publications dealing with overseas markets, contact the Bureau of Export Administration, U.S. Department of Commerce, (302) 482-2721.

10. ***Hire a public relations or advertising firm.*** To get the word out about your business, consider hiring a public relations or

advertising firm. The key to effective promotional activity is finding the right medium and the right message. Many businesses make the mistake of spending too much of their promotional resources on expensive advertising. For example, despite attracting large audiences, radio and television advertising doesn't work for many small businesses. Advertising in local newspapers and local colleges and universities or sponsoring community events are more economical and often more successful as a source of potential sales.

11. *Make sure business systems are up to date.* Analyze your business systems (computer hardware and software, cash receipt machines, facsimile and photocopy equipment, etc.) to determine if they're up to date. When it comes to technology, the sky's the limit in terms of what you can spend to be cutting edge. Therefore, be prepared to spend big money if you want the most advanced equipment.

Keep in mind, however, that not all businesses need to keep up with the latest technology. Take computers, for example: If all you need is simple word processing—letters, brief reports, and memos—there are many basic programs available, so you needn't maintain or invest in an elaborate system. Regarding other electronic gadgets, it's possible to be economical and still keep current. Quality plain paper fax machines cost as little as $400 (assuming you don't need a unit that combines expanded memory, an answering machine, and copy capabilities). All you want to do is maintain cost-effective systems that permit you to operate your business efficiently.

12. *Update your business plan.* In this chapter, we've discussed the need for a solid business plan. After your plan is finalized, you must revise it constantly to reflect changes in your business. Because your business plan will project where you want your business to be in the next three to five years, it's a good idea to constantly check actual performance against projections. By checking every month or two, you'll get a clear picture of how

your business is growing. More important, you'll be in a position to make changes as your business needs them.

13. ***Consider direct mail marketing, and don't forget to explore online opportunities.*** A recent Gallup study suggests that 28 percent of small businesses are on the Internet and another 39 percent are considering getting onto it. Although these numbers are on the rise, the dollars spent on on-line options fall far short of what's spent on the more traditional methods of reaching customers, such as direct mail, direct sales, newspapers, television, and magazines. Yet don't discount the cyberspace options available to small business. They can be an extremely effective, cost-efficient method of increasing sales.

14. ***Maintain relationships with key employees.*** Maintaining a solid relationship with key employees is important to the short- and long-term success of your business. It's often best to resist the impulse to make drastic changes in personnel in the first several weeks. In fact, key employees may enjoy special relationships with customers and suppliers. You'll need to rely on these for a smooth transition and to keep business in the future. Take the time to meet all employees. Ask them if they have any ideas on how the business could be improved.

15. ***Enlist the help of the old owner to maintain relationships with key customers and suppliers (reach out).*** As discussed in Chapter 7, customers and suppliers are the lifeblood of any business. Because in most instances the old owner had a special relationship with the business's customers and suppliers, enlisting her help (to make introductions or to provide endorsements) will prove most valuable.

You also should consider taking steps to reach out to customers and suppliers to make them feel comfortable doing business with you. Special promotions, prices, or delivery services can be an excellent way to convey to customers that you value their business. For suppliers, you might consider hosting an event where you can introduce yourself in an informal atmosphere. Arrange for the previous owner to appear and assist with the introductions. These strategies will help instill confidence in customers and suppliers and assure them that they'll receive the same level of service and commitment that the old owner provided.

The Finish Line Becomes the Starting Gate

You've done it. You're an entrepreneur. The acquisition process was, at times, grueling. Still, as you were searching out prospects, forcing yourself to ask family and friends for capital, exhausting yourself in the research and negotiations, you also were spending gratifying hour after gratifying hour dreaming about what you'd do with your business when you finally owned it. Now, having read this chapter, you have (quite sensibly) organized all those dreams into a plan for re-engineering the business in your image. You mean to run your new venture with more zest, zeal, and intelligence—and make it more profitable—than the previous owner did.

At this point, someone will probably give you a bottle of champagne. With bottle in hand, get into your car and drive to your new business. Then pop the cork and have a few prudent sips. Take a deep breath. Put the key into the lock and open the door. Look around. This is your business. The whole process has been leading up to this moment—and there's nothing like it.

Source Directory (SBA, SBDCs and S.C.O.R.E.)

SMALL BUSINESS ADMINISTRATION FIELD LOCATIONS

Reg/Loc.	Type*	City	State	Zip Code
0100	RO	Boston	MA	02222-1093
1010	DO	Boston	MA	02222-1093
0172	DO	Augusta	ME	04330
0189	DO	Concord	NH	03301
0156	DO	Hartford	CT	06106
0150	DO	Montpelier	VT	05602
0165	DO	Providence	RI	02903
0130	BO	Springfield	MA	01103
0200	RO	New York	NY	10278
0296	DO	Buffalo	NY	14202
0299	DO	Newark	NJ	07102
0202	DO	New York	NY	10278
0252	DO	Hato Rey	PR	00918
0248	DO	Syracuse	NY	13260
0206	BO	Elmira	NY	14901
0235	BO	Melville	NY	11747
0219	BO	Rochester	NY	14614

*See page 208 for an explanation of the Type codes.

Address	Telephone Number	Fax Number
10 Causeway Street, Suite 812	(617) 565-8415	(617) 565-8420
10 Causeway Street, Room 265	(617) 565-5590	(617) 565-5598
40 Western Avenue, Room 512	(207) 622-8378	(207) 622-8277
143 North Main Street, Suite 202	(603) 225-1400	(603) 225-1409
330 Main Street, 2nd Floor	(203) 240-4700	(203) 240-4659
87 State Street, Room 205	(802) 828-4422	(802) 828-4485
380 Westminister Mall, 5th Floor	(401) 528-4561	(401) 528-4539
1550 Main Street, Room 212	(413) 785-0268	(413) 785-0267
26 Federal Plaza, Suite 3108	(212) 264-1450	(212) 264-0038
111 West Huron Street, Room 1311	(716) 551-4301	(716) 551-4418
Two Gateway Center, 4th Floor	(973) 645-2434	(973) 645-6265
26 Federal Plaza, Suite 31-00	(212) 264-2454	(212) 264-4963
252 Ponce De Leon Blvd., Suite 201	(809) 766-5572	(809) 766-5309
100 South Clinton St., Suite 1071	(315) 448-0423	(315) 448-0410
333 East Water Street, 4th Floor	(607) 734-8130	(607) 733-4656
35 Pinelawn Road, Suite 207w	(516) 454-0750	(516) 454-0769
100 State Street, Suite 410	(716) 263-6700	(716) 263-6700

Reg/Loc.	Type*	City	State	Zip Code
0253	POD	St. Croix	VI	00820
0254	POD	St. Thomas	VI	00802
0300	RO	King of Prussia	PA	19406
0373	DO	Baltimore	MD	21201-2525
0390	DO	Clarksburg	WV	26301
0303	DO	King of Prussia	PA	19406
0358	DO	Pittsburgh	PA	15222
0304	DO	Richmond	VA	23229
0353	DO	Washington	DC	20005
0325	BO	Charleston	WV	25301
0316	BO	Harrisburg	PA	17101
0318	BO	Wilkes-Barre	PA	18701-3589
0341	BO	Wilmington	DE	19801-3011
0400	RO	Atlanta	GA	30309
0405	DO	Atlanta	GA	30309
0459	DO	Birmingham	AL	35203-2398
0460	DO	Charlotte	NC	28202-2137
0464	DO	Columbia	SC	29201
0470	DO	Jackson	MS	39201
0491	DO	Jacksonville	FL	32256-7504
0457	DO	Louisville	KY	40202
0455	DO	Coral Gables	FL	33146-2911
0474	DO	Nashville	TN	37228-1500
0438	BO	Gulfport	MS	39501-7758
0500	RO	Chicago	IL	60606-6617
0507	DO	Chicago	IL	60601-2511
0549	DO	Cleveland	OH	44114-2507
0593	DO	Columbus	OH	43215-2592
0515	DO	Detroit	MI	48226
0562	DO	Indianapolis	IN	46204-1873
0563	DO	Madison	WI	53703

*See page 208 for an explanation of the Type codes.

Address	Telephone Number	Fax Number
3013 Golden Rock, Suite 165	(809) 778-5380	(809) 778-1102
3800 Crow Bay	(809) 774-8530	(809) 776-2312
475 Allendale Road, Suite 201	(610) 962-3700	(610) 962-3743
10 S. Howard Street, Suite 6220	(410) 962-4392	(410) 962-1805
168 West Main Street, 5th Floor	(304) 623-5631	(304) 623-0023
475 Allendale Road, Suite 201	(610) 962-3800	(610) 962-3795
960 Penn Avenue, 5th Floor	(412) 644-2780	(412) 644-5446
1504 Santa Rosa Road, Suite 200	(804) 771-2400	(804) 771-8018
1110 Vermont Avenue N.W., Suite 900	(202) 606-4000	(202) 606-6225
550 Eagan Street, Room 309	(304) 347-5220	(304) 347-5350
100 Chestnut Street, Room 309	(717) 782-3840	(717) 782-4839
20 N. Pennsylvania Ave., Room 2327	(717) 826-6497	(717) 826-6287
824 North Market Street, Suite 610	(302) 573-6294	(302) 573-6060
1720 Peachtree Road, N.W., Suite 496	(404) 347-4999	(404) 347-2355
1720 Peachtree Road, N.W., 6th Floor	(404) 347-4749	(404) 347-4745
2121 8th Avenue, North, Suite 200	(205) 731-1344	(205) 731-1404
200 North College Street, Suite A2015	(704) 344-6563	(704) 344-6769
1835 Assembly Street, Room 358	(803) 765-5377	(803) 765-5962
101 West Capitol Street, Suite 400	(601) 965-4378	(601) 965-4294
7825 Baymeadows Way, Suite 100-8	(904) 443-1900	(904) 443-1980
600 Dr. M.L. King Jr. Place, Room 188	(502) 582-5971	(502) 582-5009
1320 South Dixie Highway, Suite 501	(305) 536-5521	(305) 536-5058
50 Vantage Way, Suite 201	(615) 736-5881	(615) 736-7232
One Hancock Plaza, Suite 1001	(601) 863-4449	(601) 864-0179
300 S. Riverside Plaza, Suite 1975S	(312) 353-0357	(312) 353-3426
500 West Madison Street, Suite 1250	(312) 353-4528	(312) 886-5688
1111 Superior Avenue, Suite 630	(216) 522-4180	(216) 522-2038
2 Nationwide Plaza, Suite 1400	(614) 469-6860	(614) 469-2391
477 Michigan Avenue, Suite 515	(313) 226-6075	(313) 226-4769
429 North Pennsylvania, Suite 100	(317) 226-7272	(317) 226-7259
212 East Washington Ave., Room 213	(608) 264-5261	(608) 264-5541

Reg/Loc.	Type*	City	State	Zip Code
0508	DO	Minneapolis	MN	55403-1563
0545	BO	Cincinnati	OH	45202
0543	BO	Milwaukee	WI	53203
0547	BO	Marquette	MI	49885
0517	BO	Springfield	IL	62704
0600	RO	Ft. Worth	TX	76155
0682	DO	Albuquerque	NM	87102
0610	DO	Ft. Worth	TX	76155
0677	DO	El Paso	TX	79935
0671	DO	Houston	TX	77074-1591
0669	DO	Little Rock	TX	72202
0639	DO	Harlingen	TX	78550-6855
0678	DO	Lubbock	TX	79401-2693
0679	DO	New Orleans	LA	70130
0680	DO	Oklahoma City	OK	73102
0681	DO	San Antonio	TX	78206-1204
0637	BO	Corpus Christi	TX	78476
0700	RO	Kansas City	MO	64105-1500
0736	DO	Cedar Rapids	IA	52401-1806
0761	DO	Des Moines	IA	50309-2186
0709	DO	Kansas City	MO	64105
0766	DO	Omaha	NE	68154
0768	DO	St. Louis	MO	63101
0767	DO	Wichita	KS	67202
0721	BO	Springfield	MO	65802-3200
0800	RO	Denver	CO	80202-2599
0897	DO	Casper	WY	82602-2839
0811	DO	Denver	CO	80202-2599
0875	DO	Fargo	MD	58108-3086
0885	DO	Helena	MT	59626
0883	DO	Salt Lake City	UT	84138-1195

*See page 208 for an explanation of the Type codes.

Address	Telephone Number	Fax Number
100 North 6th Street, Suite 610	(612) 370-2324	(612) 370-2303
525 Vine Street, Suite 870	(513) 684-2814	(513) 684-3251
310 West Wisconsin Avenue, Suite 400	(414) 297-3941	(414) 297-1377
228 West Washington, Suite 11	(906) 225-1108	(906) 225-1109
511 West Capitol Avenue, Suite 302	(217) 492-4416	(217) 492-4867
4300 Amon Carter Blvd., Suite 108	(817) 885-6581	(817) 885-6588
625 Silver Avenue, S.W., Suite 320	(505) 766-1870	(505) 766-1057
4300 Amon Carter Blvd., Suite 114	(817) 885-6500	(817) 885-6516
10737 Gateway West, Suite 320	(915) 540-5676	(915) 540-5636
9301 Southwest Freeway, Suite 550	(713) 773-6500	(713) 773-6550
2120 Riverfront Drive, Suite 100	(501) 324-5871	(501) 324-5199
222 East Van Buren Street, Room 500	(210) 427-8625	(210) 427-8537
1611 Tenth Street, Suite 200	(806) 743-7462	(806) 743-7487
365 Canal Street, Suite 2250	(504) 589-6685	(504) 589-2339
210 Park Avenue, Suite 1300	(405) 231-5521	(405) 231-4876
727 E. Durango Boulevard, Room A-527	(210) 229-5900	(210) 229-5937
606 N. Carancahua, Suite 1200	(512) 888-3331	(512) 888-3418
323 West 8th Street, Suit 307	(816) 374-6380	(816) 374-6339
215 4th Avenue, S.E., Suite 200	(319) 362-6405	(319) 362-7861
210 Walnut Street, Room 749	(515) 284-4422	(515) 284-4572
323 West 8th Street, Suite 501	(816) 374-6708	(816) 374-6759
11145 Mill Valley Road	(402) 221-4691	(402) 221-3680
815 Olive Street	(314) 539-6600	(314) 539-3785
100 East English Street, Suite 510	(316) 269-6616	(316) 269-6699
620 South Glenstone Street, Suite 110	(417) 864-7670	(417) 864-4108
721 19th Street, Suite 400	(303) 844-0500	(303) 844-0506
1 East 9th Street, Room 4001	(307) 261-6500	(307) 261-5499
721 19th Street, Suite 426	(303) 844-3984	(303) 884-6468
657 2nd Avenue, North, Room 219	(701) 239-5131	(701) 239-5645
301 South Park, Room 334	(406) 441-1081	(406) 441-1090
125 South State Street, Room 2237	(801) 524-5804	(801) 526-4160

Reg/Loc.	Type	City	State	Zip Code
0876	DO	Sioux Falls	SO	57102-1109
0900	RO	San Francisco	CA	94105-2939
0942	DO	Fresno	CA	93727-1547
0951	DO	Honolulu	HI	96850-4981
0944	DO	Las Vegas	NV	89101
0914	DO	Glendale	CA	91203-2304
0988	DO	Phoenix	AZ	85004-1093
0954	DO	San Diego	CA	92188-3540
0912	DO	San Francisco	CA	94105-1988
0920	DO	Santa Ana	CA	92701
0995	BO	Agana	GU	96910
0931	DO	Sacramento	CA	95814-2413
1000	RO	Seattle	WA	98101-1128
1084	DO	Anchorage	AK	99513-7559
1087	DO	Boise	ID	83702-5745
1086	DO	Portland	OR	97201-6695
1013	DO	Seattle	WA	98101-1128
1094	DO	Spokane	WA	99204-0317
9010		Niagara Falls	NY	14303-1192
9020		Atlanta	GA	30308
9030		Ft. Worth	TX	76155
9040		Sacramento	CA	95825
0429	HLSC	Birmingham	AL	35202-2247
0626	CLSC	Little Rock	AR	72202
0631	HLSC	El Paso	TX	79935
0228	HLSC	New York	NY	10014
0927		Santa Ana	CA	92701
0992	CLSC	Fresno	CA	93727-1547

Type codes

RO = Regional Office	DAO = Disaster Area Office
DO = District Office	HLSC = Home Loan Service Center
BO = Branch Office	CLSC = Commercial Loan Service Center
POD = Post of Duty	

Address	Telephone Number	Fax Number
110 South Phillips Avenue, Suite 200	(605) 330-4231	(605) 330-4215
71 Stevenson Street, 20th Floor	(415) 975-4859	(415) 975-4825
2719 North Air Fresno Drive, Suite 107	(209) 487-5189	(209) 487-5292
300 Ala Moana Boulevard, Room 2314	(808) 541-2990	(808) 541-2976
301 East Stewart Avenue, Room 301	(702) 388-6611	(702) 388-6469
330 North Brand Boulevard, Suite 120	(818) 552-3210	(818) 552-3260
2828 North Central Avenue, Suite 800	(602) 640-2316	(602) 640-2360
550 West "C" Street, Suite 550	(619) 557-7250	(619) 557-5894
211 Main Street, 4th Floor	(415) 744-6820	(415) 744-6812
200 West Santa Ana Boulevard, Suite 700	(714) 550-7420	(714) 550-0191
238 Archbishop F.C. Flores St., Room 508	(671) 472-7277	(200) 550-7365
660 J Street, Suite 215	(916) 498-6410	(916) 498-6422
1200 Sixth Avenue, Suite 1805	(206) 553-5676	(206) 553-4155
222 West 8th Avenue, Room A36	(907) 271-4022	(907) 271-4545
1020 Main Street, Suite 290	(208) 334-1696	(208) 334-9353
222 S. West Columbia Street, Suite 500	(503) 326-2682	(503) 326-2808
1200 Sixth Avenue, Suite 1700	(206) 553-7310	(206) 553-7099
West 601 First Avenue, 10th Floor	(509) 353-2810	(509) 353-2829
360 Rainbow Boulevard South, 3rd Floor	(716) 282-4612	(716) 282-1472
One Baltimore Place, Suite 300	(404) 347-3771	(404) 347-4183
4400 Amon Carter Boulevard, Suite 102	(817) 885-7600	(817) 885-7616
1825 Bell Street, Suite 208	(916) 566-7243	(916) 566-7280
2121 8th Avenue North, Suite 200	(205) 731-0441	(205) 731-1404
2120 Riverfront Drive, Suite 100	(501) 324-5871	(501) 324-6072
10737 Gateway West, Suite 320	(915) 540-5110	(915) 540-5185
201 Varrick Street, Room 628	(212) 620-3722	(212) 620-3730
200 West Santa Ana Boulevard	(714) 550-6037	(714) 550-0810
2719 North Air Fresno Drive, Suite 107	(209) 487-5785	(209) 487-5803

Small Business Development Centers

Region I (Boston)

University of Southern Maine
96 Falmouth Street
Portland, ME 04103
(207) 780-4420
Fax: (207) 780-4810

Byrant College
1150 Douglas Pike
Smithfield, RI 02917
(401) 232-6111
Fax: (401) 232-6416

University of Massachusetts
School of Management, Room 205
Amherst, MA 01003-4935
(413) 545-6301
Fax: (413) 545-1273

Vermont Technical College
P.O. Box 422
Randolph Center, VT 05060
(802) 728-9101
Fax: (802) 728-3026

University of Connecticut
Box U-41, Room 422
368 Fairfield Road
Storrs, CT 06269-2041
(203) 486-4135
Fax: (203) 486-1576

University of New Hampshire
108 McConnell Hall
Durham, NH 03824
(603) 862-2200
Fax: (603) 862-4468

Region II (New York)

Rutgers University
Ackerson Hall, Third Floor
180 University Street
Newark, NJ 07102
(973) 648-5950
Fax: (973) 648-1110

State University of New York
SUNY Downstate
SUNY Plaza, S-523
Albany, NY 12246
(518) 443-5398
Fax: (518) 465-4992

State University of New York
SUNY Upstate
SUNY Plaza, S-523
Albany, NY 12246
(518) 443-5398
Fax: (518) 465-4992

University of the Virgin Islands
8000 Nisky Center, Suite 202
Charlotte Amalie
St. Thomas, Virgin Islands
00802-5804
(809) 776-3206
Fax: (809) 775-3756

University of Puerto Rico
Box 5253, College Station
Building B
Mayaguez, PR 00681
(809) 834-3590
Fax: (809) 834-3790

Region III (Philadelphia)

University of Pennsylvania
The Wharton School
444 Vance Hall
Philadelphia, PA 19104
(215) 898-1219
Fax: (215) 573-2135

Howard University
2600 6th Street, N.W., Room 128
Washington, D.C. 20059
(202) 806-1550
Fax: (202) 806-1777

University of Delaware
Suite 005, Purnell Hall
Newark, DE 19711
(302) 831-2747
Fax: (302) 831-1423

**Governor's Office of Community
and Industrial Development**
1115 Virginia Street, East
Charleston, WV 25301
(304) 558-2960
Fax: (304) 558-0127

**Department of Economic and
Employment Development**
217 East Redwood Street
Ninth Floor
Baltimore, MD 21202
(410) 333-6995
Fax: (410) 333-4460

**Department of Economic
Development**
1021 East Cary Street
Richmond, VA 23206
(804) 371-8258
Fax: (804) 371-8185

Region IV (Atlanta)

University of South Carolina
College of Business Administration
1710 College Street
Columbia, SC 29208
(803) 777-4907
Fax: (803) 777-4403

University of West Florida
19 West Garden Street, Third Floor
Pensacola, FL 32501
(904) 444-2060
Fax: (904) 444-2070

University of Alabama
1717 11th Avenue South, Suite 419
Birmingham, AL 35294
(205) 934-7260
Fax: (205) 934-7645

University of Georgia
Chicopee Complex
1180 East Broad Street
Athens, GA 30602
(706) 542-6762
Fax: (706) 542-6776

University of Kentucky
College of Business and Economics
225 Business and Economics Building
Lexington, KY 40506-0034
(606) 257-7668
Fax: (606) 258-1907

University of Mississippi
Old Chemistry Building, Suite 216
University, MS 38677
(601) 232-5001
Fax: (601) 232-5650

Memphis State University
South Campus
Getwell Road, Building #1
Memphis, TN 38152
(901) 678-2500
Fax: (901) 678-4072

University of North Carolina
4509 Creedmoor Road, Suite 201
Raleigh, NC 27612
(919) 571-4154
Fax: (919) 571-4161

Region V (Chicago)

University of Wisconsin
432 North Lake Street, Room 423
Madison, WI 53706
(608) 263-7794
Fax: (608) 262-3878

Department of Trade and Economic Development
500 Metro Square
121 Seventh Place East
St. Paul, MN 55101-2146
(612) 297-5770
Fax: (612) 296-1290

Wayne State University
2727 Second Avenue
Detroit, MI 48201
(313) 964-1798
Fax: (313) 964-3648

Department of Commerce and Community Affairs
620 East Adams
Springfield, IL 62701
(217) 524-5856
Fax: (217) 785-6328

Economic Development Council
One North Capitol
Suite 420
Indianapolis, IN 46204
(317) 264-6871
Fax: (317) 264-3102

Department of Development
77 South High Street
Columbus, OH 43226-1001
(614) 466-2711
Fax: (614) 466-0829

Region VI (Dallas)

University of Arkansas
Little Rock Technology Center
Building
100 South Main, Suite 401
Little Rock, AR 72201
(501) 324-9043
Fax: (501) 324-9049

Northeast Louisiana University
College of Business Administration
700 University Avenue
Monroe, LA 71209
(318) 342-5506
Fax: (318) 342-5510

SE Oklahoma State University
517 West University
Stanton A, Box 2584
Durant, OK 74701
(405) 924-0277
Fax: (405) 924-7471

University of Houston
1100 Louisiana, Suite 500
Houston, TX 77002
(713) 752-8444
Fax: (713) 756-1500

University of Texas at San Antonio
Cypress Tower, Suite 410
1222 North Main Street
San Antonio, TX 78212
(210) 558-2450
Fax: (210) 558-2464

Texas Tech University
2579 South Loop 289, Suite 114
Lubbock, TX 79423-1637
(806) 745-3973
Fax: (806) 745-6207

Dallas County Community College
1402 Corinth Street
Dallas, TX 75215
(214) 565-5833
Fax: (214) 565-5815

Santa Fe Community College
P.O. Box 4187
Santa Fe, NM 87502-4187
(505) 438-1362
Fax: (505) 438-1237

Region VII (Kansas City)

University of Nebraska at Omaha
60th & Dodge Streets
CBA Room 407
Omaha, NE 68182
(402) 554-2521
Fax: (402) 554-3747

Iowa State University
137 Lynn Avenue
Ames, LA 50010
(515) 292-6351
Fax: (515) 292-0020

University of Missouri
Suite 300, University Place
Columbia, MO 65211
(314) 882-0344
Fax: (314) 884-4297

Wichita State University
1845 Fairmount
Wichita, KS 67260-0148
(316) 689-3193
Fax: (316) 689-3647

Region VIII (Denver)

University of Utah
102 West 500 South
Salt Lake City, UT 84101
(801) 581-7905
Fax: (801) 581-7814

Department of Commerce
1424 Ninth Avenue
Helena, MT 59620
(406) 444-4780
Fax: (406) 444-2808

University of South Dakota
School of Business, 414 East Clark
Vermillion, SD 57069
(605) 677-5498
Fax: (605) 677-5427

Office of Business Development
1625 Broadway, Suite 1710
Denver, CO 80202
(303) 892-3809
Fax: (303) 892-3848

University of North Dakota
Gamble Hall, University Station
Grand Forks, ND 58202-7308
(701) 777-3700
Fax: (701) 777-3225

University of Wyoming
P.O. Box 3622
Laramie, WY 82071-3622
(800) 348-5194

Region IX (San Francisco)

University of Nevada in Reno
College of Business Administration
Room 411
Reno, NV 89557-0100
(702) 784-1717
Fax: (702) 784-4337

University of Hawaii at Hilo
523 West Lanikaula Street
Hilo, HI 96720
(808) 933-3515
Fax: (808) 933-3683

Maricopa County Community College
2411 West 14th Street
Tempe, AZ 85281-6941
(602) 731-8720
Fax: (602) 731-8729

California Trade and Commerce Agency
801 K Street, Suite 1700
Sacramento, CA 95814
(916) 324-5068
Fax: (916) 322-5084

Region X (Seattle)

Washington State University
College of Business and Economics
245 Todd Hall
Pullman, WA 99164
(509) 335-1576

Lane Community College
99 West 10th Avenue, Suite 216
Eugene, OR 97401
(503) 726-2250
Fax: (503) 345-6006

Boise State University
1910 University Drive
Boise, ID 83725
(208) 385-1640
Fax: (208) 385-3877

University of Alaska/Anchorage
430 West 7th Avenue, Suite 110
Anchorage, AK 99501
(907) 274-7232
Fax: (907) 274-9524

S.C.O.R.E. Chapter Directory (alphabetical by state)

City	Address	Tel.	Fax
North Alabama	1601 11th Avenue South Birmingham, AL 35294-4552	(205) 934-6868	(205) 934-0538
Tuscaloosa	2200 University Boulevard Tuscaloosa, AL 35402	(205) 758-7588	N/A
Mobile	c/o Mobile Area Chamber of Commerce P.O. Box 2187 Mobile, AL 36652	(334) 433-6951	N/A
Shoals	P.O. Box 1331 Florence, AL 35631-1331	(205) 764-0244	N/A
Alabama Capitol	c/o Montgomery Area Chamber of Commerce 41 Commerce Street, Box 79 Montgomery, AL 36101-1114	(334) 240-9295	N/A
Baldwin County	327 Fairhope Avenue Fairhope, AL 36532	(334) 928-8799	N/A
East Alabama	P.O. Box 2366 Opelika, AL 36803	(334) 745-4861	N/A
Northeast Alabama	P.O. Box 1087 Anniston, AL 36202	(205) 237-5637	(205) 237-4338
Anchorage	c/o il SBA, #67 222 W. 8th Avenue Anchorage, AK 99513-755	(907) 271-4022	N/A
Phoenix	2828 N. Central Avenue, #800 Central & One Thomas Phoenix, AZ 85004	(602) 640-2329	N/A
Tucson	P.O. Box 2143 Tucson, AZ 85702	(520) 670-5008	N/A
East Valley	Federal Building Room #104, 26 N. MacDonald Mesa, AZ 85201	(602) 379-3100	(602) 379-3143
Prescott	101 W. Goodwin Street P.O. Building, Suite 307 Prescott, AZ 86303	(520) 778-7438	N/A

City	Address	Tel.	Fax
Lake Havasu	P.O. Box 2049 Lake Havasu City, AZ 86405	(520) 453-5951	N/A
Flagstaff	1 West Route 66 Flagstaff, AZ 86001	(520) 556-7333	N/A
Little Rock	2120 Riverfront Drive SBA Room 100 Little Rock, AR 72202-1747	(501) 324-5893	(501) 324-5199
Northwest Arkansas	#4 Glenn Haven Drive Fort Smith, AR 72901	(501) 783-3556	N/A
Ozark	c/o Margaret Parrish 1141 Eastwood Drive Fayetteville, AR 72701	(501) 442-7619	N/A
Garland County	1412 Airport Road, B10 Hot Springs, AR 71913	(501) 321-1700	N/A
South Central	210 N. Jackson Avenue El Dorado, AR 71730-5803	(870) 863-6113	(870) 863-6115
Southeast Arkansas	P.O. Box 6866 Pine Bluff, AR 71611	(870) 535-7189	(870) 535-1643
Los Angeles	330 North Brand Boulevard Suite 190 Glendale, CA 91203-2304	(818) 552-3206	(818) 552-3323
San Francisco	455 Market Street, 6th Floor San Francisco, CA 94105	(415) 744-6827	(415) 744-6812
Orange City	200 W. Santa Ana Blvd. Suite 700 Santa Ana, CA 92701	(714) 550-7369	(714) 550-0191
San Diego	550 West C Street, Suite 550 San Diego, CA 92101-3500	(619) 557-7272	(619) 557-5894
Santa Barbara	P.O. Box 30291 Santa Barbara, CA 93130	(805) 563-0084	N/A
Ventura	5700 Ralston Street, Suite 310 Ventura, CA 93001	(805) 658-2688	N/A
Pomona	c/o Pomona Chamber of Commerce 485 N. Garey Avenue P.O. Box 1457 Pomona, CA 91769-1457	(909) 622-1256	N/A

City	Address	Tel.	Fax
Palm Springs	555 South Palm Canyon Room A206 Palm Springs, CA 92264	(619) 320-6682	N/A
Central California	2719 N. Air Fresno Drive Suite 200 Fresno, CA 93727-1547	(209) 487-5605	(209) 487-5636
Santa Clara	280 South 1st Street, Room 137 San Jose, CA 95113	(408) 288-8479	(408) 535-5541
Sacramento	660 J Street, Suite 215 Sacramento, CA 95814-2413	(916) 498-6420	(916) 498-6422
Santa Rosa	777 Sonoma Avenue, Room 115E Santa Rosa, CA 95404	(707) 571-8342	(707) 541-0331
Stockton	401 N. San Joaquin Street Room 215 Stockton, CA 95202	(209) 946-6293	N/A
Central Coast	2524 South LaCosta Drive Santa Maria, CA 93455	(805) 934-4146	N/A
Hemet	1700 E. Florida Avenue Hemet, CA 92544-4679	(909) 652-4390	(909) 929-8543
East Bay	519 17th Street Oakland, CA 94612	(510) 273-6611	(510) 273-6015
Shasta	c/o Cascade SBDC 737 Auditorium Drive Redding, CA 96099	(916) 247-8100	N/A
Yosemite	c/o SCEDCO 1012 11th Avenue, Suite 300 Modesto, CA 95354	(209) 521-9333	N/A
Golden Empire	1706 Chester Ave., #200 Bakersfield, CA 93301	(805) 327-4421	N/A
Steinbeck-Roecker	Monterey Peninsula Chamber of Commerce 380 Alvarado Monterey, CA 95926	(408) 649-1770	N/A
Greater Chico Area	1324 Mangrove Street, Suite 114 Chico, CA 95926	(916) 342-8932	N/A
Antelope Valley	445 W. Palmdale Blvd., Suite N Palmdale, CA 93551	(805) 265-7733	(805) 265-7712

City	Address	Tel.	Fax
Toulumne County	222 S. Shepherd Street Sonora, CA 95370	(209) 532-4212	N/A
San Luis Obispo	3566 South Hiquera, #104 San Luis Obispo, CA 93401	(805) 547-0779	N/A
Denver	U.S. Customs House, 4th Floor 721 19th St. Denver, CO 80201	(303) 844-3985	(303) 844-6490
Pueblo	c/o Chamber of Commerce 302 N. Santa Fe Pueblo, CO 81003	(719) 542-1704	(719) 542-1624
Grand Junction	c/o Chamber of Commerce 360 Grand Avenue Grand Junction, CO 81501	(970) 242-3214	N/A
Colorado Springs	2 North Cascade Avenue Suite 110 Colorado Springs, CO 80903	(719) 636-3074	N/A
Fairfield City	24 Belden Avenue, 5th Floor Norwalk, CT 06850	(203) 847-7348	(203) 849-9308
Greater Hartford City	330 Main Street Hartford, CT 06106	(860) 240-4700	N/A
New Haven	25 Science Park Bldg. 25/Room 366 New Haven, CT 06511	(203) 865-7645	N/A
Greater Bridgeport	10 Middle Street, 14th Floor Bridgeport, CT 06604	(203) 335-3800	(203) 366-0105
Old Saybrook	Old Saybrook Chamber of Commerce P.O. Box 625 146 Main Street Old Saybrook, CT 06475	(860) 388-9508	N/A
Greater Danbury	100 Mill Plain Road Danbury, CT 06811	(203) 791-3804	N/A
Wilmington	824 Market Street, Suite 610 Wilmington, DE 19801	(302) 573-6552	(302) 573-6092
Washington, DC	1110 Vermont Avenue, NW 9th Floor, P.O. Box 34346 Washington, DC 20043	(202) 606-4000	(202) 606-4225

City	Address	Tel.	Fax
Ft. Lauderdale	299 East Broward Blvd. Federal Bldg., Suite 123 Ft. Lauderdale, FL 33301	(954) 356-7263	(954) 356-7145
Dade	1320 South Dixie Hwy. 3rd Floor Coral Gables, FL 33146	(305) 536-5521	(305) 536-5058
Jacksonville	7825 Baymeadows Way, 100-B Jacksonville, FL 32256	(904) 443-1911	N/A
Daytona Beach	921 N. Nova Rd., Suite A Holly Hills, FL 32117	(904) 255-6889	(904) 255-0229
Suncoast/ Pinellas	Airport Business Center 4707 140th Avenue North, #311 Clearwater, FL 34622	(813) 532-6800	(813) 532-6800
Manasota	2801 Fruitville Road, Suite 280 Sarasota, FL 34237	(941) 955-1029	N/A
Central Florida	404 North Ingraham Avenue Lakeland, FL 33801	(941) 687-4403	N/A
Orlando	80 N. Hughey Avenue Room 455, Federal Bldg. Orlando, FL 32801	(407) 648-6476	(407) 648-6425
Hillsborough	4732 Dale Mubry Highway North Suite 400 Tampa, FL 33614-6509	(813) 870-0125	N/A
Southwest Florida	The Renaissance 8695 College Pkwy, Suites 345 & 346 Fort Myers, FL 33919	(941) 489-2935	N/A
Palm Beach	500 Australian Avenue South Suite 100 West Palm Beach, FL 33401	(561) 833-1672	(561) 833-1712
South Broward	3475 Sheridian Street, Suite 203 Hollywood, FL 33021	(954) 966-8415	N/A
Treasure Coast	Professional Center, Suite 2 3220 South US #1 Ft. Pierce, FL 34982	(407) 489-0548	N/A
Charlotte County	Punta Gorda Professional Center 201 W. Marion Avenue, #211 Punta Gorda, FL 33950	(941) 575-1818	N/A

City	Address	Tel.	Fax
Space Coast	Melbourne Professional Complex 1600 Sarno, Suite 205 Melbourne, FL 32935	(407) 254-2288	(407) 254-2288
Gainesville	101 SE 2nd Place, Suite #104 Gainesville, FL 32601	(904) 375-8278	N/A
South Palm Beach	1050 S. Federal Highway Suite 132 Delray Beach, FL 33483	(561) 278-7752	(561) 278-0288
Lake-Sumter	First Union National Bank 122 East Main Street Tavares, FL 32778-3810	(352) 365-3556	N/A
Pasco County	6014 US Highway 19, Suite 302 New Port Richey, FL 34652	(813) 842-4638	N/A
Ocala	110 E. Silver Spring Blvd. Ocala, FL 34470	(352) 629-5959	N/A
Naples of Collier	Barnett Bank 3285 Tamiami Trail East Naples, FL 34112	(941) 417-1280	(941) 417-1281
Tallahassee	c/o Leon County Library 200 W. Park Avenue Tallahassee, FL 32302	(904) 487-2665	N/A
Atlanta	1720 Peachtree Road, NW 6th Floor Atlanta, GA 30309	(404) 347-2442	(404) 347-1227
Savannah	111 E. Liberty Street, Suite 103 Savannah, GA 31401	(912) 652-4335	(912) 652-4184
Dalton-Whitfield	P.O. Box 1941 Dalton, GA 30722	(706) 279-3383	N/A
Guam	Pacific News Building, Room 103 238 Archbishop Flores Street Agana, GU 96910-5188	(671) 472-7308	N/A
Hawaii, Inc.	130 Merchant Street Suite 1030 Honolulu, HI 96813	(808) 522-8130	(808) 522-8135
Maui, Inc.	590 E. Lipoa Parkway, Suite 227 Kihei, HI 96753	(808) 875-2380	N/A

City	Address	Tel.	Fax
Treasure Valley	1020 Main Street, #290 Boise, ID 83702	(208) 334-1696	(208) 334-9353
Eastern Idaho	2300 N. Yellowstone, Suite 119 Idaho Falls, ID 83401	(208) 523-1022	(208) 528-7127
Chicago	Northwest Atrium Center 500 W. Madison Street, #1250 Chicago, IL 60661	(312) 353-7724	(312) 886-5688
Peoria	c/o Peoria Chamber of Commerce 124 SW Adams, Suite 300 Peoria, IL 61602	(309) 676-0755	(309) 676-7534
Fox Valley	40 W. Downer Place P.O. Box 277 Aurora, IL 60507	(630) 897-9214	(630) 897-7002
Decatur	Milliken University 1184 W. Main Street Decatur, IL 62522	(217) 424-6297	(217) 424-3993
Southern Illinois	150 E. Pleasant Hill Road, Box 1 Carbondale, IL 62901	(618) 453-6654	(618) 453-5040
Greater Alton	5800 Godfrey Road Alden Hall Godfrey, IL 62035-2466	(618) 467-2280	(618) 466-8289
Quad Cities	c/o Chamber of Commerce 611 19th Street Moline, IL 61265	(309) 797-0082	(309) 757-5435
Quincy Tri-State	c/o Chamber of Commerce 300 Civic Center Plaza, Suite 245 Quincy, IL 62301	(217) 222-8093	(217) 222-3033
Springfield	511 West Capitol Avenue Suite 302 Springfield, IL 62704	(217) 492-4359	(217) 492-4867
Northern Illinois	515 North Court Street Rockford, IL 61103	(815) 962-0122	(815) 962-0122
Indianapolis	429 N. Pennsylvania Street Suite 100 Indianapolis, IN 46204	(317) 226-7264	N/A
Fort Wayne	1300 S. Harrison Street Fort Wayne, IN 46802	(219) 422-2601	(219) 422-2601

City	Address	Tel.	Fax
South Bend	300 N. Michigan Street South Bend, IN 46601	(219) 282-4350	N/A
Evansville	Old Post Office Place 100 NW 2nd Street, #300 Evansville, IN 47708	(812) 421-5879	N/A
Gary	973 West 6th Avenue, Room 326 Gary, IN 46402	(219) 882-3918	N/A
Southeast Indiana	c/o Chamber of Commerce 500 Franklin Street, Box 29 Columbus, IN 47201	(812) 379-4457	N/A
Anderson	c/o Chamber of Commerce 205 W. 11th P.O. Box 469 Anderson, IN 46015	(765) 642-0264	N/A
S. Central Indiana	4100 Charleston Road New Albany, IN 47150-9538	(812) 945-0266	N/A
Bloomington	Star Center 216 West Allen Bloomington, IN 47403	(812) 335-3744	N/A
Kokomo/ Howard County	106 North Washington Street Kokomo, IN 46901	(765) 457-5301	(765) 452-4564
Marion/Grant	215 S. Adams Marion, IN 46952	(765) 664-5107	N/A
Elkhart	418 S. Main Street P.O. Box 428 Elkhart, IN 46515	(219) 293-1531	(219) 294-1859
Logansport County	Chamber of Commerce 300 East Broadway, Suite 103 Logansport, IN 46947	(219) 753-6388	N/A
Des Moines	Federal Building/Room 749 210 Walnut Street Des Moines, IA 50309-2186	(515) 284-4760	N/A
Sioux City	Federal Building 320 6th Street Sioux City, IA 51101	(712) 277-2324	N/A
Council Bluffs	Chamber of Commerce P.O. Box 1565 Council Bluffs, IA 51502-1565	(712) 325-1000	N/A

City	Address	Tel.	Fax
Cedar Rapids	Lattner Building 215 4th Avenue, SF, #200 Cedar Rapids, IA 52401-1806	(319) 362-6405	(319) 362-7861
River City	15 West State Street P.O. Box 1128 Mason City, IA 50401	(515) 423-5724	N/A
Waterloo	Chamber of Commerce 215 East 4th Waterloo, IA 50703	(319) 233-8431	N/A
Burlington	Federal Building 300 N. Main Street Burlington, IA 52601	(319) 752-2967	N/A
Dubuque	c/o Northeast Iowa Community College 10250 Sundown Road Pcosta, IA 52068	(319) 556-5110	N/A
Fort Dodge	Federal Building, Room 436 205 South 8th Street Fort Dodge, IA 50501	(515) 955-2622	N/A
Iowa Lakes	P.O. Box 7937 122 West 5th Street Spencer, IA 51301	(712) 262-3059	N/A
South Central	SBDC, Indian Hills Community College 525 Grandview Avenue Ottumwa, IA 52501	(515) 683-5127	N/A
Iowa City	210 Federal Building P.O. Box 1853 Iowa City, IA 52440-1853	(319) 338-1662	N/A
Central Iowa	Fisher Community College 709 South Center Marshalltown, IA 50158	(515) 753-6645	N/A
Southwest Iowa	Chamber of Commerce 614 W. Sheridan, Box 38 Shenandoah, IA 51601	(712) 246-3260	N/A
Illowa	333 4th Avenue South Clinton, IA 52732	(319) 242-5702	N/A

City	Address	Tel.	Fax
Northeast Iowa	3404 285th Street Cresco, IA 52136	(319) 547-3377	N/A
Keokuk	c/o Keokuk Area Chamber of Commerce 401 Main Street, Pierce Bldg. #1 Keokuk, IA 52632	(319) 524-5055	N/A
Vista	Storm Lake Chamber of Commerce 119 West 6th Street Storm Lake, IA 50588	(712) 732-3780	N/A
Wichita	SBA/100 East English Suite 510 Wichita, KS 67202	(316) 269-6273	N/A
Salina	130 W.18th P.O. Box 642 Concordia, KS 66901	(913) 243-4290	N/A
Emporia	Chamber of Commerce 719 Commercial P.O. Box 703 Emporia, KS 66801	(316) 342-1600	N/A
Ark Valley	Box 314 Winfield, KS 67156	(316) 221-1617	N/A
Topcka	1700 College Topeka, KS 66621	(913) 231-1010	N/A
Hays	c/o Emprise Bank NA P.O. Box 400 Hays, KS 67601	(913) 625-6595	N/A
Hutchinson	One East 9th Hutchison, KS 67501	(316) 665-8468	N/A
Southwest Kansas	Dodge City Chamber of Commerce P.O. Box 939 Dodge City, KS 67801	(316) 227-3119	N/A
Golden Belt	Chamber of Commerce 1307 Williams Great Bend, KS 67530	(316) 792-2401	N/A
Southeast Kansas	P.O. Box 342 Girard, KS 66743	(316) 724-6100	N/A

City	Address	Tel.	Fax
McPherson	Chamber of Commerce 306 N. Main McPherson, KS 67460	(316) 241-3303	N/A
Louisville	600 Dr. Martin Luther King Jr. Place 188 Federal Office Bldg. Louisville, KY 40202	(502) 582-5976	N/A
Paducah	Federal Office Building 501 Broadway, Room B-36 Paducah, KY 42001	(502) 442-5685	N/A
Lexington	410 W. Vine St. Suite 290, Civic C Lexington, KY 40507	(606) 231-9902	(606) 253-3190
New Orleans	365 Canal Street, Suite 3100 New Orleans, LA 70130	(504) 589-2356	(504) 589-2339
Baton Rouge	564 Laurel Street P.O. Box 3217 Baton Rouge, LA 70801	(504) 381-7130	(504) 336-4306
Lake Charles	120 W. Pujo Street Lake Charles, LA 70601	(318) 433-3632	N/A
Shreveport	400 Edwards Street Shreveport, LA 71101	(318) 677-2536	(318) 677-2541
Lafayette	804 St. Mary Blvd. Lafayette, LA 70505-1307	(318) 233-2705	(318) 234-8671
Central Louisiana	802 Third Street P.O. Box 992 Alexandria, LA 71309	(318) 442-6671	N/A
North Shore	P.O. Box 1458 Hammond, LA 70404	(504) 345-4457	(504) 345-4749
Portland	66 Pearl Street, Room 210 Portland, ME 04101	(207) 772-1147	N/A
Augusta	40 Western Avenue Augusta, ME 04330	(207) 622-8509	N/A
Central & North Aroostook	111 High Street Caribou, ME 04736	(207) 492-8010	N/A
Bangor	Husson College One College Circle Peabock Hall, Room 229 Bangor, ME 04401	(207) 941-9707	N/A

City	Address	Tel.	Fax
Lewiston-Auburn	BIC of Maine-Bates Mill Complex 35 Canal Street Lewiston, ME 04240-7764	(207) 782-3708	(207) 783-7745
Maine Coastal	Box 1105, Mill Mall Ellsworth, ME 04605-1105	(207) 667-5800	N/A
Oxford Hills	166 Main Street South Paris, ME 04281	(207) 743-0499	N/A
Western Mountains	c/o Fleet Bank P.O. Box 400 108 Congress Street Rumford, ME 04276	(207) 364-3735	N/A
Baltimore	The City Crescent Bldg. 6th Floor 10 South Howard Street Baltimore, MD 21201	(410) 962-2233	(410) 962-1805
Salisbury	c/o Chamber of Commerce 300 E. Main Street Salisbury, MD 21801	(410) 749-0185	N/A
Southern Maryland	2515 Riva Road, Suite 110 Annapolis, MD 21401	(410) 266-9553	(410) 573-0981
Hagerstown	111 W. Washington Street Hagerstown, MD 21740	(301) 739-2015	(301) 739-1278
Upper Shore	c/o Talbot City Chamber of Commerce P.O. Box 1366 Easton, MD 21601	(410) 822-4606	(410) 822-7922
Frederick County	43A South Market Street Frederick, MD 21701	(301) 662-8723	(301) 846-4427
Boston	10 Causeway Street Room 265 Boston, MA 02222-1093	(617) 565-5591	(617) 565-5598
Worcester	33 Waldo Street Worcester, MA 01608	(508) 753-2929	(508) 754-8560
Cape Cod	270 Communications Way Independence Park, Suite 5B Hyannis, MA 02601	(508) 775-4884	N/A

City	Address	Tel.	Fax
Springfield	1350 Main Street Springfield, MA 01103	(413) 785-0314	N/A
Northeast Massachusetts	Danvers Savings Bank 1 Conant Street Danvers, MA 01923	(508) 772-2200	N/A
Southeast Massachusetts	60 School Street Brockton, MA 02401	(508) 587-2673	(508) 587-1340
Bristol/ Plymouth	c/o Fall River Chamber of Commerce 200 Pocasset Street Fall River, MA 02722	(508) 676-8226	N/A
Detroit	477 Michigan Avenue Room 515 Detroit, MI 48226	(313) 226-7947	(313) 226-3448
Upper Peninsula	c/o Chamber of Commerce 2581 1-75 Business Spur Sault Ste. Marie, MI 49783	(906) 632-3301	N/A
Kalamazoo	128 North Kalamazoo Mall Kalamazoo, MI 49007	(616) 381-5382	(616) 343-0430
Traverse City	P.O. Box 387 202 East Grandview Parkway Traverse City, MI 49685-0387	(616) 947-5075	N/A
Petoskey	401 E. Mitchell Petoskey, MI 49770	(616) 347-4150	N/A
Minneapolis	5217 Wayzata Blvd North Plaza Bldg., Suite 51 Minneapolis, MN 55416	(612) 591-0539	(612) 544-0436
Southwest Minnesota	Box 999 112 Riverfront Street Mankato, MN 56001	(507) 345-4519	(507) 345-4451
St. Paul	Lowry Professional Bldg. 350 St. Peter Street, #295 St. Paul, MN 55102	(612) 223-5010	(612) 223-5048
Southeast Minnesota	Rochester Chamber of Commerce 220 S. Broadway, Suite 100 Rochester, MN 55901	(507) 288-1122	(507) 282-8960
Central Area	1527 Northway Drive St. Cloud, MN 56303	(320) 240-1332	(320) 255-9050

City	Address	Tel.	Fax
South Metro	101 West Burnsville Pkwy #150 Burnsville, MN 55337	(612) 898-5645	(612) 435-6972
Duluth	4879 Adrian Lane Hermantown, MN 55811	(218) 723-2701	(218) 723-2712
Gulfcoast	One Government Plaza 2909 13th Street, Suite 203 Gulfport, MS 39501	(601) 863- 4449	N/A
Jackson	First Jackson Center, Suite 400 101 W. Capitol Street Jackson, MS 39201	(601) 965-4378	N/A
Delta	Greenville Chamber 915 Washington A P.O. Box 933 Greenville, MS 38701	(601) 378-3141	N/A
Kansas City	323 W. 8th Street, Suite 104 Kansas City, MO 64105	(816) 374-6675	(816) 374-6759
St. Louis	815 Olive Street, Room 242 St. Louis, MO 63101-1569	(314) 539-6970	(314) 539-3785
Springfield	620 S. Glenstone, #110 Springfield, MO 65802-3200	(417) 864-7670	(417) 864-4108
Tri-Lakes	HCR3 Box 3475 Shell Knob, MO 65757	(417) 858-3412	(417) 858-3412
Southeast Missouri	Route 1, Box 280 Neelyville, MO 63954	(573) 989-3577	N/A
Mexico	c/o Dennis Dexter 531 Fox Pointe Drive St. Charles, MO 63304	(314) 928-6153	N/A
Mid-Missouri	c/o Milo Dahl 1705 Halsted Court Columbia, MO 65203	(573) 874-1132	N/A
St. Joseph	Chamber of Commerce 3003 Frederick Avenue St. Joseph, MO 64506	(816) 232-4461	N/A
Ozark- Gateway	1102 Oak Hill Road Cuba, MO 65453	(573) 885-4954	N/A
Lewis & Clark	425 Spencer Road St. Peters, MO 63376	(314) 928-2900	(314) 928-2900

City	Address	Tel.	Fax
Poplar Bluff Area	c/o James W. Carson, Chair Route 1, Box 280 Neelyville, MO 63954	(573) 989-3577	N/A
Lake Ozark	Univ. Extension P.O. Box 1405, 113 Kansas Street Camdenton, MO 65020	(573) 346-2644	(573) 346-2694
Great Falls	P.O. Box 2127 Great Falls, MT 59403	(406) 761-4434	N/A
Missoula	802 Normans Lane Missoula, MT 59803	(406) 543-6623	N/A
Butte	2950 Harrison Avenue Butte, MT 59701	(406) 494-4495	N/A
Bozeman	1205 East Main Street Bozeman, MT 59715	(406) 586-5421	N/A
Helena	301 South Park/Federal Building Helena, MT 59626-0054	(406) 449-5381	N/A
Billings	815 S. 27th Street Billings, MT 59101	(406) 245-4111	N/A
Kalispell	2 Main Street Kalispell, MT 59901	(406) 756-5271	N/A
Lincoln	800 East O Street Lincoln, NE 685208	(402) 437-2409	N/A
Omaha	11145 Mill Valley Road Omaha, NE 68154	(402) 221-3606	(402) 221-3680
Norfolk	504 Pierce Street Norfolk, NE 68701	(402) 371-0940	N/A
Columbus	c/o Wayne R. Davy 41 Stires Lake Columbus, NE 68601	(402) 564-2769	N/A
North Platte	414 E. 16th Street Cozad, NE 69130	(308) 784-2590	N/A
Hastings	c/o James Svoboda 1338 West 12th Street Hastings, NE 68901	(402) 463-5818	N/A
Panhandle	c/o Marvin Harms 150549 CR 30 Minatare, NE 69356	(308) 632-2133	N/A

City	Address	Tel.	Fax
Fremont	Chamber of Commerce 92 West 5th Street Fremont, NE 68025	(402) 721-2641	N/A
Las Vegas	301 F. Stewart, Box 7527 Las Vegas, NV 89125	(702) 388-6104	N/A
Northern Nevada	785 W. 6th Street Reno, NV 89503-4315	(702) 324-2902	N/A
Lakes Region	67 Water Street, Suite 105 Laconia, NH 03246	(603) 524-9168	N/A
Upper Valley	Citizens Bank Bldg. 20 W. Park Street, 316 First Lebanon, NH 03766	(603) 448-3491	N/A
Seacoast	195 Commerce Way, Unit A Portsmouth, NH 03801-3251	(603) 433-0575	N/A
Merrimack Valley	275 Chestnut Street, Room 618 Manchester, NH 03103	(603) 666-7561	(603) 666-7925
Monadock	34 Mechanic Street Keene, NH 03431-3421	(603) 352-0320	N/A
Concord	143 N. Main Street, Room 202A Concord, NH 03301	(603) 225-1400	N/A
Somerset	Raritan Valley Community College Box 3300 Somerville, NJ 08876	(908) 218-8874	N/A
Newark	2 Gateway Center, 4th Floor Newark, NJ 07102	(973) 645-3982	(973) 645-2375
North West	c/o Bob Kopchains, Chair 25 Tannery Hill Drive Hamburg, NJ 07419	(973) 209-8525	N/A
Monmouth	Brookdale Community College Career Services 765 Newman Springs Road Lincroft, NJ 07738	(732) 224-2573	N/A
Bergen City	327 E. Ridgewood Avenue Paramus, NJ 07652	(201) 599-6090	N/A
Ocean County	33 Washington Street Toms River, NJ 08754	(732) 505-6033	N/A

City	Address	Tel.	Fax
S. New Jersey	c/o United Jersey Bank 4900 Rte. 70 Pennsauken, NJ 08109	(609) 486-3421	N/A
Greater Princeton	216 Rockingham Row Princeton Forrestal Village Princeton, NJ 08540	(609) 520-1776	(609) 520-9107
Albuquerque	Silver Square, Suite 330 625 Silver Avenue, SW Albuquerque, NM 87102	(505) 766-1900	(505) 766-1833
Roswell	Federal Building, Room 237 Roswell, NM 88201	(505) 625-2112	(505) 623-2545
Santa Fe	Montoya Federal Building 120 Federal Place, Rm. 307 Santa Fe, NM 87501	(505) 988-6302	(505) 988-6300
Las Cruces	Lorelto Towne Center 505 S. Main Street, Suite 125 Las Cruces, NM 88001	(505) 523-5627	N/A
Rochester	601 Keating Federal Building 100 State Street, Room 410 Rochester, NY 14614	(716) 263-6473	(716) 263-3146
Buffalo	Federal Building, Room 1311 111 West Huron Street Buffalo, NY 14202	(716) 551-4301	N/A
Dutchess	c/o Chamber of Commerce 110 Main Street Poughkeepsie, NY 12601	(914) 454-1700	N/A
Syracuse	100 S. Clinton Street, Room 1073 Syracuse, NY 13260	(315) 448-0422	N/A
Northeast	Albany Col Chamber of Commerce 1 Computer Drive South Albany, NY 12205	(518) 446-1118	(518) 446-1228
Watertown	518 Davidson Street Watertown, NY 13601	(315) 788-1200	(315) 788-8251
Utica	SUNY Institute of Technology P.O. Box 3050 Utica, NY 13504	(315) 792-7553	N/A

City	Address	Tel.	Fax
Auburn	c/o Chamber of Commerce 30 South Street P.O. Box 675 Auburn, NY 13021	(315) 252-7291	N/A
S. Tier Binghamton	49 Court Street, P.O. Box 995 Metro Center/2nd Floor Binghamton, NY 13902	(607) 772-8860	N/A
Brookhaven	96 Jerome Drive Farmingdale, NY 11735	(516) 451-6563	N/A
Westchester	350 Main Street White Plains, NY 10601	(914) 948-3907	(914) 948-4645
Chemung	c/o SBA 333 East Water Street, 4th Floor Elmira, NY 14901	(607) 734-3358	N/A
Huntington	c/o Chamber of Commerce 151 W. Carver Street Huntington, NY 11743	(516) 423-6100	N/A
Tompkins County	c/o Tompkins Chamber of Commerce 904 E. Shore Drive Ithaca, NY 14850	(607) 273-7080	N/A
Orange County	Orange City Chamber of Commerce 40 Matthews Street Goshen, NY 10924	(914) 294-6121	N/A
Staten Island	c/o Chamber of Commerce 130 Bay Street Staten Island, NY 10301	(718) 727-1221	N/A
Ulster	Ulster City Community College Clinton Bldg., Room 107 Stone Ridge, NY 12484	(914) 687-5035	(914) 687-5015
Queens County	120-55 Queens Blvd. Room 333, Queens Borough Hall Kew Gardens, NY 11424	(718) 263-8961	(718) 263-9032
Suffolk	6 Quantuck Bay Road West Hampton Beach, NY 11978	(516) 288-6340	(516) 288-5715
New York	26 Federal Plaza, Room 3100 New York, NY 10278	(212) 264-4507	(212) 264-4963

City	Address	Tel.	Fax
Nassau County	Dept. of Commerce & Industry 400 County Seat Drive, #140 Mineola, NY 11501	(516) 571-3303	N/A
Charlotte	200 N. College Street Suite A2015 Charlotte, NC 28202	(704) 344-6576	(704) 344-6769
Raleigh	Century PO Bldg, Suite 306 P.O. Box 406 Raleigh, NC 27602	(919) 856-4739	N/A
Asheville	Federal Building, Room 259 151 Patton Asheville, NC 28801	(704) 271-4786	(704) 271-4009
Henderson	Federal Bldg., Room 108 West 4th Avenue & Church Street Hendersonville, NC 28792	(704) 693-8702	N/A
Greensboro	400 W. Market Street, Suite 410 Greensboro, NC 27401-2241	(910) 333-5399	N/A
Wilmington	Alton Lennon Fed. Bldg. 2 Princess Street, Suite 103 Wilmington, NC 28401	(910) 815-4576	(910) 256-5150
High Point	High Point Chamber of Commerce 1101 N. Main Street High Point, NC 27262	(910) 882-8625	N/A
Unifour	c/o Catawba County Chamber of Commerce P.O. Box 1828 Hickory, NC 28603	(704) 328-6111	N/A
Durham	411 W. Chapel Hill Street Durham, NC 27707	(919) 541-2171	N/A
Sandhills Area	c/o Sand Hills Area C of C 1480 Hwy 15-501, P.O. Box 458 Southern Pines, NC 28387	(910) 692-3926	N/A
Chapel Hill	c/o Chapel Hill/Carboro Chamber of Commerce 104 S. Estes Drive, P.O. Box 2897 Chapel Hill, NC 27514	(919) 967-7075	N/A

City	Address	Tel.	Fax
Outer Banks	c/o Outer Banks of Chamber of Commerce P.O. Box 1757 Kill Devil Hills, NC 27948	(919) 441-8144	N/A
Down East	P.O. Box 95 New Bern, NC 28560	(919) 633-6688	(919) 633-9608
Fargo	P.O. Box 3086 657 2nd Avenue, Room 225 Fargo, ND 58108	(701) 239-5677	N/A
Minot	P.O. Box 507 Minot, ND 58702-0507	(701) 852-6883	(701) 852-6905
Upper Red River	4300 Technology Drive P.O. Box 8372 Grand Forks, ND 58202	(701) 777-3051	N/A
Bismarck-Mandan	P.O. Box 5509 Bismarck, ND 58502-5509	(701) 250-4303	N/A
Columbus	2 Nationwide Plaza, Suite 1400 Columbus, OH 43215-2542	(614) 469-2357	N/A
Cleveland	1100 Superior Avenue, Suite 620 Eaton Center Cleveland, OH 44114-2507	(216) 522-4194	(216) 522-4844
Cincinnati	525 Vine Street Ameritrust Bldg., Room 850 Cincinnati, OH 45202	(513) 684-2812	(513) 684-3251
Toledo	1946 N. 13th St., Suite 367 Toledo, OH 43624	(419) 259-7598	N/A
Akron	c/o Regional Dev. Board One Cascade Plaza, 7th Floor Akron, OH 44308	(330) 379-3163	(330) 379-3164
Dayton	Federal Building, Room 505 200 W. 2nd Street Dayton, OH 45402-1430	(513) 225-2887	(513) 225-7667
Youngstown	306 Williamson Hall Youngstown University Youngstown, OH 44555	(330) 746-2687	N/A
Mansfield	Chamber of Commerce 55 N. Mulberry Street Mansfield, OH 44902	(419) 522-3211	N/A

City	Address	Tel.	Fax
Licking County	50 West Locust Street Newark, OH 43055	(614) 345-7458	N/A
Canton	116 Cleveland Avenue, NW Suite 601 Canton, OH 44702-1720	(330) 453-6047	N/A
Heart of Ohio	377 West Liberty Street Wooster, OH 44691	(330) 262-5735	(330) 262-5745
Tulsa	Chamber of Commerce 616 S. Boston, Suite 406 Tulsa, OK 74119	(918) 581-7462	(918) 581-6908
Oklahoma	c/o SBA, Oklahoma Tower Bldg. 210 Park Avenue, #1300 Oklahoma City, OK 73102	(405) 231-5163	(405) 231-4876
Lawton	4500 W. Lee Blvd. Bldg, 100, Suite 107 Lawton, OK 73505	(405) 353-8727	(405) 250-5677
NE Oklahoma	201 S. Main Grove, OK 74344	(918) 786-6284	(918) 786-9841
Ardmore	P.O. Box 1585 Ardmore, OK 73402-1585	(405) 223-7765	N/A
Portland	1515 SW Fifth Avenue Suite 1050 Portland, OR 97201-5494	(503) 326-3441	(503) 326-2501
Southern Oregon	Valley of the Rogue Bank P.O. Box 969 Medford, OR 97502	(541) 776-4220	N/A
Willamette	1401 Willamette Street P.O. Box 1107 Eugene, OR 97401-4003	(541) 465-6600	(541) 484-4942
Salem	P.O. Box 4024 Salem, OR 97302-1024	(503) 370-2896	N/A
Bend	c/o Bend Chamber of Commerce 63085 North Highway 97 Bend, OR 97701	(541) 382-3221	(541) 382-3221
Pittsburgh	1000 Liberty Avenue, Room 112 Pittsburgh, PA 15222	(412) 395-6560	(412) 395-6562
Reading	c/o Chamber of Commerce 645 Penn Street Reading, PA 19601	(610) 376-6766	N/A

City	Address	Tel.	Fax
Lancaster	118 West Chestnut Street Lancaster, PA 17603	(717) 397-3092	N/A
Harrisburg	4211 Trindle Road Camp Hill, PA 17011	(717) 761-4304	(717) 761-4315
Philadelphia	1315 Walnut Street, Suite 500 Philadelphia, PA 19107	(215) 790-5050	(215) 790-5016
Lehigh Valley	Rauch Bldg., 37 Lehigh University 621 Taylor Street Bethlehem, PA 18015	(610) 758-4496	(610) 758-5205
Erie	120 West 9th Street Erie, PA 16501	(814) 871-5650	N/A
N. Central PA	Federal Building, Room 304 240 W. 3rd Street P.O. Box 725 Williamsport, PA 17703	(717) 322-3720	(717) 322-1607
Scranton	Kane Professional Bldg. 116 N. Washington Ave., Suite 211 Scranton, PA 18503	(717) 347-4611	N/A
Wilkes-Barre	20 N. Pennsylvania Avenue Wilkes-Barre, PA 18702	(717) 826-6502	N/A
York	Cyber Center 1600 Pennsylvania Avenue York, PA 17404	(717) 845-8830	(717) 845-9333
Uniontown	P.O. Box 2065 DTS Pittsburgh Street, Federal Building Uniontown, PA 15401	(412) 437-4222	N/A
Mon-Valley	435 Donner Avenue Monessen, PA 15062	(412) 684-4277	N/A
E. Montgomery County	Baederwood Shopping Center 1653 The Fairways, Suite 204 Jenkintown, PA 19046	(215) 885-3027	N/A
Cumberland Valley	Chambersburg Chamber of Commerce 75 S. Second Street Chambersburg, PA 17201	(717) 264-2935	N/A
Monroe-Stroudsburg	556 Main Street Stroudsburg, PA 18301	(717) 421-4433	N/A

City	Address	Tel.	Fax
Chester County	Government Service Center Suite 281 601 Westtown Rd. West Chester, PA 19382-4538	(610) 344-6910	(610) 793-2780
Westmoreland County	St. Vincent College 300 Fraser Purchase Road Latrobe, PA 15650-2690	(412) 539-7505	N/A
Bucks County	c/o Chamber of Commerce 409 Hood Boulevard Fairless Hills, PA 19030	(215) 943-8850	(215) 943-7404
Altoona-Blair	c/o Altoona-Blair Chamber of Commerce 1212 12th Avenue Altoona, PA 16601-3493	(814) 943-8151	N/A
Warren County	Warren County Chamber of Commerce P.O. Box 942 315 Second Avenue Warren, PA 16365	(814) 723-9017	N/A
Tri-County	238 High Street Pottstown, PA 19464	(610) 327-2673	N/A
Central PA	200 Innovation Blvd., #242-B State College, PA 16803	(814) 234-9415	(814) 238-9686
PR & VI	Citibank Towers Plaza 252 Ponce de Leon Ave., 2nd Floor San Juan, PR 00918-2041	(809) 766-5001	N/A
JGE Knight	380 Westminster Street Providence, RI 02903	(401) 528-4571	(401) 528-4539
Midlands	Strom Thurmond Bldg. 1835 Assembly Street, Room 358 Columbia, SC 29201	(803) 765-5131	(803) 765-5962
Piedmont	Federal Bldg., Room B-02 300 E. Washington Street Greenville, SC 29601	(864) 271-3638	N/A
Coastal	284 King Street Charleston, SC 29401	(803) 727-4778	(803) 853-2529
Grand Strand	P.O. Box 2468 Myrtle Beach, SC 29578	(803) 918-1079	N/A

City	Address	Tel.	Fax
Sioux Falls	First Financial Center 110 South Phillips Ave., Suite 200 Sioux Falls, SD 57102-1109	(605) 330-4231	N/A
Rapid City	444 Mt. Rushmore Road, #209 Rapid City, SD 57701	(605) 394-5311	N/A
Memphis	Federal Building 167 N. Main Street, Suite 390 Memphis, TN 38103	(901) 544-3588	N/A
Nashville	50 Vantage Way, Suite 201 Nashville, TN 37228-1500	(615) 736-7621	N/A
Chattanooga	Federal Building 900 Georgia Avenue, Room 26 Chattanooga, TN 37402	(423) 752-5190	(423) 752-5335
Greater Knoxville	530 South Gay Street Farragot Bldg., Suite 224 Knoxville, TN 37902	(423) 545-4203	N/A
Jackson	c/o Chamber of Commerce P.O. Box 1904, 194 Auditorium Street Jackson, TN 38302	(901) 423-2200	N/A
Kingsport	c/o Chamber of Commerce 151 East Main Street Kingsport, TN 37662	(423) 392-8805	N/A
Northeast Tennessee	1st Tennessee Bank Bldg. 2710 S. Roan Street, Suite 584 Johnson City, TN 37601	(423) 929-7686	(423) 461-8052
Dallas	Comerica Bank, 2nd Floor 6260 E. Mockingbird Dallas, TX 75214-2619	(214) 828-2471	(214) 828-2803
Houston	9301 Southwest Freeway Suite 550 Houston, TX 77074	(713) 773-6565	(713) 773-6550
Fort Worth	100 East 15th Street, #24 Ft. Worth, TX 76102	(817) 871-6002	(817) 871-6031
San Antonio	c/o SBA, Federal Building 727 E. Durango, Room #A527 San Antonio, TX 78206	(210) 472-5931	(210) 472-5937
L. Rio Grande Valley	222 E. Van Buren, Suite 500 Harlingen, TX 78550	(956) 427-8533	(956) 427-8537

City	Address	Tel.	Fax
Corpus Christi	651 Upper North Broadway Suite 654 Corpus Christi, TX 78477	(512) 888-4322	(512) 888-3418
El Paso	10737 Gateway West, Suite 320 El Paso, TX 79935	(915) 534-0541	(915) 540-5155
Lubbock	1611 10th Street, Suite 200 Lubbock, TX 79401	(806) 472-7462	(806) 472-7487
Abilene	2106 Federal Post Office & Court Abilene, TX 79601	(915) 677-1857	N/A
Austin	2501 S. Congress Austin, TX 78701	(512) 442-7235	(512) 442-7528
East Texas	RTDC 1530 SSW Loop 323, Suite 100 Tyler, TX 75701	(903) 510-2975	N/A
Texarkana	P.O. Box 1468 Texarkana, TX 75504	(903) 792-7191	(903) 793-4304
Waco	401 Franklin Avenue Waco, TX 76701	(817) 754-8898	(817) 756-0776
Brazos Valley	Norwest Bank Building 3000 Briarcrest, Suite 302 Bryan, TX 77802	(409) 776-8876	N/A
Wichita Falls	Hamilton Building P.O. Box 1860 Wichita Falls, TX 76307	(817) 723-2741	N/A
Golden Triangle	P.O. Box 3150 Beaumont, TX 77704	(409) 838-6581	(409) 833-6718
Salt Lake	169 E. 100 South Salt Lake City, UT 84111	(801) 364-1331	(801) 364-1310
Ogden	324 25th Street 6104 Ogden, UT 84401	(801) 625-5712	N/A
Central Utah	1275 N. University, Suite 8 Provo, UT 84604	(801) 373-5300	N/A
Southern Utah	c/o Dixie College 225 S. 700 East St. George, UT 84770	(801) 652-7741	N/A

City	Address	Tel.	Fax
Northern Utah	c/o Cache Valley Chamber of Commerce 160 N. Main Logan, UT 84123	(801) 752-2161	N/A
Montpelier	c/o SBA P.O. Box 605 87 State Street, Room 205 Montpelier, VT 05601	(802) 828-4422	N/A
Champlain Valley	11 Lincoln Street, Room 106 Winston Prouty Fed Bldg. Essex Junction, VT 05452	(802) 951-6762	N/A
Northeast Kingdom	c/o NCIC/20 Main Street P.O. Box 904 St. Johnsbury, VT 05819	(802) 748-5101	N/A
Marble Valley	256 N. Main Street Rutland, VT 05701-2413	(802) 773-9147	N/A
Richmond	1504 Santa Rosa Road Dale Building, Suite 200 Richmond, VA 23229	(804) 771-2400	(804) 771-8018
Roanoke	250 Franklin Road Federal Building, Room 716 Roanoke, VA 24011	(540) 857-2834	(540) 857-2043
Hampton Roads	Federal Building, Room 737 200 Granby Street Norfolk, VA 23510	(757) 441-3733	(757) 441-3733
Peninsula	c/o Peninsula Chamber of Commerce P.O. Box 7269, 6 Manhattan Square Hampton, VA 23666	(804) 766-2000	N/A
Bristol	20 Volunteer Parkway P.O. Box 519 Bristol, VA 24203	(423) 989-4850	N/A
Shenandoah Valley	c/o Waynesboro Chamber of Commerce 301 W. Main Street Waynesboro, VA 22980	(540) 949-8203	N/A
Central Virginia	918 Emmet Street North Suite 200 Charlottesville, VA 22903	(804) 295-6712	(804) 295-7066

City	Address	Tel.	Fax
Greater Lynchburg	Federal Building 1100 Main Street Lynchburg, VA 24504-1714	(804) 846-3235	N/A
Greater Prince William Co.	Prince William Chamber of Commerce 4320 Ridgewood Center Drive Prince William, VA 22192	(703) 590-5000	N/A
Martinsville	115 Road Street P.O. Box 709 Martinsville, VA 24112-0709	(540) 632-6401	N/A
Williamsburg	c/o Chamber of Commerce 201 Penniman Road Williamsburg, VA 23185	(757) 229-6511	N/A
Tri-Cities	c/o Chamber of Commerce 108 N. Main Street Hopewell, VA 23860	(804) 458-5536	N/A
Seattle	1200 6th Avenue, Suite 1700 Seattle, WA 98101	(206) 553-7320	(206) 553-7044
Spokane	Business Information Center 1020 W. Riverside Avenue Spokane, WA 99201	(509) 353-2820	(509) 353-2600
Tacoma	1101 Pacific Avenue Tacoma, WA 98402	(206) 274-1288	(206) 274-1289
Ft. Vancouver	1200 Ft. Vancouver Way P.O. Box 8900 Vancouver, WA 98668	(360) 992-3241	N/A
Mid-Columbia	c/o SBDC P.O. Box 1647 Yakima, WA 98907-1647	(509) 574-4944	(509) 574-4943
Bellingham	Fourth Corner Economic Dev. Group P.O. Box 2803 1203 Cornwall Ave. Bellingham, WA 98227	(360) 676-4255	(360) 647-9413
Charleston	1116 Smith Street Charleston, WV 25301	(304) 347-5463	N/A
Wheeling	1310 Market Street Wheeling, WV 26003	(304) 233-2575	N/A

City	Address	Tel.	Fax
Huntington	1101 6th Avenue, Suite 220 Huntington, WV 25701-2309	(304) 523-4092	N/A
U Monongahela VA	1000 Technology Drive Suite 1111 Fairmont, WV 26555	(304) 363-0486	N/A
Milwaukee	310 W. Wisconsin Avenue, #425 Milwaukee, WI 53203	(414) 297-3942	(414) 297-1377
Madison	c/o M&I Bank 7448 Hubbards Avenue Middleton, WI 53562	(608) 831-5464	N/A
Eau Claire	Federal Building, Room B11 510 South Barstow Street Eau Claire, WI 54701	(715) 834-1573	N/A
Fox Cities	227 S. Walnut Street P.O. Box 1855 Appleton, WI 54913	(414) 734-7101	(414) 734-7161
La Crosse	712 Main Street P.O. Box 219 La Crosse, WI 54602-0219	(608) 784-4880	N/A
Wausau	300 Third St., Suite 200 P.O. Box 6190 Wausau, WI 54402-6190	(715) 845-6231	N/A
Green Bay	835 Potts Avenue Green Bay, WI 54304	(414) 496-8930	(414) 496-6009
Central Wisconsin	1224 Lindberg Avenue Stevens Point, WI 54481	(715) 344-7729	(715) 344-7729
Superior	305 Harborview Parkway Superior, WI 54880	(715) 394-7716	(715) 394-3810
Casper	Federal Building #2215 100 East B Street Casper, WY 82602	(307) 261-6529	N/A

Commercial Lease Check-Up

How long does the lease run? Can it be renewed? Is the lease assignable? You can't buy goodwill if the seller isn't able to transfer the lease or if the lease is about to expire. So if you can't answer these questions, you have no idea of what the business is actually worth. Therefore, a careful examination of the business's lease must be high on your list of priorities.

Even though you will be "inheriting" the former owner's lease when you buy his business, the transfer of the lease is often an ideal time to renegotiate with the landlord for more favorable terms. And, despite landlord's claims to the contrary, lease agreements are not etched in stone—they can be negotiated. Here are some of the key business terms you can expect to see in a typical lease as well as advice on what pitfalls to avoid:

1. *Assignability*. Make sure the seller has, and you'll have, the capability to assign the lease to another party. Without a lease for its location, there may be little value in acquiring the

business. And without the right to transfer the lease, it may impossible for you to sell the business after it's yours.

2. *Term/renewal.* Determining that the lease can be transferred is not enough. If the lease is about to expire, you and your business could be pressed to find other space. This could be costly and you might lose customers in the process. The capability to extend or renew the term of your lease can be extremely valuable to your business, especially if the former owner has built up a significant clientele. If you can't get a long-term lease, ask for a short lease with several options to renew. That way you get the best of both worlds. You'll be able to leave if necessary or stay for an extended period of time if things go well. In most instances, getting a lease with renewal options costs you nothing. And because it's likely that the landlord already has spent money to put you into the space when you first took it over, you should be able to negotiate a below market rent for the renewal term.

3. *Rent step-ups; percentage rent.* To determine whether the owner is paying a market rent for the space, you'll need to analyze what comparable space is renting for in your area. Commercial real-estate brokers can be a valuable resource in obtaining comparable rent figures. In addition, examine how rent is defined in the lease. *Fixed rent* may be a set figure that graduates over time or fluctuates in accordance with some external cost-of-living index. If an outside standard is being used, try to cap the increase in any lease year to a certain amount, say 2 to 3 percent. Many retail and shopping center leases require a tenant to pay an added rent based upon a percentage of the business's gross sales or revenues, often kicking in after the tenant has achieved a minimum sales threshold. The definition of *gross sales* should not be overly broad. It should not include refunds, returns, and other items not received in the ordinary course of business.

4. *Escalations*. Normally, a tenant will be required to pay its share of a building's increases in operating expenses. To ease the financial strain of these charges on your business, ask the landlord to cap escalations at a certain dollar amount per year. Also, try to delay when these increases kick in (so your business has a chance to get off the ground).

5. *Use/legality of use*. If possible, the lease should permit "any legal use." In any event, the "use" clause must be sufficiently broad to enable your business to use the premises for its intended purpose, to accommodate the flow of people and customers, and to permit incidental or ancillary uses related to the business. Make sure the certificate of occupancy authorizes your intended use and ask the landlord to represent that your use does not violate existing laws.

6. *Personal liability and security deposit*. Even if you're sure your business will succeed, you always should insulate yourself from personal liability. If your business is incorporated, the lease should be signed by the corporation—not by an individual. How much security deposit you pay will be a function of your business's financial strength and reputation. You also may be able to arrange for the amount of security to be reduced over time.

7. *Services such as electricity.* Be sure you know exactly what services the landlord will provide (HVAC, elevator, water, cleaning, and trash removal) and during what hours. If you anticipate needing overtime services, make sure they're available and find out the cost. Be sure the electrical capacity of your space is suitable for your business. Many old buildings are not properly equipped to handle sophisticated computer and technological systems. Make sure you pay for electricity based on your actual consumption and, if you are required to pay the landlord for providing electrical service, make certain that your costs will not be greater than if you had purchased electricity directly from the public utility.

8. *Alterations*. Make sure the lease permits you to make cosmetic, decorative, and other non-structural alterations without asking for the landlord's consent. For all other work, the landlord should agree not to unreasonably withhold or delay his consent.

9. *Repairs and maintenance*. The landlord should be required to maintain the exterior and structural portions of the building in "good working order" as well as public portions of the building and the building's plumbing, electrical, heating, air-conditioning, and ventilating systems. Make sure you have the right to a rent abatement in the event your space is not usable due to damage, delays in the landlord's making repairs, or service interruptions.

10. *Space measurement*. Most landlords characterize rent on the basis of a dollar figure per "rentable" square foot of the premises. Because there's no universally accepted definition of rentable area, space measurement often is difficult to pin down. Make sure you are only being charged for "carpetable" space, i.e., space that you actually can use.

11. *Financial stability of the landlord*. A business owner should carefully analyze the risks of entering into a long-term lease with a financially weak landlord. A landlord's financial troubles can affect the quality of building services as well as the capability of the landlord to fund construction of the space or to maintain properly the appearance of the building. To protect yourself, ask the landlord for an escrow, letter of credit, or meaningful personal guaranty to secure these obligations.

12. *Build out of space*. The lease should spell out what the landlord will do to get the space ready. The initial work should include demolition of the space, removal of hazardous materials, and installation and hook up to the building's heating, ventilation, and air-conditioning (HVAC) system. If these items were not adequately addressed by the former owner, you

should attempt to renegotiate for them as part of your purchase.

13. ***Delivery of possession.*** If you're getting a new lease or the landlord is renovating your space, the timing of when the space will be ready for you to conduct business is vital. Unexpected delays in construction or a landlord's inability to remove an existing tenant can spell disaster for your business. Make sure the lease contains an outside date for substantial completion (in the case of construction) and occupancy (if the space is occupied by an existing tenant). If the space is not delivered by that date, you should have the right to cancel the agreement.

14. ***Other clauses.*** Expect to encounter some unique issues if the business is located in a shopping center or strip mall. Check the lease to see if it includes the following:

- ***Volume kick-out clause.*** This clause would enable you to cancel the lease if sales don't reach an agreed-on amount by a specified date.

- ***Co-tenancy clause.*** This clause would enable you to cancel the lease if a certain percentage of the shopping center or mall is vacant, or if one or more major tenant closes or moves out.

- ***Common area charges.*** These clauses include charges for maintaining common areas (such as lobbies, walkways, parking lots) and for insurance and security. Some landlords tack on administrative costs or other expenses to the point that these charges no longer represent operating expense "pass-throughs" but instead become profit centers for the landlord. Try to get the landlord to agree to cap annual increases at no more than 3 to 5 percent and make sure any administrative expense is reasonable (no more than 5 to 10 percent), and that you retain the right to audit the landlord's bill for these charges.

- *Construction allowance.* If you plan to expand or renovate the space—or if you move to new unimproved space—often you can negotiate a construction allowance to help offset the cost of alterations and improvements. These typically range anywhere from $5 to $40 per square foot, depending on the amount of space you take, what rent you're paying, and how much *you* will be investing in improving the premises.

Conclusion

A business and its lease are inseparable. Knowing what to avoid as well as what to ask for will not only save you money, it could save your business.

Checklist for Evaluating a Franchise

(Developed by the U.S. Department of Commerce)

The Franchise Opportunity Itself

- Did your lawyer approve the franchise contract after he studied it paragraph by paragraph?
- Does the franchise call upon you to take any steps which are, according to your lawyer, unwise or illegal in your state, county, or city?
- Does the franchise give you an exclusive territory for the length of the franchise or can the franchisor sell a second or third franchise in your territory?
- Is the franchisor connected in any way with any other franchise companies handling similar merchandise or services?
- If the answer to the last question is yes, what is your protection against this second franchisor organization?
- Under what circumstances can you terminate the franchise and at what cost to you, if you decide for any reason at all that you wish to cancel it?

- If you sell your franchise, will you be compensated for your goodwill, or will the goodwill you have built into the business be lost by you?

The Franchisor

- How many years has the firm offering you a franchise been in operation?
- Does the franchisor have a reputation for honesty and fair dealing among the local firms holding its franchise?
- Has the franchisor shown you any certified figures indicating exact net profits of one or more going firms, which *you* have checked with the franchisee?
- Will the franchisor assist you with:

  A management training program?
  An employee training program?
  A public relations program?
  Capital?
  Credit?
  Merchandising ideas?

- Will the franchisor help you find a good location for your new business?
- Is the franchisor adequately financed so that it can carry out its stated plan of financial help and expansion?
- Is the franchisor a one person company or a corporation with an experienced management team trained in depth (so that there would always be an experienced person as its head)?
- Exactly what can the franchisor do for you that you cannot do for yourself?
- Has the franchisor investigated you carefully enough to assure itself that you can successfully operate one of its franchises at a profit both to it and to you?

- Does the state have a law regulating the sale of franchises and has the franchisor complied with the law?

You—The Franchisee

- How much equity capital will you need to purchase the franchise and operate it until your income equals your expenses?
- Where are you going to get the equity capital you need?
- Are you prepared to give up some independence of action to secure the advantages offered by the franchise?
- Do you really believe you have the innate ability, training, and experience to work smoothly and profitably with the franchisor, your employees, and your customers?
- Are you ready to spend much or all of the remainder of your business life with this franchisor, offering its product or service to your public?

Your Market

- Have you made any study to determine whether the product or service you propose to sell under franchise has a market in your territory at the prices you will have to charge?
- Will the population in the territory given you increase, remain static, or decrease over the next five years?
- Will the product or service you are considering be in greater demand, about the same, or less demand five years from now?
- What competition from nonfranchise firms and franchise firms already exists in your territory for the product or service you're contemplating selling?

Confidentiality Agreement

AGREEMENT and acknowledgment between [   ] (the "Company") and [   ] (the "Undersigned").

WHEREAS, the Company has agreed to furnish the Undersigned certain confidential information relating to the affairs of the Company for purposes of evaluating the business of the Company for purposes of prospective acquisition and/or involvement by the Undersigned, and

WHEREAS, the Undersigned agrees to review, examine, inspect or obtain such information only for the purposes described above, and to otherwise hold such information confidential pursuant to the terms of this Agreement,

BE IT KNOWN, that the Company has or shall furnish to the Undersigned certain confidential information, and may further allow the undersigned the right to inspect the business of the Company and/or to interview employees or representatives of the Company, or others, all on the following conditions:

1. The Undersigned agrees to hold all confidential or proprietary information or trade secrets including, without limitation, all financial information concerning the Company and all information concerning its operations, as well as customer lists and controls, price information, margins and development projects ("information") in trust and confidence and agrees that it shall be used only for the contemplated purpose and shall not be used or exploited for any other purpose or disclosed to any third party.

2. No copies will be made or retained of any written information disclosed or supplied, without the Company's consent.

3. At the conclusion of our discussions, or upon demand by the Company, all information, including written notes, photographs, memoranda, or notes taken by or on behalf of the Undersigned shall be returned to the Company.

4. This information shall not be disclosed to any person or entity, including, without limitation, any employee or consultant unless they agree to execute and be bound by the terms of this Agreement, and shall have done so.

5. It is understood that the Undersigned shall have no obligation with respect to any information known by the Undersigned or generally known within the industry prior to the date of this Agreement, or which becomes common knowledge within the industry thereafter.

6. The Undersigned shall defend, indemnify and hold the Company harmless from and against any costs, damages or expenses arising out of the Undersigned's breach of the terms of this Agreement.

DATED:_____, 1997

[   ]

By: _____

_____

Letter of Intent

Mr. Steven S. Seller
c/o Former Owner, Inc.
100 Post Road
White Plains, New York

Dear Mr. Seller:

I would like to take this opportunity to memorialize our discussions concerning my interest in your business, The Post Road Sales Company (the "Business"). As you are aware, it is not our intention to be bound by the terms of this letter. Instead, the purpose of this letter is to outline the manner in which we intend to pursue my interest in acquiring, and yours in selling, the Business.

I am interested in pursuing the acquisition of the Business based upon the following terms:

1.   The purchase price for the Business is to be $250,000 based on an inventory level of $125,000 wholesale cost at the time of transfer. In the event the inventory is less or more than $125,000, the difference shall be added or subtracted from the purchase price.

2.   The proposed purchase price would be paid in the following manner:

   $1,000 "good faith" deposit upon delivery of this letter of intent.

   $24,000 down payment upon signing the formal agreement.

   $25,000 by certified or cashier's check at the time of closing.

   $200,000 to be financed by you, payable in 7 years based upon a 25-year amortization schedule at an interest rate of 8 percent. The note would be secured by a lien on the assets of the Business, which you would agree to subordinate to future financing.

3.   Any adjustment based on any increase or decrease in either inventory or liabilities shall be added or subtracted from the note balance.

4.   The assets of the Business shall be sold free and clear of all claims, debts, liens, or other liabilities with the undersigned receiving good and marketable title.

5.   In the event I buy the Business, Mr. Steven S. Seller will agree as follows:

   • Not to engage in a competing business for a period of time and within a geographic area to be agreed upon and reflected in a separate agreement between us.

   • To provide full-time consulting and other requested services for a period of time and at a rate of compensation to be agreed upon and reflected in a separate agreement between us.

6.   It is understood that you shall provide me (as well as my professional advisors) with accurate information and sufficient access to the last five years of tax returns, financial statements, and books and records, as well

as other information regarding the business operations of the Business (including, with your reasonable prior approval, access to your employees, suppliers, customers and landlord), as may be necessary to conduct an appropriate investigation of the Business. To assure you that I will not disclose any of the information I obtain, nor use any of the information to compete with the Business, I have agreed contemporaneously with the execution hereof, to sign a confidentiality agreement wherein I promise to keep any information disclosed to me in the strictest confidence.

7. It is understood that any transaction wherein I acquire the Business from you is expressly conditional upon:

- My obtaining a lease on the premises on such terms, rents, and conditions as I deem acceptable.

- Our entering into an agreement on terms that is satisfactory to our respective attorneys and to us.

In the event these conditions, as well as any other contingencies specified in the formal agreement signed by us, are not fully satisfied, all deposits shall be promptly refunded.

8. Enclosed is my check for $1,000 to be held by you as a good faith deposit pending the consummation of a transaction between us. The foregoing shall be fully refundable in the event we do not enter into a mutually satisfactory agreement for the purchase and sale of the Business.

9. In consideration for the good faith deposit given herewith, you agree to keep the Business off the market and not to offer it for sale to any other person or entity for a period of thirty (30) days after the date hereof.

If you agree with the foregoing, please signify by signing where indicated and return a signed copy to me within two (2) days of your receipt of this letter of intent. If I do not hear from you within this time, I will assume that you are no longer interested in selling the Business to me, and you will immediately return the $1,000 check given herewith.

It is understood that all brokerage fees shall be paid by you and that an acceptable date of closing would be on or about thirty (30) days after we enter into a formal purchase agreement.

THE PARTIES SHALL NOT BE BOUND OR OBLIGATED TO EACH OTHER (other than with respect to the obligation of Seller to provide accurate information and access to me regarding matters pertaining to the Business, as well as with respect to my obligation to keep such information in the strictest confidence as set forth in the confidentiality agreement signed in connection herewith).

Very truly yours,

NEWCO., INC.

By:_____

The foregoing is acknowledged and agreed to:

FORMER OWNER, INC.

By:_____

_____

Steven S. Seller, as an individual

Asset Purchase Agreement

AGREEMENT made this 15th day of April, 1998, by and between FORMER OWNER, INC., a New York corporation with its principal offices at 100 Post Road, White Plains, New York and STEVEN S. SELLER, residing at 90 Robert Drive, New Rochelle, New York (hereinafter collectively referred to as "Seller"), and NEWCO., INC., a New York corporation, with an address at c/o Newco's counsel, 300 Park Avenue, New York, New York (hereinafter referred to as "Purchaser").

WHEREAS, Seller is the owner of a retail hardware and home improvement business located at 100 Post Road, White Plains, New York operated under the registered trade name of "The Post Road Sales Company" (the "Business"); and

WHEREAS, Seller desires to sell and Purchaser desires to purchase all of the assets of the Business on the terms as herein contained.

NOW, THEREFORE, for good and valuable consideration receipt whereof is hereby acknowledged and in consideration of the covenants, agreements, terms and provisions as herein contained mutually agreed by and between the parties as follows:

SECTION 1: SALE OF ASSETS

Seller agrees to sell to Purchaser and Purchaser agrees to buy the following described business: Retail Hardware and Home Improvement Store known as and by the name: THE POST ROAD SALES COMPANY located at 100 Post Road, White Plains, New York including the stock in trade, fixtures, equipment, accounts receivable, contract rights, lease, good will, licenses, rights under any contract for telephone service or other rental, maintenance or use of equipment, machinery and fixtures at the above location, free and clear of any debts, mortgages, security interests or other liens or encumbrances except as herein stated (collectively referred to herein as the "Purchased Assets").

SECTION 2: PURCHASE PRICE

The purchase price to be paid by the Purchaser shall by TWO HUNDRED FIFTY THOUSAND ($250,000.00) DOLLARS based upon an inventory value of $125,000.00 wholesale cost at the time of Closing, as more particularly described herein.

SECTION 3: TERMS OF PAYMENT

The terms of payment are as follows:

- TWENTY-FIVE THOUSAND ($25,000.00) DOLLARS upon execution hereof, receipt of which is hereby acknowledged, which sum shall be held in escrow by Seller's attorney, Lawrence J. Lawyer, Esq., until Closing or earlier termination hereunder;

- TWENTY-FIVE THOUSAND ($25,000.00) DOLLARS by certified or cashier's check on the Closing Date;

- FIFTY THOUSAND ($50,000.00) DOLLARS ("Escrow Fund") by certified or cashier's check payable to Purchaser's attorney, Brian A. Barrister, Esq. ("Escrow Agent");

- The balance of ONE HUNDRED FIFTY THOUSAND ($150,000.00) DOLLARS, to be adjusted to reflect the wholesale cost of remaining inventory as hereinbelow described is to be paid by execution and delivery by Purchaser of a promissory note, a copy of which is annexed hereto as Exhibit B (the "Promissory Note"); and

- As security for the payment of the Promissory Note, Purchaser agrees to grant Seller a security interest in the goods and chattels and all other personal property of the Business mentioned in Exhibit A hereof. Purchaser agrees to perfect such security interest by executing and delivering to Seller a Security Agreement and a Financing Statement, in accordance with the provisions of the Uniform Commercial Code.

  At Purchaser's request, Seller agrees that it shall subordinate its security interest to any future financing for the Business.

- The wholesale cost of remaining inventory shall be valued (for purposes of determining the balance of the purchase price due hereunder) in the following manner: On the morning of the Closing, a physical inventory of the premises shall be taken and priced by representatives of the Seller and Purchaser. The inventory is to be jointly prepared and shall be in writing, and shall show the quantity of each item, the wholesale value per unit, and the total value. In valuing the inventory for this purpose, the parties shall use the Seller's cost or the fair market value, whichever is less. Any dispute hereunder shall be resolved pursuant to the rules of the American Arbitration Association.

SECTION 4: ALLOCATION OF PURCHASE PRICE AMONG PURCHASED ASSETS

The parties agree that the purchase price of $250,000.00 shall be allocated among the assets conveyed hereby as follows and that each party shall complete their respective tax returns in a manner consistent with the following allocation:

- Lease $20,000.00;

- Inventory $50,000.00;

- Furniture, fixtures & equipment $5,000.00;

- Covenant Not to Compete $150,000.00; and

- Goodwill $25,000.00.

SECTION 5: CLOSING DATE

The closing of title shall take place on June 22, 1997 at 10:00 A.M. at the office of Purchaser's attorney, Brian A. Barrister, Esq., 300 Park Avenue, New York, New York.

SECTION 6: LIABILITIES

Seller shall furnish to the Purchaser, in accordance with the requirements of any applicable Bulk Sales Law and/or the Uniform Commercial Code, a list of Seller's existing creditors, signed and sworn to by the Seller, it containing the names and business addresses of all existing creditors of the Seller, with the amounts due to each creditor and also the names of all persons who are known to the Seller to assert claims against the Seller even though such claims are disputed. Seller understands that in accordance with the provisions of any applicable Bulk Sales Law and/or the Uniform Commercial Code, the Purchaser intends to deliver or send appropriate notice to all the persons shown on the list of creditors furnished by the Seller and to other persons, if any, who are known to the Purchaser to hold or assert claims against the Seller. Seller shall fully comply with any applicable Bulk Sales Law and/or Uniform Commercial Code with regard to the payment of all creditors. Further, Seller shall indemnify and hold Purchaser harmless from and against any liabilities arising as a result of any inaccuracies in said list, such as omitted names or incorrect information. The terms of this provision shall survive the Closing.

SECTION 7: SELLER'S REPRESENTATIONS AND WARRANTIES

Seller, jointly and severally, makes the following representations and warranties to Purchaser:

- That as of the date hereof, there are no proceedings, violations or governmental orders issued in connection with Seller's operation of the Business and that the operation of the Business is not in violation of law.

- That as of the date hereof, the Lease is in full force and effect without default or modification thereunder, all payments due have been made, and there has been no event which with notice or lapse of time or both would constitute a default.

- That the Seller is a corporation duly organized in accordance with the laws of the State of New York and is in good standing.

- That as of the date hereof Seller has, and at the time of the closing, Seller shall have, good title to the assets which are being transferred hereunder, free of all liens and encumbrances, except as set forth herein.

- There is no litigation or proceeding pending or to Seller's knowledge threatened against or relating to the Seller, its properties or business, which shall in any way restrict or inhibit the Seller's ability to enter into and complete this transaction, or effect Purchaser's ability to use the assets purchased hereunder.

- That Seller is duly authorized to complete this transaction.

- That there are no leases or contracts, employment, service or otherwise, affecting the business being sold except as set forth herein.

- That the premises are currently covered by adequate insurance.

- That Exhibit C annexed hereto is a true, correct and complete copy of the Lease and all amendments thereto.

- That the equipment, machinery, furniture, inventory and other tangible assets will be in good working order on the date of closing.

- That the Seller has no subsidiaries or interest in other businesses that conduct part of the Seller's Business.

- That the Seller has no business dealings or interests in any customers or supplier's businesses that aren't arms length.

- That the financial statements (given to Purchaser previously) are complete, accurate, have been prepared in accordance with generally accepted accounting principles applied consistently and fairly present the financial condition of the Seller for the periods covered.

- That all taxes, including income, sales and withholding taxes owed by the Seller have been paid in full.

- That after this Agreement has been signed and prior to Closing, the Seller will conduct the Business in the ordinary course, maintain its assets in good condition, use its best efforts to maintain good relations with customers, employees and suppliers and refrain from taking any actions that would be adverse to Purchaser's interests.

- That Purchaser and Purchaser's representatives shall be given full access to Seller's employees, books and records and contracts and that Seller and its accountant shall cooperate with Purchaser and supply such information as Purchaser may reasonably request prior to closing.

- All of the representations and warranties shall survive the Closing.

SECTION 8: PURCHASER'S REPRESENTATIONS AND WARRANTIES

Purchaser makes the following representations and warranties to Seller as follows:

- That if the Purchaser is a corporation, same shall be duly organized, validly existing and in good standing under the laws of the State of New York. The Purchaser has the power ("corporate" or otherwise), to carry on its business as now conducted and to own its assets and to acquire all of the Purchased Assets and to operate the Business.

- That the Purchaser has all requisite power and authority to enter into this Agreement and to carry out its obligations hereunder including, without limitation the purchase of the Purchased Assets and the execution and delivery of a note evidencing the purchase money indebtedness and the documents creating the related purchase money security interests in the Purchased Assets. The execution and delivery of this Agreement and the consummation of the transactions contemplated hereby have been duly authorized by the Board of Directors of the Purchaser and consented to by its shareholders and no other corporate proceedings on the part of the Purchaser are necessary to authorize the execution and delivery of this Agreement and the consummation of the transactions contemplated hereby.

- That the inventory to be purchased will be purchased for resale, and that Purchaser has applied, or will immediately apply, to the proper authorities of the State of New York for a registration certificate under the New York State sales tax laws. The Purchaser will indemnify Seller against all claims for any New York State sales tax on such merchandise arising from this sale. Seller will indemnify Purchaser against all claims for sales tax arising prior to Closing.

SECTION 9: CONDITIONS PRECEDENT TO THE OBLIGATIONS OF PURCHASER TO CLOSE

The obligation of the Purchaser to purchase and pay for the Purchased Assets is subject to the fulfillment, prior to or on the Closing Date, of each of the following conditions:

- All representations and warranties of the Seller contained in this Agreement shall be true and correct as of the Closing Date, as if made at the Closing.

- The Seller shall have performed and complied with all covenants and agreements required by this Agreement to be performed by it prior to Closing.

- No material adverse change (financial or otherwise) in or to the Business or the Purchased Assets.

- Seller shall have obtained all required consents for the transfer to Purchaser of all leases, licenses, contracts and permits necessary to conduct the Business at the Premises.

SECTION 10: DOCUMENTS TO BE DELIVERED BY SELLER AT CLOSING

On the Closing Date, Seller will execute and deliver to the Purchaser, the following:

- An assignment of all Seller's right, title and interest in the Lease covering the Premises.

- A Bill of Sale in proper legal form to transfer all the Purchased Assets which will contain the usual warranties and affidavit of title.

- A Non-Competition Agreement, a form of which is annexed hereto as Exhibit D.

- A Consulting Agreement, a form of which is annexed hereto as Exhibit E.

SECTION 11: DOCUMENTS TO BE DELIVERED BY PURCHASER AT CLOSING

On the Closing Date, Purchaser will execute and deliver the following documents:

- An assumption agreement whereby the Purchaser will accept and assume all of the terms, covenants and provisions of the Lease covering the Premises.

- The Promissory Note, evidencing principal indebtedness in the amount of $150,000.00 (as may be adjusted as provided herein) in the form annexed hereto as Exhibit B.

- The Security Agreement in the form as annexed hereto as Exhibit F.

- Two (2) counterpart forms of UCC-1 Financing Statement, in the form and containing the content as set forth in Exhibit G hereto, all relating to the Purchased Assets.

- Board of Directors resolution and shareholders' consent as to Purchaser consenting to and authorizing the execution and delivery of the foregoing documents.

SECTION 12: INDEMNIFICATION OF PURCHASER BY SELLER

Seller, jointly and severally, hereby agrees to indemnify and hold Purchaser harmless from and against any and all claims, actions, proceedings, expenses, reasonable legal fees and judgments of third parties arising out of or related to the Purchased Assets to be conveyed hereunder or in any way related to the conduct of Seller's Business prior to the Closing Date (including, without limitation) any and all liabilities for taxes of whatever nature or kind. The provisions of this Section shall survive the Closing.

SECTION 13: INDEMNIFICATION OF SELLER BY PURCHASER

Purchaser hereby agrees to indemnify and hold Seller harmless from and against any and all claims, actions, proceedings, expenses, reasonable legal fees and expenses and judgments of third parties arising out of or related to the Purchased Assets to be conveyed hereunder in any way related to the conduct of the Business from and after the Closing Date (including, without limitation) any and all liabilities for taxes of whatever nature or kind, but excluding from such indemnity any claims arising by reason of Seller's operations prior to Closing.

SECTION 14: ESCROW

- The $50,000.00 ("Escrow Fund") to be deposited with the Escrow Agent at Closing shall be held by the Escrow Agent for a period of twelve (12) months after the date of Closing. At the expiration of such period, the Escrow Agent shall pay to Seller $50,000.00 less any amounts paid by the Corporation (upon presentation to Escrow Agent of appropriate evidence thereof) prior to the expiration of such period for liabilities or obligations other than those to which the Purchaser has agreed to take subject to or as have been adjusted for between the parties.

- Any portion of the $50,000.00 held by the Escrow Agent which is not to be paid to the Seller in accordance with the foregoing provision shall be paid to the Purchaser. In determining his obligations under this paragraph, the Escrow Agent shall be entitled to rely completely upon (i) a writing signed by both Seller and Purchaser; or (ii) a writing signed by Purchaser and/or the Corporation, authorizing release of the Escrow Fund.

- If either party gives Notice to Escrow Agent demanding payment of the Escrow Fund, Escrow Agent shall give prompt Notice to the other party of such demand. If Escrow Agent does not receive Notice of objection from such other party to the proposed payment within seven (7) business days after the giving of such Notice, Escrow Agent is hereby authorized and directed to make such payment. If Escrow Agent does receive such Notice of Objection within such seven (7) day period or if for any other reason, Escrow Agent in good faith shall elect not to make such payment, Escrow Agent shall continue to hold such amount until otherwise directed by Notice from the parties hereto or a final, nonappealable judgment, order or decree of a court. However, Escrow Agent shall have the right at any time to deposit the Escrow Fund with the clerk of a court in the county in which the Premises are located and shall give Notice of such deposit to Seller and Purchaser. Upon such deposit or other disbursement in accordance with the terms of this paragraph, Escrow Agent shall be relieved and discharged of all further obligations and responsibilities hereunder.

SECTION 15: SELLER'S COVENANT NOT TO COMPETE

Simultaneously with the execution of this Agreement, Seller and Purchaser have entered into a Non-Competition Agreement whereby Seller has agreed not to engage directly or indirectly in any business that competes with the Business being conducted by Seller. A copy of the foregoing agreement is annexed hereto as Exhibit H.

SECTION 16: SELLER'S AGREEMENT TO PERFORM CONSULTING SERVICES FOR THE BUSINESS

Simultaneously with the execution of this Agreement, Seller and Purchaser have entered into a Consulting Agreement whereby Seller has agreed to provide consulting and other services as requested by Purchaser from and after the Closing Date. A copy of the foregoing agreement is annexed hereto as Exhibit I.

SECTION 17: RISK OF LOSS FROM CASUALTY

Risk of loss or damage by fire, prior to Closing of this transaction, shall be borne by the Seller. In the event such loss or damage is both uninsured and substantial, either of the parties hereto may, at his option, cancel this Agreement, in which event the Purchaser shall be entitled to the return of the monies paid hereunder and thereupon neither of the parties shall have any further claims as against the other.

SECTION 18: BROKERS

The parties represent that this transaction was not brought about or influenced in any way by any broker or brokerage agency. Each party covenants and agrees to indemnify and hold the other harmless from any and all claims for brokerage commissions that may be brought or asserted by any broker for bringing about this sale, based upon the acts of Seller or Purchaser, as the case may be.

The provisions of this Section shall survive the Closing.

SECTION 19: NOTICES

All notices, demands, consents, statements and other communications hereunder shall be in writing and shall be deemed given (a) when delivered personally or delivered by telecopier (if a contemporaneous telecopier confirmation is received upon dispatch and with a copy sent by Federal Express or equivalent or by mail) or delivery by overnight courier service such as Federal Express to the parties on a business day during normal business hours at the address set forth above.

SECTION 20: GOVERNING LAW; JURISDICTION

This Agreement shall be governed by, and construed in accordance with the laws of the State of New York applicable to agreements made and to be performed entirely within that State, excluding the choice of laws rules thereof. Unless otherwise set forth herein, the parties consent to the exclusive jurisdiction of the Courts of the State of New York for adjudication of all disputes and controversies arising out of this Agreement and the transactions contemplated herein.

SECTION 21: ENTIRE AGREEMENT; MODIFICATION

This Agreement represents the entire understanding of the parties and no modifications thereof, or additions thereto, have been agreed to or will be binding hereafter unless executed in writing by all of the parties hereto.

SECTION 22: WAIVER

No delay or failure by either party to exercise any right hereunder, and no partial or single exercise of any such right shall constitute a waiver of that or any other right unless otherwise expressly provided herein.

SECTION 23: BINDING EFFECT

This Agreement shall be binding upon and inure to the benefit of the parties hereto, and their respective successors and assigns.

IN WITNESS WHEREOF, the parties hereto have caused this Agreement to be executed this 15th day of April, 1997.

FORMER OWNER, INC.
STEVEN S. SELLER

By:_____

_____

NEWCO, INC.

By:_____

Non-Competition Agreement

AGREEMENT made this 15th day of April, 1998 by and between BUYER, INC., a New York corporation with offices at 100 Post Road, White Plains, New York (the "Company") and STEVEN S. SELLER and FORMER OWNER, INC., residing at 90 Robert Drive, New Rochelle, New York (collectively, the "Seller").

RECITALS

WHEREAS, Seller has established, owned and operated the business known as The Post Road Sales Company;

WHEREAS, the Company has on this date entered into an agreement with Seller and Seller's company, Former Owner, Inc., to purchase the entire business and assets of The Post Road Sales Company (the "Purchase Agreement"); and

WHEREAS, as a material inducement to the Company to enter into the Purchase Agreement, Seller has agreed to enter into this Non-Competition Agreement (the "Agreement") with the Company.

NOW, THEREFORE, in consideration of the mutual covenants here-inafter contained, it is agreed as follows:

1. *TERM AND NATURE OF AGREEMENT.* Seller and Former Owner, Inc. jointly and severally agree and covenant that for a period of five (5) years following the date of execution of this Agreement, none of Seller, Former Owner, Inc. or any affiliate thereof shall:

- directly or indirectly, as proprietor, stockholder, principal, partner, director, officer, agent, employee, consultant or otherwise, engage in any business or activity in competition with the Company.

- directly or indirectly (i) employ, solicit for employment, or advise or recommend to any other person that they employ or solicit for employment any person employed by the Company, or (ii) solicit, recommend or invite the patronage of any customers or suppliers of the Company.

The restrictions contained in this paragraph shall apply anywhere within the Continent of North America.

Seller acknowledges that the restrictions contained in this Paragraph, in view of the nature of the business in which the Company is engaged, are reasonable and necessary in order to protect the legitimate interests of the Company, and that any violation thereof would result in irreparable and substantial harm to the Company for which the Company does not have an adequate remedy at law, and Seller therefore acknowledges that, in the event of his violation of any of these restrictions, the Company shall be entitled to obtain from any court of competent jurisdiction temporary, preliminary and permanent injunctive relief as well as damages and equitable accounting of all earnings, profits and other benefits arising from such violation, which rights shall be cumulative and in addition to any other rights or remedies to which the Company may be entitled.

If any of the time periods or the geographical areas specified throughout this paragraph should be adjudicated as unreasonable in any court or governmental proceeding then the time period shall be reduced by the elimination of such portion thereof or both so that such restrictions may be

enforced for such time period in and such geographical area as is adjudicated to be reasonable.

2. *SELLER'S NON-DISCLOSURE COVENANT.*

* *Non-Disclosure of Information by Seller.* It is understood that certain aspects of the business of the Company is of a confidential
nature. Prior to the expiration of the term hereof, there may have
been revealed to Seller, or Seller through his ownership of The
Post Road Sales Company may have prior knowledge of,
Confidential Information (as hereinafter defined) concerning the
business of the Company. Seller, for himself and his affiliates (the
term "affiliate" to mean any entity in which Seller may have any
direct or indirect interest), agree that during the five (5) year term
hereof, and for a period of one (1) year following the expiration
hereof, he will not divulge or appropriate to his own use, or to the
use of any third party, any Confidential Information.

* *Definition of Confidential Information.* As used herein, the term
"Confidential Information" means the following oral or written
information relating to the Company: information, plans, products, sales or manufacturing data, customer lists, supplier lists or
any other trade secrets or confidential materials or information of
the Company, or of any enterprise, controlled by or under common control of the Company or its principals, *provided that*, the
term "Confidential Information" as used herein shall not include:
any such information that, prior to its use or disclosure by Seller
or any of his affiliates, can be shown to have been in the public
domain or generally known or available in the industry in which
the Company is or has been involved, or to customers, suppliers or
competitors of the Company through no breach by Seller of the
provisions of this Section 2.2 or breach by any other person subject to any non-disclosure obligations to the Company.

3. *INJUNCTIVE RELIEF.* The parties hereto acknowledge and agree
that a breach by Seller or any of his affiliates of the restrictive covenants
contained in this Agreement would cause irreparable injury to the
Company and that the remedy at law for any such breach would be inadequate and the Seller agrees and consents that, in addition to any other

available remedy, temporary and permanent injunctive relief may be sought in any proceeding which may be brought by Company or any of its shareholders to enforce such restrictive covenants without necessity of proof that any other remedy at law is inadequate.

4.   *SUCCESSORS AND ASSIGNS*. This Agreement shall inure to the benefit of the parties, their heirs, successors and assigns.

5.   *APPLICABLE LAW.* This Agreement shall be governed by the laws of the State of New York.

6.   *ENTIRE AGREEMENT.* This Agreement supersedes all prior understandings and agreements between the parties, and may not be amended orally, but only by a writing to be signed by the parties hereto.

IN WITNESS WHEREOF, the parties have caused this Agreement to be executed as of the day and year first above written.

SELLER:

_____

STEVEN S. SELLER

FORMER OWNER, INC.

By:_____

COMPANY:

BUYER, INC.

By:_____

Consulting Agreement

Agreement made this 15th day of April, 1998 by and between Buyer, Inc., a New York corporation, with offices at 100 Post Road, White Plains, New York (the "Company") and Steven S. Seller residing at 90 Robert Drive, New Rochelle, New York (the "Consultant").

WHEREAS, the Consultant has established, owned and operated the business known as The Post Road Sales Company;

WHEREAS, the Company has entered into an agreement with the Consultant and Consultant's company, Former Owner, Inc., to purchase the entire business and assets of The Post Road Sales Company; and

WHEREAS, the Company and Consultant wish to assure the continuance of the Consultant's services in connection with such business.

NOW, THEREFORE, in consideration of the mutual covenants herein contained, the parties agree as follows:

1. *TERM.* The term of this Agreement shall continue for a period of three (3) years commencing upon the effective date of the acquisition by the Company of the business and the assets of Former Owner, Inc.

2. *COMPENSATION.* As compensation for the services to be rendered to Company by Consultant, Company shall pay to Consultant an annual compensation of $50,000, payable in equal monthly installments, subject to applicable withholding.

3. *DUTIES.* The services to be performed by the Consultant hereunder shall include the following:

- To coordinate and supervise the sales operations of the business.

- To consult with and to render opinions to the Company on new products and strategies.

- To introduce Company and its employees and representatives to, and to interface with, suppliers, customers and employees of the business in order to maintain and facilitate the Company's relations with the foregoing.

- To assist Company in maintaining existing customers and in pursuing new ones.

- To consult with the Company on any and all other matters affecting the business.

In performing these services, the Consultant agrees that he shall always be subject to the direction and control of the Company.

4. *DEVOTION OF TIME AND EXTENT OF SERVICES.* The Consultant shall devote sufficient time and attention to the Company's business to allow him to properly perform his duties hereunder. The Consultant shall be obligated to perform his services "on-site" at the Company's business location, unless otherwise instructed by the Company, for a minimum of five (5) days per week (Monday through

Friday), eight hours per day. The Consultant shall assume and perform all additional responsibilities and duties that the Company may from time to time assign to him.

5. *RESTRICTIVE COVENANT.* Contemporaneously with the execution of this Agreement, the Company and Consultant have entered into an agreement whereby the Consultant (along with his company, Former Owner, Inc.) has agreed not to compete, directly or indirectly, with Company or to have any interest in or to be otherwise involved in any way whatsoever with any person or entity that competes, directly or indirectly with the Company (the "Non-Competition Agreement"). A copy of the Non-Competition Agreement is annexed hereto as Exhibit A. In the event Consultant breaches any of the terms and conditions of the Non-Competition Agreement, Company shall not be obligated to pay Consultant the compensation set forth herein. The foregoing remedy shall be in addition to those remedies set forth in the Non-Competition Agreement, as well as in Paragraph 6 of this Agreement.

6. *REMEDIES FOR BREACH.* The Company and Consultant recognize that the services to be performed by Consultant hereunder are special and unique. Accordingly, in the event Consultant breaches or threatens to breach any of the terms and conditions of this Agreement, Company shall be entitled to an injunction restraining such breach or threatened breach. Nothing herein prohibit the Company from pursuing any other remedy available to the Company, including without limitation, an action for damages for such breach or threatened breach.

7. *SUCCESSORS AND ASSIGNS.* This Agreement shall inure to the benefit of the parties, their heirs, successors and assigns, however this Agreement may not be assigned by the Consultant.

8. *APPLICABLE LAW.* This Agreement shall be governed by the laws of the State of New York.

9. *ENTIRE AGREEMENT.* This Agreement supersedes all prior understandings and agreements between the parties, and may not be amended orally, but only by a writing to be signed by the parties hereto.

IN WITNESS WHEREOF, the parties have executed this Agreement as of the day and year first above written.

COMPANY:

BUYER, INC.

By:_____

CONSULTANT:

By:_____

STEVEN S. SELLER

About the Author

MITCHELL B. STERN HAS BEEN IN THE PRIVATE PRACTICE OF law since 1984. In addition to advising clients on the creation, acquisition, sale, and management of small and medium-sized businesses, his expertise includes the acquisition, leasing, and financing of commercial and residential real estate as well dealings in general business and corporate matters. He also provides counsel with respect to commercial and civil litigation, intellectual property, and employment- and entertainment-related contracts and transactions.

Mr. Stern has made several appearances on national television as a legal expert for CNBC to discuss real estate as well as other business and personal finance matters. He has also written numerous articles for magazines—including *Working Woman, Personal Finance,* and *New York*—on matters involving entrepreneurship, small business, real estate, and personal finance. He is also a contributing author to *Beat the System,* a book published by Rodale Press in 1997. Mr. Stern lives in New York City with his wife and two children.

Index